Exvantage

By P.K. Perkins

P.K. Perkins
Add me on Facebook as PK.PERKINS

Follow me on INSTAGRAM: @P.K.PERKINS

TWITTER:@KHYAILPIERRE
YOUTUBE : HHHL PROJECT
Printed in the United States of America

First Printing: November 2013

ISBN- 978-1493670710

THERE IS NOTHING LIKE THE LOVE AND HELP I HAVE RECEIVED
FROM MY FAMILY...

BUT MOST OF ALL FROM MY PARENTS ...

THANK YOU FOR ALL THE SUPPORT AND PATIENCE

SLACKING IS FOR THOSE WHO DO NOT BELIEVE IN THE REWARD
OF THEIR WORKS....

P.K.PERKINS

ALL PRAISES BE TO GOD

1

Austin Wells

-Wish me good luck.-

Is what I text my best friend Camry as I was approaching my girlfriend's apartment.

-Welcome to manhood bro! I'm so proud of you-

He replied as I approached her apartment door.

Today was the day I carried out my plan to ask my girlfriend of one year and five months to marry me. I had been planning this day all week all the way down to the forecast. The day was perfect, clear skies and lovely Atlanta weather brought the time for things like this to happen. I just couldn't believe that I was finally at this point in my life where I was ready to be with one woman. I really had second thoughts when I went down to Peach street to Vemans jewelry and saw how much money I was about to spend all for one ring. It wasn't even the wedding ring either it was just the engagement ring. Twenty – five hundred dollars to declare my love up until the wedding day where I was probably going to have to spend another twenty-five hundred dollars for a wedding ring that was nothing but a circle of precious metal with no stones that was probably worth half of the engagement ring but the jewelers charged the same price simply because of the occasion. But I guess this is what I wanted.... Nothing was going to mean more to me than the smile that I was going to put on Tonya's face. It was only going to prove to me that my short comings were worth every penny. I wasn't going to do it this early but we had got into this big fight about a week ago that was basically was about this very subject and I kind of lost it. I hated being pressured into anything especially when it came to commitment. The idea of a long term commitment reminded me of a prison or something for some reason. I think it was when I went to jail for one night and the long and stocky officer had come to my cell and said something that I will never forget. He said, "If you ever planned on getting married, this is what it feels like."

Then he slammed the barred doors and walked away with his head down as if he was a victim of his own words. Ever since then I had been very cautious about taking any relationship out of the girlfriend stage. I was so cautious that I was already a victim of my own paranoia by giving up the perfect girl before Tonya, and I wish that I could have her back. But I guess you live and you learn. It took me a long time to finally get over my fears and to finally get to this point. Tonya wasn't perfect but she was worth a shot in the dark. I would be a fool to let her get away like I did Marie Lovejoy. I owed it to myself to at least try and commit to someone other than the man in the mirror.

I hadn't seen Tonya since the fight almost a week ago but it was because I needed my space to think so I stayed away from her at my place and didn't bother checking on her because I feel she needed time to think things out too. I mean I texted her and everything but as far as physically seeing her, I just wasn't ready. It wasn't like we were avoiding each other because she had a key to my place and I had one to hers so it was kind of like we both had this mutual respect for each other when it came to our space.

I stood outside of her apartment door, pulled the engagement ring out of my pocket and gave it one last look before taking a long deep breath. The one large diamond in the middle sparkled from the light of the sun while the numerous smaller diamonds that circled it twinkled behind its bright shine.

"There is no way that any woman can say no to this." I said to myself putting the ring back in my pocket and pulling out the key to her apartment.

"The rest of my life is gone!" I said to myself out loud as I put the key into the keyhole and opened the door.

Austin!" Tonya shouted looking up at me like a deer caught in the head light. She covered up her breast and hopped up off the large dark guy that she was having sex with.

"What the hell, Tonya!?" I shouted covering my eyes a little bit as if I had caught my mother having sex. "Who the hell is this?" I shouted dropping my hands from my face and aggressively taking a step toward the large half naked man who was pulling up his pants and scrambling to his feet from the couch.

"Austin! Don't!" Tonya shouted running in between us still trying to stay covered as if either one of us hadn't already seen everything she had to offer.

"What do you mean don't? Who the hell is this Tonya? What is going on? One little fight and you're going to go and do this?!" I shouted grabbing her by the arm and pushing her out of the way.

"What u want to do?!" the large dark skinned guy shouted as all of the sudden there was no more obstacles in between us. It was just air and opportunity.

Tonya had landed hard on the couch and balled up into a fetal position to try and protect her body from the expected fight.

Now I'm no punk or nothing but I really did expect to fight the guy but now that we were standing with each other face to face, I was getting a better look at him and I wasn't beginning to feel too good about the odds of me winning anything that had to do with combat. I was in good shape I thought at 6'0 180pounds but clearly this guy took being in shape to a totally different level. He was maybe 5'9 give an inch or two but at least 220 pounds. I was seeing muscles on him that I didn't know that humans had. I couldn't help but notice his large shoulders and chest because it was like they had their own area code. His abs looked like paved bricks and his arms; well they were too big for me to wrap both my hands around. I couldn't help but look down and notice his post erection poking out the bottom half of his jeans right below his left pocket.

"IS THAT REAL?" I thought to myself clearly giving his body too much of a look over.

If I was going to fight this guy I needed to be thinking about how I was going to get his big ass down to the ground because clearly things weren't looking too good for me by just pure size and strength. Deep down inside a piece of me had already given up on any consideration of fighting him just based off the sure size of his physique. It wasn't only his size that was intimidating but also his black timberland boots and baggy blue jeans, no shirt and black Du-rag covered up by a black Detroit tigers hat, that only proved the fact that he wasn't an ordinary

Atlanta thug. This guy was clearly from out of state and if u asked me those were the most dangerous type of people around because nobody knew them. So, in an area where they didn't have anywhere to lay there head for long like this one they really didn't have too much to lose. He could kill us both and go back to wherever he came from as if nothing happened. If I was going to do anything I needed to be smart about it and what I mean by that was I needed to resolve this situation by creating a peaceful exit for either myself or him without feeling like I had sacrificed an ounce of my pride in front of Tonya.

I looked him up and down one more time trying to find a flaw in his posture and his toned body but I couldn't find anything; then suddenly a break

"Who the hell has sex with a hat on?" I wanted to say but couldn't find it in me to blurt out.

"Austin please calm down... Just let me explain!' Tonya said frantic

"Yeah you better calm your ass down before I cool your ass off"

"Khyel shut up please!" Tonya interrupted getting back to her feet and standing between us again. "I'm sorry baby I didn't mean for any of this to happen... We were just talking and..."

"And what you just so happened to find his dick up in you?! That didn't look like that wasn't supposed to happen Tonya! It looked like u was happy that it was happening!" I exclaimed taking a couple of steps backward.

"It wasn't like that."

"Yeah whatever Tonya... Aye look here homeboy you got to go! Get your shit bro and get the hell out of here!" I yelled.

"I'll leave as soon as I get the rest of my stuff from upstairs" he replied walking through the living room and up the steps up to her bedroom.

"The rest of his things? What is he talking about Tonya? You have this fool staying here?" I yelled cutting my eyes into hers.

"Austin please just calm down..... You remember Khyel, my best friend from Detroit? He flew all the way out here to help me get through the horrible feelings I was experiencing from our fight and..."

"Hold on wait! Khyel Porter? Your ex-boyfriend that you had told me about; the one who cheated on you with your cousins?" I exclaimed.

"That was a misunderstanding and yes my ex... he was here to help me"

"Wow... yeah he was clearly here to help you alright. Help you do what Tonya? Come to your senses, get some relief? Help you work out some stress. Reevaluate your options? Wait....No, I know. Fuck your brains out!!! That's what he's here for and clearly that's what your slut hoe ass wanted! I can't believe this shit here!" I exclaimed pacing back and forth across the living room floor.

"Austin please just stop okay...Just let me explain." she interrupted again.

Before she could say anything else the big incredible hulk built like ex- boyfriend came walking down the steps with a black gym bag in his right hand full of his belongings.

"Oh...so he stayed here? Is this why I haven't been hearing from you Tonya?!" I shouted in disdain as he casually walked across the living room past me and set his bag on the brown leather couch.

"Look man you need to lower your tone before the neighbors file a complaint" he demanded.

"What neighbors? You don't have any neighbors! You don't know anybody out here to be concerned about any damn neighbors!" I yelled.

"Actually, Tierra and Chris are pretty cool people. They invited me over for dinner last night...We would have went but we couldn't get it together soon enough to make it there." he replied as he gave Tonya a slight grin.

"Austin..." She pleaded.

"You have to be fucking kidding me...he knows your damn neighbors?! I don't know your neighbors! They never invited us to shit! He's been here that long Tonya?! Are you fucking serious? What the fuck?! Did you have him come out here as soon as we got into a fight?!"

"It wasn't like that Austin..." She replied frantically.

"Then what the hell was it like?!? This man has a duffle bag and is getting invites to dinner and you mean to tell me it isn't like that? Why am I even still standing here listening to this bullshit?"

"I told you to calm down didn't I?! I think you need to leave before I make you leave." The big shirtless gorilla built man said aggressively.

"Look man I don't know how they do it in Detroit or wherever you from but down here in the A all that tough guy shit will get you put in an early grave. You aren't from here! This is my turf and I'll make sure you never make it out of here shawty! One phone call and you're done!" I blurted out shocking myself. I mean I was pissed so I guess I didn't care anymore about my safety.

"Austin shut up please! Khyel please don't hurt him, he's probably been drinking" Tonya begged keeping her body as a blockade between us two.

"One phone call? Well go ahead and make yours and I'll make mines but I'm pretty sure once I finish talking to Dinero that you're not going to want to waste your time dying."

"Dinero?" I said under my breath to myself.

"Yeah, Dinero fool! He's one of my clients and a really close friend of the family. He owes me a bunch of favors too...I'm sure he wouldn't mind handling a small problem like yourself."

I knew I should have just shut my mouth and left when I saw Khyel's big black husky ass. Khyel alone gave me doubts but Dinero wasn't anyone to play with. He was one of the biggest gangsta's in the city. In the last ten years the man had beat eight murder cases and lord knows what else. If Khyel really knew Dinero then I just needed to do what was best and leave like I originally planned on doing. But I wasn't about to go out like no punk after all I did just walk in on him and MY girl having sex.

"You know what...Tonya I'm just going to leave. It was good while it lasted I guess but clearly I can't do this anymore...Just let me run upstairs and grab a couple of my things and I'll be on my way."

"All of your stuff is in a box in the corner already packed...I did it the other day when I was mad." She replied in extreme discomfort.

"Cold blooded!" I replied running up the steps to her room. She wasn't lying! All my stuff was in a pile in a box waiting on me. Two pairs of shoes, some shorts, undershirts, boxers, DVD's, and a set of five pound weights that I had bought because I called myself really trying to get into the whole super body thing, but I guess my efforts were pointless.

I picked the box up and left out her bedroom back down the stairs into the living room.

"You need help with that little man!" Khyel asked walking towards me as if he was actually going to help me. This was one of those days sarcasm was going to cost his ass because once he got in arms reach I grabbed one of the steel five pound dumbbells out the box and quickly went across his jaw with it.

"Help that fool!" I shouted as he fell down onto the floor. I dropped the box and tried to prepare myself for an attack from him. However, to my surprise, it wasn't him I had to worry about I soon found out as a remote control to her T.V. came flying towards my head.

"Stop! Don't be hitting on him! Just leave!" Tonya shouted as she grabbed her cordless house phone and hurled it at me right over my head into the wall.

I started to charge towards her but I saw that the big black gorilla was recovering from his sudden sleep. I knew I couldn't fight two people and besides hitting women wasn't my thing.

"I don't know what I bought this for..." I yelled pulling the ring out of my pocket and showing it to her. I guess the sudden shine from the diamonds was enough to freeze her in place for a second. She gasped for air as she stared at the ring then back at me.

"Austin!" she exclaimed.

As soon as I saw the look of regret on her face I put the ring back into my pocket and quickly grabbed my things.

"It was nice while it lasted but later for you" I replied hurrying out of the apartment door.

"Austin...no...wait..." She yelled as I made my way to my car suddenly on a high horse.

"Deuces!" I shouted throwing up two fingers.

I quickly got into my 2005 black ram truck and sped off, sure that I had left a tire mark on the pavement of her parking lot. But I didn't go far. Matter of fact I only made it to the red light before I had to pullover in a McDonald's parking lot and reassess how I really felt about what I had just lost.

There was only one person I could call and have advice that I respected and felt was genuine and that was my best friend Camry. He was the one person that convinced me that taking my relationship to the next level was a good idea because his life was so good. He was the same age as me, married and successful, so if anybody could help me it was him.

2

Camry Carter

"You are just so beautiful! I guess that's why I married your sexy self..." I exclaimed slapping my wife, Linda, on her full robust behind as she got up and prepared for a shower.

We were using half of our time share down in Orlando, Florida. A beautiful condo on the beach that was fit for a King as it always brought the term R &R to a reality. Things couldn't be any better for me right now. My beautiful chocolate covered wife and dream getaway made me not want to go back to the busy home I called Atlanta. I wish I could do like six months back home and six months here and maybe then the constant change of environment would make me appreciate home more. I love constantly going to and from around the country, especially when I had the time. I know the economy is in a downward spiral right now especially in my field of work with real estate but I have been one of the fortunate ones to not feel any real effects to my pockets.

I looked at the bedroom's patio doors onto the beach from my bed and took a large deep breath as I watched the waves rise up on the glistening sand and back into the ocean. If heaven was anything like this then I needed to figure out why I wasn't there yet and how to get there. Nothing could mess up this time I was having with my gorgeous wife and beautiful scenery.

Brrr...Brrr...Brrr... My phone violently vibrated on the wooden lamp desk next to the bed.

"Who could this be" I thought to myself grabbing my phone and looking at the large screen.

"Austin? What's up?' I said in my relaxed tone.

"Man, I can't believe I listened to you! I done spent all this money on this bitch and this shit happens! I'm so mad I can't even drive!" Austin yelled into the phone.

"What! Wait man what are you talking about?" I replied scratching my head.

"What am I talking about?! Tonya man! I did what you said and got the ring!" He yelled.

"Ok...I know all of that, so what's wrong?"

"I went to her place to propose but instead of kissing and making up, I walked in on her fucking some big black dude who looked like the incredible hulks black protégé. This is all your fault man I swear man this shit hit me hard."

"So wait...who was the guy? He's from the A?"

"That's the worst part man...This cat from Detroit or something."

"So why didn't you call the goons and stomp him out?!" I replied getting hype in my bed.

"Because he claimed he knew Dinero. He said they were good friends."

"Oh... That's crazy... So you walk in and see your girl getting hammered by an oversized beast. Don't tell me you had the wedding ring in your hand like baby will you marry me?!" I replied lightly chuckling.

"You find this funny? Bro are you serious?" I said getting irritated.

"My bad bro; I just got caught in the moment trying to picture everything... What else happened?"

"What you think happened?! I squared off with the oversized gorilla; you know I've never been a punk."

"So y'all fought? You ok?"

"Am I ok? You asking me like I got beat up or something or like I can't fight."

"Come on man with all the emotions...You know you have never been a hell of a fighter, you're a ladies man. You must have gotten beat up?"

"Hell no man! That dude didn't want to fight me. I just went and got my stuff then pretty much knocked old dude out."

"Knocked the dude out!?! So y'all did fight?"

"No, I hit him and he was knocked out cold...I mean he was snoring and everything."

"Man you lying! As long as I have known you and threw punches back and forth! I've never seen you hurt a fly when trying to kill it. Matter of fact, I saw you punch a dude back in high school and he kept going about his business as if you were never there. My wife hits harder than you. My kids will probably hit harder than you at six months and I know for a fact my 98 year old grandma hits harder than you and she has osteoporosis."

"Are you done yet? You over exaggerate everything I swear. First of all, that fly was fast and on steroids or something. I'm not afraid to beat no six month old baby's ass and your grandma has 98 years of built up strength. She's probably stronger than some body builders."

"Oh my God are you serious?!"

"I'm just saying man....I swear it was a program on T.V. talking about the strongest people on earth were the active elderly because they have matured muscle tissue or something like that."

"Man, get the hell outta here....I'm about to hang up."

"Ok...Ok...I did knock the dude out but I hit him with a five pound dumbbell to the jaw to make it possible."

"Man, I knew it had to be something because I swear being hit by you is like getting hit by a roll of tissue being thrown from six inches away." I said erupting in laughter.

"Are you done yet?"

"I'm just saying bro...how did your hands get so soft? A balled up fist on your body feels equivalent to a bowl of pudding. Do you know Bill Cosby? I bet he would sponsor your bowl of pudding fists." I said laughing even harder.

"Come on man, damn! I'm trying to tell you what happened and you trying to joke...Will you just listen?!"

"You right, I should just listen.... I'm just finding it hard not to laugh imagining you throwing a bowl of pudding in the guy's face."

"What?! Bowl of pudding? What are you talking about? Look man... Call me back when you are back in the city. I see you're on some silly shit right now."

"Alright man... I'll see you in a couple of days." I replied hanging up the phone.

I was like family to Austin and he was definitely my right hand man but I must say his love life is always messed up. He just never could seem to pick the right one. I think he may have had one or two good girls as girlfriends but the rest of them were the neighborhood freaks. Or they were the obvious pass around to your friends so he could experience in the bedroom what you experienced when you were with her. Austin would keep all the girls he should be with as friends and all the girls he should keep as an associate he would try to wife. That's why I didn't ask him anymore about him walking in on Tonya having sex with another man because it wasn't a total surprise. First of all, he met Tonya on Facebook and she had a boyfriend when he met her for the first time in person. But the killer is that the exact same day he met her, he had sex with her in his car a block away from her boyfriend's house. The broad had the nerve to tell her boyfriend that she was at choir rehearsal. All Austin kept saying was how well she could hit all these high notes. I warned him then that the girl was scandalous but he really didn't care. All he kept saying was she was his little "good thing." A couple months later this clown was telling me that she broke up with her boyfriend for him. I could tell that made him feel like a big man for some egotistical reason.

The "big man ego" that was a horrible feeling that numerous people of both genders felt they needed to feel for a boost or to just validate themselves all together. In this case the big man ego fed on the satisfaction of taking someone else's girl through sex and a bunch of sweet nothings in her ear. I say sweet nothing talks because at first Austin had no intentions of being with Tonya. He would just tell her what she wanted to hear to get what he wanted from her when he wanted it. Every time Tonya gave in and laid down with him the bigger his ego got and the better he felt about himself. What made his head blow up even more was learning facts about her boyfriend; mainly the physical like, the size of his penis. Austin asked her why she kept running to him for sex instead of her boyfriend and she would tell him it was because he felt better. So Austin proceeded to ask, "What is it specifically? He has a little dick or something?"

Austin asked her this in hopes that she would say no and that his was bigger to make him feel like the more dominant man but instead she replied:

"No, his dick is huge and much bigger than yours but it hurts sometimes and it's like he doesn't know what to do with it to stop hurting me. Yours feels perfect like it just fits and it was made to make me feel good. I don't know it's like you went and studied my vagina while he just ignored what I liked...."

Now at first Austin was kind of down by the "his dick is bigger than yours" answer but once she clarified her answer he found new satisfaction within himself.

"So you're saying size doesn't matter?" he asked.

"It does...it's not like you're little Austin, you're a nice size but his is too big.... So yeah I guess size does matter and in your case, you're the perfect size and you pay attention enough to what I like to give me all the right moves. You have an amazing stroke..." She replied reassuring him that he was safe in the games they played.

Her words only took his ego to another level now knowing that he had the smaller package but the better grade for pleasing her. Just knowing that was equivalent to having the biggest dick or in his case the better one. Austin was a victim of societies cliché's about men just like so many other people. Growing up most of the time, especially in high school, one of the main things guys hear when it comes to sexuality is that the man with the biggest penis is the most desired. But who really set that rule? I have been trying to figure that out for the longest because most of the women I talked to that had been with a guy who was packing would tell me that the sex hurt. So it just makes me think how big is too big and how many guys had the woman who started that cliché been with? Was she saying that because she really meant it or because she had been with so many guys that the normal sized man couldn't please her anymore because she was physically worn down by so much sexual activity? I came to that conclusion because throughout history a lot of the highly sex charged women were the ones who had the most popular influence.

Let me reassure you that I was blessed below the belt but that doesn't stop me from wondering. Sometimes I wish Austin would have my eye for women so he could experience the joy I feel every time I look at my chocolate queen. I met Linda back in my freshman year of college. From the day I met her, I just knew that she was the one. We both graduated from college the same day and I proposed to her on the stage at graduation. It was one of those moments I'll never forget. It was just something about her full lips, chocolate skin covering her perfectly coke bottle shaped body that I couldn't resist. I felt she would be perfect for me. Not to mention, the brains she has matched my own and she uses her ability to think on her own. She has a degree in engineering and works at the airport in the city. Her good paying job was another reason to wrap her up in my arms because the real estate business I was in could go from sugar to shit in seconds. Linda was the best choice for me and trusts me when I say that I had hundreds of options to choose from. For some reason women are highly attracted to my 6'3" frame. My mother was white and my dad was black so they left me with a high yellow complexion and dark hair. My body is pretty muscular considering I don't play any sports anymore and I only hit the gym three times a week. Wait a minute, a grown black man, great job, no kids, college graduate, and a great body? Now that I think about it like that, I would be attracted to me too! I see how I could be such a hot commodity. If I want to sit here and be arrogant I would say that I'm most black women's dream especially when it comes to how faithful I am in my relationship. I don't even watch pornos. To me, it's pointless because nothing turns me on like the sight of my gorgeous wife. I've never been one to sleep around while in a relationship or even think about stepping out on my wife. I mean if it ever got to that point then I would rather end the relationship then sleep around and risk getting caught. My wife calls me the perfect man and so does her family members and some of her friends but I just call it being a man. After all, someone has to do it.

Even though I was on my vacation I couldn't help but wonder what was going through Austin's mind. I knew he was heartbroken and probably on the brink of questioning his manhood because Tonya decided to go be with another man. I was just hoping that he wasn't going to go too hard on himself over this. I remember the last time he was so heartbroken by his high school sweetheart that he was thinking about going gay. It was crazy to me because he called me at like three in the morning to get me to talk him out of it as if he was about to commit suicide or something. I guess for a man like Austin going gay was the new suicide. I can't wait to get home and see for myself what's going on with him. As of right now there is no telling what's happening. He could be butt naked running around in the street yelling "FUCK LOVE" or something I don't know. Austin was the unpredictable type like that so it wouldn't surprise me if when I got back I had to bail him out of jail. Or catch him with a house full of dwarfs dressed in Santa's helper outfits. But until I landed back in the "A", I guess I was obligated to enjoy this beautiful place and my beautiful wife I thought to myself as my wife walked back into the room wrapped in a white towel and dripping wet from her shower.

"Ready for another round", I exclaimed hopping off my bed and charging towards her on a mission to clear my mind by exercising my right as her husband.

3

Crystal Wilks

I didn't know how much my twelve hundred dollar stilettos or my five thousand dollar dress was going to matter to me after today. Both my shoes and dress were gifts from my ex-husband. He loved me so much that he would spend his last on me. Terrence was a powerful man just by his presence alone. 6'6", dark skinned with long dread locks and about 350 pounds of muscle on his powerful frame. He played professional football in Oklahoma for a little while before he was cut from the team. Meeting him was like a dream because everything with us happened so fast. After the first date we had went to Vegas and eloped after just three months. Everybody said that it was too fast and it would never work but they didn't understand the love Terrance and I shared. It was magical. We were planning on opening up a couple of businesses together and having a bunch of kids but I guess some things weren't meant to be.

Thoughts raced through my mind as I looked over at my attorney in his black Armani suit and fresh cut fade as he shuffled through his papers to make sure they were neatly piled and in order. He looked over at me and winked with confidence sure that we had the case in the bag. But I wasn't too sure of that by the way the black male judge was dictating the whole case as if he wanted me to burn in prison. Good thing I went with a jury trial because if I didn't I'm sure I would be in jail no questions asked. However, since I went with the jury trial I think I might have a chance.

The court room was full of friends and family members all hoping for justice and demanding their feeling of justice to be announced. The room was tense and almost immobile without the threat of stumbling over the shared tension in the air. The thing that I didn't understand was why I was feeling the most tension from the prosecutor? You would swear that I was being tried for a crime against her. She said over and over again that if I got another day outside this courtroom then it would be an injustice to not only the victim's family but also the entire United States penal system. But that was nothing compared to the last line she was almost held in contempt for during her closing arguments. She said even if I was found guilty it still would be beneficial to my wellbeing because a person like me deserved to be in a lava pit with the devil himself and raped until Satan began to have mercy on his own actions. Once she said that I swear the whole courtroom gasped and the judge damn near broke his gavel because he had banged it so hard on his desk.

Regardless of what the judge had stopped, the prosecutor had convinced me that I was going to be buried under the prison just like the media had been saying all this time. "It's going to be okay Mrs. Wilks." My lawyer said touching my hand. But in the back of my mind it seemed like we both knew better. He was just saying things to soothe me because he was my representative and he had to act like he was on my side.

Sitting there waiting on the jury to come with their verdict seemed to take forever but it was really only two hours to be exact. My lawyer said that was pretty fast for this type of case with major concern showing on his face.

"Has the jury reached a verdict?" The judge asked taking a sip of his coffee and pushing his reading glasses up on his nose.

"Yes your honor." One of the jury members said standing up nervously with a piece of paper in her hand. The fairly large white woman had stained armpits in her red dress that informed me that it was either too hot in here or it got really intense back there. Just looking at her sweaty armpits made me begin to feel the heat my damn self as if it was a transfer of energy. Everything after that point was a blur up until I heard the words of the sweaty pits woman say, "We the people find Mrs. Crystal Wilks not guilty of second degree murder due to self-defense."

"Oh hell no!" A man yelled from the up roaring crowd behind me.

"Congratulations Mrs. Wilks, enjoy your freedom…..call me." My lawyer said in the utter chaos of emotions, handing me his card as if I was going to forget his information after I left out the court room.

I sat there in the chair for a minute in disbelief but at the same time relieved that all this was soon going to be over and I could move on with my life. I thanked God and Jesus and took a deep breath.

"She probably fucked the judge right along with that lawyer of hers and that bitch in the red dress with the sweaty armpits! That's how she got my brother! You're going to pay you dirty slut. You pretty woman!" Terrence brother yelled as the guards grabbed him up and hauled him out the courtroom.

"You're going to pay for killing my brother bitch!"

I sat in my ex- husband's black Ferrari 458 Halia and took another deep breath so relieved that all this was over. No more reporters, no cameras, no nothing. Despite the fact that I had to wait three hours and go through the back entrance to avoid them amongst Terrance angry family, I was glad it was over. But the point was I could finally begin a new life.

Terrance had died six months ago but the case was just now coming to an end so that meant that it was six months of extra hell that I had to go through all because people had to state their own horrible opinions. Where was the compassion nowadays for people who were victims like myself and totally innocent? It seemed like the media only wanted to report bad news because good news didn't last enough. The bad thing about always reporting good news was if it was said too much then people would take it as if that individual was boasting. But let the same network or person always speak on negativity then everybody seems to be alright with that. I guess the saying is true; nobody likes to see or hear good news especially when it has nothing to do with them. If this is what the world has come to then I'm not sure I wanted to be here anymore.

I couldn't wait to get back home to my mansion in always pleasant Hollow, Texas and finally get some rest. It had just felt like a ton of weight had left my shoulders now that the trial was finally over with. To think a couple of months ago Terrence and I were sneaking off and having wild sex in the team locker room and now he was dead. It was crazy how everyone blamed me for his death when it was his own actions that killed him. A woman can only take so much before she just snaps. All the cheating and lonely nights weighed down on my body and soul. Not to mention, everything I was hearing on the many social networks about him being with this girl and that girl. However, the worst was the proof of his dirty deeds. He had the nerve to record his unjustified actions and put them all over the internet. I don't know how many computer screens I had damaged because of the Terrance Wilks sex tape that kept popping on my screen. But through all his mess I still stuck by his side. It was all the days I had to wear big sunglasses to cover my black eyes he would give me or the days I couldn't leave my house because he had whooped my ass so bad that it began to take its toll on me.

Terrance was a giant compared to my little 5'2" frame and high yellow complexion. My hair used to be long and vibrant but I had to cut it all off and start from scratch because he pulled a patch of it out. Do you know how many people I had believing that I was fighting cancer once they discovered that I was wearing a wig? I was keeping my mouth shut and dealing with all his bullshit all because I loved him and wanted to protect his image. I was such a fool. Then one day it finally hit me that I couldn't take anymore. I contemplated and prayed for months trying to figure out what to do. I was hoping God helped our love to be restored but it never happened. Instead he kept on cheating and beating me over and over again at his will. I don't know where I got the idea or the strength from but I conjured enough bad to relieve myself of his no longer needed services.

One day he came home and I purposely started a fight with him. I let him beat me bloody all over the house so it was evidence of actual abuse. It started in the living room and ended in the kitchen where I stabbed him in the neck with the biggest knife in my reach. I wanted to cut his head off but I knew there was no way in hell I was going to be able to get away with self-defense if I did that so instead I just watched him bleed to death while calling the police in dire need for help.

Watching him die was nothing like the movies. I was expecting him to drop dead after I stabbed him with the large knife in his neck. But it didn't happen that way. He beat me for another two or three minute after pulling the knife out of his neck. It was almost as if he didn't realize until the last minute. But when he did he made some of the most horrible noises that I ever heard as he was gasping for air. I was relieved but saddened by his suffocating death and a little about my own future seeing that I was so badly beaten that I had to be taken to the hospital and admitted there for almost two weeks.

4

Austin Wells

I can't believe she did me so wrong. Tonya had yet to call me and apologize let alone return any of my phone calls. It had been a couple of days since I had seen her getting hammered by the hard body warrior and she still had been keeping her distance. It wasn't like an apology was going to make what happened go away but....then again what the hell do apologies do anyway? Who came up with the term? I don't know how many times in my life I heard someone say to me, "I just want an apology" as if that was the band aid for all disasters and bad decisions. That word is only appropriate for true accidents but not horrible decisions like the one Tonya made. Even if she did apologize I wouldn't be able to stop thinking back to the moment I heard her hollering in all bare ass while she was riding the black super hero like his name was Mr. Ed. If she was smart she wouldn't have let it go that far. So I guess the word sorry was perfect now. Now that I was sitting here thinking about it there was nothing an apology could do. The damage was already done. The only problem was if that was the case then why was I still looking for her to call me? Was it love?

I want to blame it on love but in my young life I've experienced some heart breaking relationships and I learned that even after I am hurt or heartbroken it isn't the love that keeps me going after the heart break but more possibly a habit of being around them or talking to them all the time. It's very easy to control love if you ask me but ten times harder to control a habit because most of the time the habit is in control.

"I was going to marry that girl!" I said out loud to myself as I sat in my bed and looked around my horribly organized room.

Normally I'm a clean freak but in this case I'm at peace in funk. Why clean when I'm not going to have any company over?

Ever since I had my own place I had been with Tonya and she had this pet peeve about things lying around everywhere. So I guess I can credit her for turning me into a clean freak. This was my "Fuck you Tonya" behavior maybe...I wasn't sure what it was but I knew I needed a break from everything for a while just until I figured it all out. I was even thinking about relocating but I wasn't sure I had enough money to just end my six month lease early and still be able to pay the deposit at some other place.

Truth is I had seven grand to my name that I had been saving for almost eight months now. I had one full time job as a security guard at a chain of banks and a weekend job with my uncle who had a lawn service. Both the jobs were temporary of course until I could find a good job in the field I got my degree in which was computer engineering. After I graduated, I had a job that actually paid great and seemed like a perfect fit for me. But just as I started to get comfortable the company somehow needed to downsize and had to let me go. I haven't been able to recover ever since that happened so I've been making do with what I could.

Beyond all my relationship problems and messy habitat one thing I know for sure was if I had called another day off work to soak in my misery then I was definitely going to get fired. I usually loved my job but this week I had to work at a bank that was in the same plaza where Tonya worked. She worked at a pharmacy not even a hundred feet away from the bank. Every time I worked there we would go on a lunch break together and have wild sex wherever we saw fit. It didn't matter if it was in the alley behind the plaza or in the car or even in the plaza restroom; we always found a way to make things interesting.

"Oh sweet Jesus! The memories are too much to bear!!!" I shouted out loud to the silent white walls that seemed to be the perfect listener to all my venting. I didn't understand why I wanted to hear from Tonya but couldn't deal with the idea of seeing her. I knew where to find her, where she stayed, and how to approach her. But then again, that was when I thought I knew her. The Tonya I fell in love with wouldn't have let no big black gorilla built man from Detroit be her saddle.

Boom! Boom! Boom! Boom! Boom!

I jumped from the sudden banging on my front door. I wanted to just continue in my thoughts and lay in the bed because I didn't feel like being bothered but at the same time I was hoping it would be someone I could talk to other than these walls. I hopped up out the bed and quickly walked to the door and looked through the peephole.

"Tonya!" I said under my breath as I looked at her standing in the hallway in her white work jacket.

"Austin open up! I know you're in there...I know your car outside....Come on now...You know I have to go back to work!" She yelled banging on the door a couple more times.

I wanted to say something but I quickly caught myself and continued to stare at her through the peephole. She had her huge Louis Vuitton Handbag that I had bought her for her birthday hanging from her wrist with a folded piece of paper in her other hand. Damn! Even in her work clothes she looked amazing. I was starting to get aroused looking at her lips through the door. She had on my favorite lip gloss I loved for her to wear. It was just something about lip gloss on a woman's lips that were so inviting in so many different aspects.

I put my hand on the door knob and was about to turn it to open the door but I stopped myself again as a flash of the face Tonya was making while she was riding the incredible hulks daddy, oddly crossed my mind. I stepped back away from the door and dropped my head discouraged. As I did so, a folded piece of paper slid in my apartment from underneath the door. I walked back up to the door and looked out the peep hole and saw that Tonya was gone. I picked the folded paper up and unfolded it and began to read.

Austin,

I'm not trying to make any excuses for what I've done. I feel so foolish for doing it in the first place. I was wrong but I needed some space and some type of relief that you weren't willing to provide at the time. Khyel had just showed up at the right time. He knows me very well and I had just let him take advantage of my vulnerability. I'm sorry… If it means anything to you, I love you so much and I miss you beyond reasoning. I pray and hope that you forgive me and if not then I wish you the best. If you don't want to be with me anymore at least I hope we can be friends. I need you in my life Austin…Please give me another chance.

Love…Tonya

As soon as I got done reading the letter I was startled by four more loud knocks at the door.

Boom! Boom! Boom! Boom!

"Austin?! Open up boy...I know you're in there, I smell you all the way from out here!" Camry shouted through the door.

"Go away!" I yelled back.

"Man hell no! Open the door and stop acting like a bitch!"

"Oh now I'm a bitch!"

"Not like that man but you know what I mean....You don't have to act like that towards me...I haven't even done shit to you."

"You weren't there when I needed you!"

"What?! I was on vacation!"

"And I was watching my girl get banged by Godzilla."

"Man, open the door!" Camry yelled kicking it at the same time.

I unlocked the door and let him see his self in as I made my way to the couch.

"Damn! What did you just get done eating sardines and spoiled milk with a side of fresh shit?!" He exclaimed while he shut the door behind him as he pinched his nostrils.

"It's not that bad...Is it? I was thinking more like an open bag of sour cream chips." I replied sniffing the air as he came into the living room and sat down.

"Man I can't believe your living like this…What happened to you…?"

"This happened!" I replied handing him the letter I had just received from Tonya.

"What is this? A letter?" He asked grabbing the letter and reading it.

"Austin, why is she talking to you as if y'all are still together? What would make her think you were still with her after you caught her getting hammered by Donkey Kong? By the way who is this guy again?"

"You want to see him?"

"What? You have pictures of him or something? Don't tell me you took pictures of him bro…I swear I'll walk out and then break into your room while you're not here just to see if you have pictures of me laying around here." Camry said looking around the room all suspiciously.

"Man shut up!" I replied going to Khyel Porter's website. "Look."

"Bro…he has his own website? This guy looks like he sleeps in the gym but oddly he's not gruesome big. He is perfect in every way, form and fashion. This guy has muscles I never knew existed before….Bro…No homo but I would have cheated on your ass too with this dude…catch me on a drunk night and I might pay him to fuck my wife just so I can watch!" He exclaimed adjusting his jeans as if he was getting an erection while keeping his eyes locked on the computer screen.

"Pause!" I yelled yanking the laptop away from him.

"What?" he replied coming out of the temporary trance he was in while admiring his body.

"What's wrong with you man? That's a boy!"

"Man I wasn't looking at him like that...he has a lot of females on there...that's all I was looking at." He replied wiping the look of guilt off his face.

"There aren't any females on his page fool...You sure you're happily married?"

"Don't cut into me like that man."

"I'm just saying...you're the one talking about; "He does have a nice body...Oh my God he has muscles I've never seen before" or no wait here's the gayest one you said.... "No homo Austin but if I wasn't me I would fuck him too." Who says that shit and can still feel confident about being a man in the morning? No homo Austin, I would lick every inch of his body if my tongue wasn't in my mouth but if it was in somebody else's mouth I would suck him like my favorite flavored Blow Pop sucker...No homo though"...I said in a tone that was mocking Camry's but with a hint of femininity.

"You're going way too far Austin!!" Camry replied with the serious look on his face.

"I'm going too far or you're acting too gay? You can't say no homo after saying all that gay shit! Don't be mad at me for addressing your homotude. You should be happy I'm catching it and addressing it instead of your wife."

"Bro change the subject before I punch you in the mouth" He demanded sitting up on the couch as if he was actually going to get up and hit me in the mouth.

"You know there was a study somewhere that I read about men who were overly aggressive were really trying to mask their own gayness." I blurted out.

"Shut the fuck up!"

"I'm just saying you need to check that attitude bro...I don't see why you're mad anyways. After all I'm the one going through all the drama."

"Yeah you're right...my bad....No wait just a minute...What the hell is homotude?"

"Look it up."

"Man that's not a word. I'm not even about to waste my time straining my eyes looking for a word that doesn't exist." Camry said skeptically.

"It is in one of those dictionaries bro...Homotude is homosexual attitude or behavior. Everybody knows that bro." I replied in confidence knowing I probably had made that word up.

"Yeah sure tell me anything. I only graduated from one of the best schools in the country."

"I can't argue with that one bro."

"So anyway what are you going to do about Tonya? When did she bring you this letter?"

"Right before you came. I'm surprised you didn't see her on your way up here."

"I think I did but I wasn't sure that was her because I was getting out of my car when the girl I thought was her was getting in hers. Plus I just knew that you weren't dumb enough to take her back after what she did... Right? You're not thinking about taking her back are you?"

The room got silent for a minute as I thought about answering his questions.

"Austin? What's taking you so long to say no? Don't tell me that you are actually considering getting back with her?" He went on to say in disbelief.

"We never broke up we just stopped talking that's all." I replied clearly unsure about what to do.

"What?! Austin you saw another man not just smashing your girl but super smashing her ass! How much more information do you need to know that she isn't the one? I can't believe you're having such a hard time; its common sense bro. I mean weren't you talking about marrying this chick? I hope that you aren't anymore because now you know for sure she is a hoe or should I say every body's girl?"

"Come on man watch your mouth."

"What are you serious? You're ready to fight me over her? Well look man, I'm going to go and I guess when you calm down then we can hook up later when you have thought this out. It seems like you're starting to forget who has been there for you after all this time through thick and then." Camry replied standing up and walking towards the door.

"No man, don't go bro... My bad I'm tripping but you know it's because I'm not good with dealing with stuff like this. I bought her a ring and everything, those feelings aren't that easy to let go."

"Wait, you bought her the ring?" Camry asked stopping and turning around. The look on his face changed after I told him and clearly it stopped him from his dissent. He sat back down on the couch.

"Yeah I told you I was going to marry her. You're the one who talked me into doing it!"

"I did?"

"Yeah?"

"Why did I do that? Especially knowing Tonya originally was looser than a knot tied by a nine month old baby."

"Come on man."

"Don't get mad at me bro. You knew before y'all got together that she was faster than Hussein Bolt in the hundred yard dash. We know at least eleven guys that she has been with and I'm not talking about dating. I'm talking about fucked all in the same year. I told you to do what the other guys did but you refused to listen and decided to do the dumbest shit by making her your lady."

"Eleven guys?"

"And that's just the ones that we know of. She is probably been with more guys than the both of us have been with women. I don't really see how you're so confused by her actions." Camry said folding his arms and reclining back on the couch.

"Confused? Cam we were together happily for two years; why wouldn't I be confused?"

"Because she was that way before y'all got together so what makes you think that she is going to be any different now?"

"So what are you saying that people don't change?"

"No I am saying that just because you fell in love doesn't mean that she was going to stop loving what she was doing in the process. Her loving you was just an addition to the things that she loves to do and was already in love with. You're just one added piece to the puzzle."

"Who do you think you are?"

"I'm Cam your right hand man; the only true friend that you have ever had. Don't get mad at me bro but I'm just trying to get you to see what is real. If you don't want to hear what's real then I'll stop talking or better yet you can go back to bed and dream of that fake reality that you so desire to be in."

"So you don't think that I should be with her?"

"Hell no, I've been saying that from the beginning but her super sucker lips and thunder clap ass has you all fucked up."

"Man ... I guess you are right ... Well at least I can get my money back for that damn ring I bought her...you want to see it?"

"Man hells no; just get your money back and call it done before you do something stupid like put it on her finger. Matter of fact let's do that right now, get up and put some clothes on and lets go return the damn thing."

"No man I'm not ready to go out there."

"What? What do you need; for your house to catch on fire for you to leave it? Go get your clothes on and let's get out of here Austin. Maybe then we can get some fresh air and possibly get you some more women to get your mind off Tonya."

"That does sound good but no thanks... I need more time." I replied content with my decision.

"You sound like a female right now. You want to act that way staying here in this entire funk and get yourself together. I'll get at you later. But before I go think about this, If I could take back anything it would be all those times that I wasted sulking over a female or anybody for that matter. The only person worth that much time and effort isn't even visible to any eyes. So if you're not going to give Him that time then what makes you think that someone who constantly hurts you deserves it?... get it together bro; who knows maybe this will work out for the best. If you ask me the ex-always has it better than any person affiliated with relationships. The ex is like a hybrid of a single person. Being the ex you have all the same freedom of a single person but all the advantages you had when you weren't single with the person that you broke up with."

"What?" I asked clearly confused.

"Just because you two are broken up doesn't mean the feelings that she had for you or the way that you make her feel has to be broken or forgotten too. Just play the game and you will be one happy, free, ex-boyfriend with an all access pass to all your ex-girlfriends just like how Khyel was with your girl Tonya."

"Come on man you don't have to use that as an example... and how am I supposed to do that. I'm not Khyel, I don't look like that."

"I'm married bro how am I supposed to know? Maybe you should get Khyel's number and ask him." He replied cracking a huge smile. "No but really I believe that you will figure it out. You're smart." He replied getting up shaking my hand and walking out the front door leaving me to ponder on what he had threw in my ear.

I don't know why it seemed like Camry had all the answers to all my problems but he did. He was very smart and able to apply his logic to every situation especially in my case. I could be totally lost and bothered with something for days but once he got an ear to my problem it was nothing for him to come up with a solution. As long as I can remember he had no more than three maybe four serious girlfriends in his life but he seemed to handle and pick better women than myself. Like the one he is married to now I would die to have her by my side. She is beautiful and super smart but most of all she has her own money. I believe there are more women out here like that than men nowadays but a lot of them come with a ton of problems and no manual on how to fix them. As far as trying to make me feel better about being single or the so called ex, I think that he was on to something; I'm just not sure exactly what.

5

Leon didn't have the best looking body that I had ever seen, nor did he have the cutest smile or the cleanest look that I usually went for and found in Terrence. But Leon understood me and I was just comfortable with him. We had dated for almost two years back in high school but once it was time to go off to college we had went our separate ways. His light skin and scrubby beard made him look ten times more intimidating than what he really was and his pudgy belly and disappointment of a frame made it clear that he was as soft as a teddy bear. He didn't look like this bad back in high school when we dated. Back then he was muscular and the captain on the football team; he used to make me feel so lucky. What's crazy to me is when we kiss and I close my eyes he makes me feel like I'm in high school again. I can't seem to figure out how that feeling from ten years ago is still there. Does that feeling mean that I never let go of what we had or does it mean I'm reading into the moment the wrong way. The last thing that I want to do is start to feel something that really isn't there causing me to fall too fast for somebody I know isn't right for me.

"Are you going to let me take the Ferrari on the road today?" Leon asked as he rolled over to what used to be Terrance's side of the bed.

"Drive on the main road?" I replied catching my breath.

"Yes on the main road Crystal, I'm sick of driving the car around the property. I want to take it on the road and see what the car can really do."

"I told you Leon it's too soon. If anyone saw you in that car and knew that it was mines then it would be all over the news and internet."

"It's too soon? The trial has been over with for two months stop being so uptight. I'm sick of having to hide and having to sneak in and off the property like I'm somebody you're embarrassed to see. Terrance has been dead long over a year when will you let it go? When is it just going to be me and you, you know, just enjoying life?"

"Leon please don't start with this fantasy shit! Let's get real for a second. Yes there are feelings still there for you and I'm comfortable with you but you are still legally married with 4 kids and one on the way. Live on with our lives? Yeah we can do that but not publically and together. If we are going to do anything together it's going to be in this house Leon; that's where I'm going to draw the line for the sake of my own feelings."

"What about my feelings Crystal! Answering to you every beckon call? I'm sneaking over here at all odd times of the night. I don't even know what to do about all these feelings that constantly go through my head."

"Feelings? What feelings?"

"Crystal I still love you ok! I never stopped loving you and have missed you every day that you have been gone."

Before replying I took a minute to regain control of my tongue before I blurted out a response based off emotional impulse due to the moment. You know the whole I miss you too Leon and I still love you so much response. I've found myself looking at people who say that to their old fling or boyfriend

45

and I've always said I wasn't going to be the one because there is no geniality in those words; it's the history and habitual familiarity of that person that makes us say some of the dumbest things we clearly don't mean. Don't get me wrong, we may feel that way a little bit because of some false hope that we can get that old thing back but mark my words when I say it isn't real.

"Miss me every day I was gone Leon? Can we please get real for a second, you cheated on me back in high school with the woman you're with now and married to with four kids. Let me say this one more time Leon, you're married with four kids. Please miss me with that love song shit and just keep fucking me when I ask please. Let's just keep things simple. Now if you can't seem to do that and just that alone then maybe you need to keep your ass at home with your family where you belong." I replied rolling over on my side of the bed and folding my arms.

A sudden pause filled the air as I settled into my warm spot in the bed.

"Wow... Crystal don't act like that baby. I told you Chanel and I were going through some things and getting a divorce and that I wanted to work things out with you..."

"Save it Leon clearly you have missed my point. I think that it's time for you to leave. This conversation is making me uncomfortable."

I could feel his eyes cutting through my back because he was staring at me so hard.

"Ok... I get it... I got it... give you what you need and get the hell out? "

"No Leon I want great sex from you and for you to be a great friend also in this house for right now but I want you to miss me with all that other mess that you're talking about right now. I'm a mess inside and I don't want my emotions jumbled around anymore than they already are."

"Ok baby I got it," He replied kissing me on my neck and running his hand down my side and across my waist line then resting it on my hip. Do you want to go for another round?" He whispered in my ear.

"Nope... I want you to go home to your wife and kids. Go be a good father to them until I call you again instead of being a cheating dead beat dad. I'm not in the mood anymore so leave!" I replied calmly but in a stern tone.

"Are you serious?" He replied sitting up and digging his eyes even deeper into my back.

"I put some money in your jeans for you and your kids. It should be enough for the money you should have made at work today if you would have went plus more... I'll call you when I need you again."

"Wow" He replied yanking the covers from his body and quickly putting on his clothes.

"Don't be mad."

"I'm not mad boss lady just enlightened that's all, see you later... Bitch!" He replied as he left my room and made his way through the mansion quickly.

I wrapped my silk sheet around my body and reached over into my drawer next to my bed on my night stand and grabbed my little twenty two caliber handgun. I got up and looked out the window to make sure that he was truly leaving my property. One thing that marriage had taught me not only from all my lonely nights but also from the days my husband was home was to stay aware of my surroundings and somehow stay protected. Stabbing a man is a lot harder than it looks on TV. It's not a smooth and easy action like you would think it was. The tearing of skin tendons and muscles are felt in my hand through every inch of the knife that's pushed through the body. I will never forget the vibration that I felt through the knife as it ripped through his body. The slower I pushed the knife into his body the more I felt his pain and that's when I learned the quicker the better. I guess right then and there I was experiencing the universal law of speed; it ignored feeling and provided adrenaline; no feelings of fear or complete control until whatever you were doing was done.

I stood in my window and watched Leon get into his car and drive off my property in a rage almost hitting my steel privacy gate as he left. What reasons did he have to be mad? Leon had his own problems to worry about in his own life and here he was lying up in bed with me wanting to share his issue with me? What could possibly make him think that I wanted to share his burden of four kids and an irritating baby mama?

I would see that type of behavior in many of my friend's lives and that's when I noticed that that's when all the fun stops. When things stop being simple and start being more complicated that's when someone needs to take control and either leave or draw the line. With Leon for example, we have a simple arrangement that works perfectly when we just do what is intended which is having sex. But once he starts expressing feelings and wanting more then that's when it gets complicated.

Complicity is the reason why so much isn't understood and we know if certain things aren't understood then nothing is going to function right. Like driving a car such as my Ferrari, it's highly complicated to a person that doesn't understand how it works and if a person that doesn't understand how to operate gets in it and tries to drive it then one of two things will happen and neither of them are good. Besides Leon making things complicated by wanting to take things to the next level. In the process he also looked incredibly trifling.

How could any man elude their responsibilities as a father and a husband to go start somewhere else?

I know that he said that he and his wife were having problems but doesn't every man have problems with the woman he is involved with the moment he sees someone else that he would like to stick his dick in. They got along well enough to have four kids together and one on the way. Men say that they are having problems to justify their cheating ways and also to make the person interested to feel a little more comfortable in the participation of his, what should be illegal activities. Don't get me wrong some people don't care but for the ones that do it's a method that works every time all the time. Trust and believe me when I say that a man looks ten times more attractive when he is honest and upfront. As quiet as it is kept all women don't like to be looked at like prey or shall I say pursued. In this day and age "the new age" women are stronger and more of a go getter than ever before so that means what used to be the prey becomes the predator. I get a rush of liberation when I'm able to pursue and conquer whatever it is that I go after and that includes my men and my money. That's what it is all about right? Let's be honest about self for a minute; if that hasn't happened then nothing will go right or be enjoyable. That's why it is important to stay in control in situations like the one with Leon because if I had let Leon take the lead I would find myself in another situation like the one I had to fight to get out of. What Leon needed to do was stay home with his damn family and start wearing a condom or have his estranged wife (let him tell it) take some birth control.

The fool in me was going to let him help me have a child because I had always wanted one so bad. The lonely feelings that I would have deep inside would often drive me to make irrational decisions but often times I would find my way back to logic and pop my birth control in my mouth and follow it with a glass of warm water; only to follow that warm water with a glass of red wine and a shot of 1800 minutes later.

Terrance and I tried to have a child throughout our whole marriage but no matter how hard we tried nothing would ever happen. I had numerous doctor visits and so did he; the doctors told us that nothing was wrong with either of us and to keep trying but just like before, nothing. We even discussed having an Invitro but just the risk involved and the idea of a child being a God given event made me not want to do it. The procedure was more of a take your destiny into your own hands type of thing instead of a glorifying event like the normal way of making a baby. I feel like instead of a child being created, we would have been customizing a child that was ours but tampered with by man. To be honest it scared me just thinking about it. Then at the same time who knows what else the doctors are doing with my precious eggs while they sit up in their labs and get toyed with. There are some sick people In the world; the doctor could be putting a little bit of his sperm in with my husband's just to make sure that a piece of his self-lives on.

I know that I didn't have relationships or men totally figured out but one thing that I was sure of was that I was tired of being alone and in this big house by myself. Maybe my time had truly run its course in Texas. Maybe it was a time for a change of scenery. I was thinking New York, Los Angeles, Miami, Atlanta or maybe even Detroit. I had family in most of those places except for Miami so I couldn't help but think maybe I would be better off moving to one of those places for support especially since the trial was over with.

Miami was always going to be an option strictly because of the scenery and the vibe that ran through the people. It seemed like a highly energetic place full of events and attractive people. I would have never wanted to move out there if Terrance was alive because it wasn't a place for couples but more so a place to explore and let go in life on numerous levels but mainly a sexual one. I could see myself waking up on the beach after a night of partying or wild sex with a Cuban named Ricardo who had swam to Florida from his communist country. New York seemed like a good choice because it was the land of opportunity. New York was all about business and big buildings. It would definitely be my first choice if I had plans to get into designing or stock or something like that but those dreams had left me a long time ago along with being a rapper, actor and any other form of entertaining. Maybe I would have those desires later on in life but for now I was looking for peace more than a career. Atlanta seemed like it would support my needs more than anywhere else. Maybe there I could buy myself a house of my choice for my small size and open up a restaurant or something. The quiet life that I had so longed for may come true there. As much as I love glamour and the big lights of the city I long for the quiet life of the country. I understand that Atlanta is a stripper city but there are plenty of places around the city where I can find my peace right? But aside from Atlanta I believe that Detroit is my first choice because that's where most of my family resides and maybe that's what I need more is family support; especially with Terrance's family members calling my house leaving death threats and having to constantly look over my shoulder when I'm out is ridiculous. Living life paranoid is no way to live life; you're not even going to want to live. I was just tired of everything from the media to death threats. Texas was a beautiful place but they carried guns freely here and Terrence's family members weren't the only ones who I think were pissed about losing their big star. Hate mail was a regular here at my household and when I say regular I mean a lot of regular by the barrel loads. Hate mail poured into my house twenty times more than a collections agency notice. It was definitely time for a change of scenery and right now the familiar faces of my family members and Detroit streets sounded good. As I sat here and thought back to my old neighborhood I didn't see any luxury in it but the comfort of being home was making me feel better about moving there.

6

It wasn't a day that went by that I wasn't thinking about what Camry had said.

"Get it together bro, who knows maybe this will work out for the best. If you ask me the ex-always has it better than any person affiliated with relationships. The ex is like a hybrid of a single person. Being an ex you have all the freedom of a single person but all the advantages that you had when you wasn't single with the person you broke up with."

It seemed like those words were meant for me to hear because they were echoing in my head on a daily basis. I was thinking that it was me trying to figure things out but it's been too persistent for it to be just a coincidence. I was beginning to feel like maybe its purpose was for me to discover my purpose. Maybe I wasn't meant to be tied down in a relationship to some woman that wasn't going to be satisfied with good. If you ask me no woman is really ever satisfied because they don't shed light on any positives when it comes to men; instead they see all the negative. Like when Tonya and I used to talk she could only seem to pick out the negatives but let me try to say something positive and she gets silent. Where they do that at?

If there are so many women like Tonya that can't find any positive about the men they chose to get with then maybe that's why so many of them are either single, lesbian or in a relationship but miserable.

Maybe it was true about relationships not being for everyone. Although, it seemed to have been working for not only my parents but my good friend Camry, I would have to consider them the lucky ones with the most tolerance. That's all relationships were to me was learning how to tolerate the next persons bullshit, so the hope of anytime sex would be a reality and the fear of being alone wouldn't manifest. Children most definitely play a part in relationship but who's to say if they add any satisfaction in being with the same never satisfied with good female for longer than one night.

My mom always told me that an ex was an ex for a reason and it was no benefit to being what was associated with what was considered wrong like the opposite of a check mark but in this case I could turn the title of an ex into something positive. Instead of it being associated with a person who failed in a relationship how about I find a way to make an X literally mark the spot.

Khyel seemed to have grasped this logic very well seeing that he was able to come all the way from Detroit to bang my girlfriend after taking advantage of her in her vulnerable state. The comfort that he seemed to provide seemed to be the key to his success which makes plenty of sense. Most women aren't going to open their legs to anybody but if they were going to do it, then who better than someone that they are familiar and at ease with would seem to be the key. But how the hell do I get on a positive note with my ex?

For all my life after I ended a relationship I tried my hardest to forget about that person and move on with my life on a peaceful note. Trying to take advantage would mean that I would have to find a way to be cool with them so they could be useful somehow. But how the hell was I going to do that? Who was I going to try that on?

Thinking about this was more complicated than I thought. So it seemed like I was just going to have to go try it out on somebody and learn from trial and error.

....

Work was the same as ever but a little more hectic because of the trying times. Summer was leaving and fall was trying to settle in with the Atlanta heat. I was so hot standing outside of the city bank in my security guard uniform I had sworn I was on fire. The dark blue collar shirt didn't help me cool off any faster; my fire arm was heavy and hot also. The steel from the gun burned my hand every time I put my hand on my hip and accidently brushed my fingers against it. Working here was cool like I really didn't have to do much but stand here and look like I wasn't about to play any games if someone tried to rob the place. However the truth was if someone robbed the place I would be the one behind the robbery because I knew the bank like the palm of my hand. If I was really pressed for money I would be in the Bahamas chilling drinking a Tahitian treat counting money right now; But I wasn't no fool. I might have been able to deceive other people but I wasn't able to deceive myself. I hated guns, just having the one on my hip made me nervous. Too many people have died from guns for no reason or accident and I wasn't trying to be one of them. A certain football player was one of the lucky ones but look how much trouble a gun brings. This man shot himself in the leg at a night club on accident; he didn't harm no one but himself and the state still threw his ass in jail as if the pain he was feeling from not only the bullet in his leg but also the embarrassment he was going to feel from not being able to participate in his professional career wasn't enough. Guns weren't anything but trouble but honestly it wasn't only the idea of what they could do to a person physically or legally because before any of that happens there is a sound that scares me before anything. It seems like the loud clap a gun provides after pulling the trigger would do just as much damage as the bullet.

I remember one time my friends and I were out joy riding and one of them had been in the back seat playing with one of his two large hand guns and in the process one of them had went off and caused the driver to slam into a tree. Now everybody survived the accident but two of the guys were deaf in one ear because the windows were up when the gun went off which gave the sound nowhere else to go. I found the whole event to be a little ridiculous but at the same time it said one thing to me and that was guns aren't nothing to play with.

"Hey, Austin?" Mrs. Jenkins said waving at me as she passed by.

"How are you doing?" I replied wiping the sweat beads from my forehead and smiling.

"Better now that I see you here… it always gets crazy around this time of year especially with the heat and all. You know us black folks can't be crowded together in this heat all at once with somebody acting a fool especially around money." She replied shaking her head as she opened the door to her red c-class Benz.

"Well I'm glad to make you feel safe Mrs. Jenkins. You have a nice day."

"Alright…" She replied sitting into her car seat then hopping back up quickly.

"What's wrong?"

"That damn leather just burned the shit out of me; it felt like I had sat my leg into a frying pan!" She exclaimed smiling and making a chuckle out of her misfortune.

"Yeah it will do that sometimes especially in this heat." I replied smiling at her.

She looked at me and paused for a second then dug in her purse and pulled out a business card.

"Do you do private events?" She asked coming up to me.

"I can but to be honest I've never done one. Why?"

"I'm having a fundraiser at my place in about a week and I want some security because I'm going to have some known jewelry designers there selling their stuff and I want them to feel safe."

"Really?"

"Yes and I figured all my lady friends wouldn't have a problem with having some eye candy to look at while they are giving away their money." She replied as she handed me the card. As I grabbed the card a bright light from her huge diamond ring slightly blinded me reminding me that she was married and not to get out of line with this married woman.

"Ok" I replied squinting my eyes.

"Call me to get the details if you're interested but I need to know before the week is out, Ok?"

"Alright." I replied as she switched back to her car. I couldn't help but admire her little frame as she walked away. Her behind looked like a medicine ball under her tight skirt and I couldn't help but notice her Vaseline rubbed legs that shined from the sun off her dark cocoa brown skin.

Mrs. Jenkins had to be in her forties but looked like twenty nine was her fitting age. She was every body's boss here at the bank and was a key person in hiring me. She was married to some white guy who owned a bunch of burger restaurants or something all around Georgia but she never really talked about him. If I didn't have such a respect for married couples then I would have been all over her trying my best to continue to be the guy that her husband clearly wasn't. I say that because security was a big thing to her as if she wasn't getting the feel that I gave her at home. It tickled my spine every time she talked about how safe I made her feel because she had no idea how fast I would be gone if somebody actually tried to rob this place. I would probably be gone as soon as it looked like someone was going to announce they were robbing the place. I know it was my job to protect the bank but nobody said anything about me dying in the orientation for damn near twelve dollars an hour. I mean If I wanted to I could be a hero and protect the bank and its money but at the same time who was going to protect me? I don't care how safe I made people feel a couple dollars an hour wasn't worth getting shot over.

I did wish that I had my own gun for that Khyel guy I walked in on fucking my ex girl. I would have shot the both of them and probably ended up in one of the racist Georgia prisons. But then again if that was the case I'm glad that I didn't have it. Plus I feel I made more of a statement handling him with my bare hands. A big dude like that probably isn't use to guys standing up to him like I did. He probably would have been more hostile and threatening if I had pulled a gun out on him to be honest.

Certain days at work time went fast and other days' time went so slow it seemed like the wheels that turned time had a flat. I had to have drunk over six twenty four ounce water bottles and used the bathroom just as many times. Standing around in all that heat was a workout. When it was time for me to leave it was like a weight off my shoulders especially when the air conditioner from my car hit my face.

For some reason I couldn't help but think about Mrs. Jenkins and her big round ass in that tiny skirt she had on, it was almost as if she was trying to tease me or something. I wasn't sure how happy she was at home but I knew she was making it hard for me to be respectful to her husband especially in the heat. I don't know what it was about hot weather that made people want to do things ten times more than they would the rest of the years and that's fight or have sex. The nice weather must have a trigger in our hormones or something that I don't know about. I know one thing; as I was driving home I couldn't seem to keep my erection down. The sight of every woman walking around the city streets in these short shorts and tight clothes only pumped more blood to the last place I needed it to be. I was so horny I was tempted to unzip my pants and pull my dick through my boxer hole and masturbate while I drove home. It was either do it while I drove or pull over to the side and pop one off. The thought seemed like a good one but once I got to a red light and decided to go through with the JWD (jacking while driving), I had looked in my rear view mirror and saw the police snug against my bumper.

"Shit!" I said out loud struggling to put my large erection back into my pants. I knew moving too much would get their attention so instead of going through the struggle of putting it back in my pants I just kind of put it under my shirt until the blood found somewhere else to go and I was able to get it back in my pants.

I couldn't believe that this is what it was coming to worrying about getting caught in the middle of a JWD. It sounded ridiculous and when I sat and thought about it I couldn't believe that I was so desperate. Who jacks off in the car? While driving?! There was a big ticket for texting while driving but I wonder what kind of ticket they would issue for jacking off at the wheel. This just wasn't something that someone like me should be doing. I should have pussy lined up by the block but I didn't. I was ready to jack off like I was in prison or something ...Pathetic...

I had devoted so much energy into making Tonya feel secure and special that I hadn't realized that I had pushed every other female I was cool with, out of my life. Because of that I had been pussy-less for I don't know how long. Tonya was the last girl I had been with. I couldn't believe that I was holding out for so long for just her and she was busy playing cowgirl with that house built like boy. Why should I suffer? As bad as I wanted to move on and forget about that bitch I couldn't. I was going to have the last word and maybe then I would be satisfied. Maybe it was wrong to have this resentment and anger towards her but who am I to suppress my feelings? Who is she to do me so wrong and expect me not to have had any feelings? She came to my house banging on my door leaving some apologetic ass note with hopes that I would forgive her and work things out or at least be friends with her; fuck that! I should go to her place right now and bust the windows out on her car with a brick attached with a note saying good riddance.

Wait a minute...

She can be my first trial; after all she is technically an ex now. Were these types of people the type that Camry wanted me to target? If it works like Camry said it would then this would be worth all the hassle. I'll be getting what I need not only sexually but also mentally with no strings attached right?

I texted Camry and told him the trial Exvantage was in effect and he quickly texted me back.

-Exvantage?!-

Little did he know that was like a light bulb going off in my head. But before I started doing anything I needed to handle some business that couldn't wait for anybody else. I was about to explode literally it seemed like. By the time I got to my place I felt like a water balloon with too much water in it. As bad as I didn't want to resort to pleasing myself I felt I had to before I lost any more blood due to the large erection I was sporting between my legs that I was trying to walk around.

....

"Thank you Mrs. Jenkins!" I yelled as what seemed like a load of bricks had been lifted from me. The image of seeing her earlier in the day stuck with me and played a big part in relieving myself; if only she knew how grateful I was that she wore that tight ass skirt. I cleaned myself up with a dirty t-shirt that was lying around in my room because I couldn't find anything else that was in arms reach.

Now that I was in my right mind I took off my work clothes and got into the shower so I could cool off and get away from the hot weather. Plus I needed to take the time out to try and figure out how I was going to approach Tonya. It had been a while since we had spoken or anything so I am totally clueless to how she would receive me once I reached out. Sitting here wondering how she was going to receive me wasn't going to get me anywhere fast so it was only one way to find out. I sat in silence anxious for her to her pick up as the phone continued to ring.

Ring……. Ring…… ring…..

"Tonya?" I said into the phone that was still dripping with suds and water. I was so eager to see what was going to happen that I didn't give myself a chance to dry off good from the shower I just took before I picked up my cell phone and started dialing her number.

"Austin?" She replied sounding surprised to hear my voice.

"Hey, how have you been?"

"I'm ok; I guess… did you get my letter?"

"Yeah I got it."

"Why haven't you called me? I've been calling you but you obviously don't want anything to do with me anymore."

As bad as I wanted to say something ignorant and go off, I decided not to. Instead of making her feel bad I bit my tongue and swallowed my pride so I wouldn't mess up what I was trying to do.

"I just had to get myself together before I got back with you that's all. I'm good now though... so what's been going on with you? Is your boyfriend still around?" I blurted out regretfully.

"Boyfriend? I don't have a boyfriend Austin... Khyel will never be my man again. He was just a reliable friend that's all."

"Hold on one second." I interrupted putting the phone on mute.

Did this stupid bitch just say reliable friend?

"What about me you dirty slut? What was I when you were slamming up and down on the hulks little brother's cock! He was more reliable than me? You dirty slut bitch! I hate you!" I yelled into the phone knowing she couldn't hear me but for some reason it just made me feel better.

"Sorry about that. I said cutting the mute off the phone and picking up where I left off. So what were you saying?"

"I forgot."

"I guess it wasn't important then."

"Don't say that, do you remember?'

"Yup."

"Then refresh my memory."

"Nope... I don't want to talk about it anymore."

"That is what I miss about you Austin, you speak your mind. All these other guys kiss my ass and let me do and say what I want which is cool but it's not really the type of guy that I can see myself with … like you."

"You're saying that you can still see yourself with me?" I replied finding myself slightly involving my emotions.

"Duh, we were just together and those feelings just don't go away,you were… never mind…" She replied obviously biting her tongue.

"I was what?" I replied anxiously awaiting her to finish her sentence.

She took a deep breath before she started her sentence. "The one I guess; you were Mr. Right! There! I said it … Are you happy now? I screwed up Austin and I'm sorry… I just miss you so much."

"Hold on again please…Just a second." I replied putting the phone back on mute. If I was the one, then why the hell would you throw away so much for a freak week with a Mr. Marcus look alike! Stupid! It's too late now. But that's ok because I'm going to teach your ass a lesson. Payback is a bitch but in this case it's me! I shouted again into the phone.

"Hello? Austin?" I heard her say.

I quickly took the phone off of mute and answered her call.

"Yeah… I'm back." I replied gathering myself together.

"Do you want me to call back? Is right now a bad time?" She asked clearly a little frustrated.

"Oh umm… no… it's just Cam, he is on his way over here and he is on some other shit right now that's all."

"Well I can call you back if you want."

"No…I mean, fuck him; he is on his way over here so I can talk to him then. What were you saying?"

There was a sudden pause and then her taking a deep breath.

"I miss you Austin, so much… I need you." She blurted out.

"Think Austin. What to say now?" I asked myself. I had two options; I could avoid the emotional side of things and change the subject or I could cater to her feelings and try to make her feel more comfortable by letting her know her feelings weren't alone. My next move was obviously crucial and if I wanted to be that guy I said I wanted to be then I needed to be smart and play the game to get my way.

"I miss you too Tonya…"

"Really?"

"Yeah … you were the one for me too… Hell I was going to ask you to marry me Tonya."

"Yeah I have been thinking about that all day… Austin can I please just see you?"

"I have a picture on my face book page that you can take a look at all day if you want to see me."

"No, I want to see you in person Austin!"

It took me a second to realize how much this was going to work in my favor... then it clicked....

"Hell yeah... when?" I blurted out clearly letting my little head have a say so.

" Preferably as soon as possible." She replied with a little bit more life in her voice.

My dick rose up immediately.

"I'm on my way over there right now!" I blurted out.

"Wait isn't Cam on his way over there right now! "She replied.

"Oh yeah." I replied, irritated by my own lies getting in my way. "O.K ... well how about tonight? I'll just call you when I'm on my way. Is that cool or do you have plans?"

"That will work... I'm not doing anything tonight. Just call before you come ok..."

"I got you... see you later." I replied trying to keep my cool.

"Ok... Bye" She replied hanging up.

"HELL YEAH!" I shouted throwing the phone on the bed and jumping in the air. "I'M BACK BABY! WE GONE GET SOME ASS... WE GONE GET SOME ASS! WE BACK... WE BACK... DADDY LONG STROKE IS BACK!" I yelled continuing my celebration.

Did that just work?

Only time will tell... wait until I tell Cam, he is going to trip.

7

Camry Carter

"But if I don't get up and go to work then your ass would be begging for more money and whatever else you were lacking!" I yelled at Linda as she followed me through our house with more complaints.

"There is no need to yell Camry; if you're going to do that then I'll talk to you later about this but just know that it's an issue and I'm reaching out to you about it." She replied following me into the bedroom and standing in the doorway while watching me flop down on the bed.

"Yeah ok."

"That's it Camry? So are you saying my issue is not an issue to you? That's what I'm talking about; you don't care about no one else's feelings but your own." She yelled.

"I thought that we weren't doing all this yelling back and forth? I'm trying to get some peace and quiet right now so I can think. I have to get up and go back to work soon and your stealing some of my valuable rest time as we speak." I replied trying not to let my temper get the best of me.

"You know what... fuck you Camry! Go ahead and get your precious sleep and I hope when you wake up you do so with some sense." She replied walking out the bed room and down the main hall.

"Thank God!" I said out loud relieved to get away from her constant nagging.

Ever since we had been back from our vacation, things had been going downhill with us because we weren't able to see each other as much. Our schedules were so much in conflict that sometimes a day or two would go by before I could see her at all. It was like we had to schedule an appointment if we wanted to see one another or something. I must admit that it wasn't totally a problem that I was ok with but I didn't see a problem with taking in more work for a month or two. I looked at it like it would make up for the days we took off on our vacation with an added bonus. I kind of see where she was coming from as far as us not spending much time together lately but I don't understand how that could be her issue. I mean we still have sex occasionally when there is time and we text throughout the day when we haven't seen each other or had much time to talk over the phone. I was actually a little re-energized by the whole over loaded days and random hours that I had to put in. It made me feel like I did when we first started out. I'm actually doing the same thing that I first started doing when I first started in the real estate business; scrambling from house to house and client to client just to make a sell. The only difference was that I was doing it with larger estate now. Every now and then I would sell an average rate property or a low income home that was going for under forty thousand dollars just to remind myself how much further I wanted to go. Plus the different people I ended up interacting with always seemed to keep me grounded.

The price of the house always determined the type of person I was going to meet. A house that cost forty thousand most likely was going to produce a first time home buyer who was young and up and coming or a dope dealers wife or girlfriend that was looking for a house to turn their dirty money into something legal . It also depended on the neighborhood as far as the ethnicity was concerned.

A house that cost one hundred thousand on up usually brought on couples who were looking to settle down with one another and start a family. These couples most of the time were married or engaged with a child or two. Oddly, I would get some single clients mainly women searching for a place to lay their head and get away from whatever home life they felt they needed to escape from. These women were usually up and comers; graduates who had come a long way and found a good job after school.

The million dollar homes were the trickiest though these homes attracted all type of people from super ghetto to super snobby. The color never really matters because when you start being in costly places the only color that ever matters is green. Guessing what type of person I was going to run into was always a roll of the dice because there were so many people getting rich overnight it seemed. There are times I would be expecting to see a very classy person and get surprised by Pooky and Ray Ray who had just struck gold signing a million dollar record deal or sports deal or better yet Sue Ann and her husband Bubba who is really her first cousin from the trailer park who suddenly lucked up and hit the lottery. I run into athletes more than I do regular people. These guys are richer than anybody else in any other profession and they love to spend their money like they never had it before because nine times out of ten they haven't. My favorite ones are the ones that want to take care of their whole family and buy up everything for everyone. That's when I usually cash in because they use me to find their families houses. That's how I have been so successful to date, word of mouth and good karma. My success is something that Linda tries to make me regret. She swears up and down its tearing down our relationship but when it comes to getting the bills paid and buying her nice things she doesn't complain. I would bet every dollar that I had if I had lost my job and worked at McDonalds that her attitude and how much she loves me would totally change. I probably would be reading some divorce papers right now as we speak if I hadn't worked this hard to get where we are today.

I hate it when women complain about how good things are when they know if things were any worse they would be more miserable than what they ever claimed to be. She was complaining about the little time that we were spending together but I was trying to figure out what was the big deal. I mean some time is better than no time right? So what, we weren't spending that much time together for this little bit of time; our bank accounts were getting fatter and with bigger accounts came so much more elbow room.

Did that sound selfish? Well to me it's not; it's just the closest thing to logic. If we are supposed to be this successful couple, no time apart should change our view of one another. It had been a month or so since we had been back from vacation and it had been hard work ever since. If this little bit of time was going to be the deal breaker then maybe the deal we made at the altar wasn't a good one.

People tend to misinterpret what commitment means nowadays as if saying " I love you" wasn't meant to be token literal anymore. Behind the word commitment is the ability to have strength to endure whatever it is that goes against you. I love you is supposed to be a feeling generated by words that helps reassure that comfort and commitment but nowadays it seems like any and everything is a deal breaker. Sometimes I almost wanted to keep up my long work days just to see how much she can take. This was nothing if you asked me but for some reason it seemed like it could turn into something that was soon going to open the both of our eyes.

I had received a text from Austin saying something about operation Ex-vantage taking place but I didn't have much time to get back with him to see what he was talking about. I was hoping that he hadn't took my advice literal and was actually thinking about playing some type of love game with any one's heart. Playing with people's hearts can get even more dangerous than cheating because so much of the unexplained is involved.

Austin had numerous exes so I was wondering if he did take what I said literal, which girl was he going to end up messing with. I just knew it wasn't Tonya especially after seeing the guy she cheated on him with. I had never seen him so hurt before about anything so Tonya would be my last guess. On the other hand he could be trying it out on her because she caused him the most pain. He could be trying to find a way to get even or come out on top of the situation the best way he thought he could. Now that I think about it, I wouldn't be surprised if Tonya was the one he chose. I was hoping that it wasn't too soon to see her because if he wasn't careful he could find himself falling for her again but even harder this time because he knows firsthand that she isn't girlfriend material.

Who was I kidding?

Knowing Austin he was at her house right now cuddled up under some Khyel cum stained blankets sucking his thumb like a little baby. When it came to women Austin was weaker than superman around some kryptonite. I would be surprised if he came out of her place the same man with the same mind as when he first went in. He probably would go to her house with operation Ex-vantage on his mind but after she throws those lips, hips and ass on him he's going to be thinking operation make up. I was hoping my boy was stronger than that but then again I know my boy.

8

There was much more thinking that I needed to do to convince myself that it was time to leave Texas. Most of my family was in Detroit, so I went back up there and called myself looking for a place around the city. It felt refreshing to be home especially in the summer sun when the best of the cars came out and people actually showed their face in the sun. I loved the early fall in the city even though it was very hot and unpredictable not only as far as the forecast but also because of the people. A peaceful outing on the city streets could quickly turn into a life changing experience that there was no preparing for.

Texas wasn't too much different. They drove old school cars down there and fixed them up just like most Detroiters did; it was just a different model that they were dumping their money into. Of course the style was the same but at a faster pace in Detroit than in Texas. In Texas the people were just animal skinned out, it didn't matter if it was alligator, bull horns, rattle snake, foxtail it didn't matter. In the city it was one of the same but strictly gator or mink. It had to be high end to be considered fashionable in Detroit or at least look high end. There were so many Africans that could get you whatever type of look-alike designer that you wanted it was ridiculous.

As long as it had been since I had been in the city, the two reasons I gladly left reoccurred and reminded me that some things will never change and it wasn't the place for me. Dealing with my family and all their begging always nagged me. Now that I was back home and on my own it seemed ten times harder than what it once was.

"Crystal can you pay for this or buy me that or loan me this?"

It seemed like that was all people were interested in; forget how I was feeling or what I was going through but more so what I could do for them. I have heard the saying F.O.E (family over everything) but I swear I couldn't stand being around my family when they acted this way. It seemed like family only acted like family when you could do something for them but until then, they were no different than a stranger I would pass by and never notice. Blood doesn't determine who my family is. It only helps me determine who I' m related to; or who I have received some traits from. Don't ever let a relative trick you into thinking they are anything more than relation and if you do fall for that trick, just don't let them abuse and use you too much before you realize what's going on.

BANG! BANG! BANG!

Shots rang outside of my window at my grand-mothers house. That was the second reason why I wasn't ready to move back to the city. The gunshots and the violence never seemed to stop. I mean I know there is violence everywhere you go but in Detroit it was like on steroids because the climate was so tense with people losing their jobs and not knowing whether or not they were going to make it to the next day. There are definitely people shooting in Texas but it's sometimes because of hunting or for the hell of it but not to kill somebody. In the city more times than likely when you hear gunshots they are hitting someone. I wasn't sure if I was ready to move back to the on again off again murder capital.

My mother told me that Atlanta was no different than the city but that wasn't what I was hearing or experienced when I had went down there by myself or with Terrence some years back. There were some similarities but there was a southern hospitality that you couldn't get anywhere else but in the south. I loved the feeling that you could only get in the south.

My eyes were leading me to Atlanta and hopefully my first class flight there will be followed by a deposit on a house, some moving trucks and a new place I can call home.....In so many words ... A new beginning.

9

Austin Wells

"Austin! Did that … Was that real? I can barely breathe and feel my legs!" Tonya exclaimed lying next to me in her queen sized bed trying to catch her breath.

"As real as it gets baby..." I replied calmly in my satisfaction and badly needed relief.

"I feel so much better … I missed you so much."

"Yeah me too" I replied a little burnt by all the reuniting words. She had been saying how much she had missed me the whole time we were having sex. She sounded like a broken record."

"Oh... Austin! I missed... you...Awe! I missed... oh my god!" She would constantly repeat and moan out with every stroke that I would deliver to her body.

I said it back a couple of times because I guess that I was caught in the moment but after saying it a couple of times I found myself actually meaning it and wanting back what I was missing all this time. Right then and there I realized that if I didn't be careful then this little plan of mines was going to back fire and set me up for more failure by allowing my emotions to lead me back into a relationship with her. The last thing that I wanted to do was get back with her, right?

"I'm so glad that we are back together Austin... I missed you so much!" Tonya exclaimed wrapping her arms around my body and placing her head on my chest.

"Whoa, back together?" I interrupted sitting up in the bed.

"Yeah... What's wrong?" She replied looking at me with a look of confusion on her face.

"Who said anything about getting back together? I thought we were just fucking?" I blurted out regretting that I had allowed such boldness to be in my tone.

Tonya cut her eyes at me and kind of jerked her head back away from me in clear disappointment but with enough patience to explain things to me.

"What makes you think that I'm like that? Why would I be having sex with you if we weren't?" She replied quickly biting her tongue as I gave her the bitch please look. "Ok ... umm well I see how things are ... I'm not stupid I get it ... I guess that I will see you later." She said instantly changing her mood from feeling disrespected to discomfort...

"You want me to leave?"

"Well if we aren't going to get back together then what do you need to be here for? You got what you wanted now it's time for you to go especially if you want to act like that." She replied doing the whole ghetto neck roll thing again.

I couldn't believe what I was hearing. How could she be talking to me this way as if she didn't care about me anymore or something? It was pissing me off that she could act so heartless. As bad as I didn't want to get back with her I didn't want to see her hurt. I couldn't help but want to be with her longer. It wasn't supposed to go like this. All I wanted was some type of gratification magnifying the love that we had with one another. I may have said differently earlier back at the apartment when my dick was harder than going on a diet but now that I was here in the bed next to what was supposed to be my victim, I mean ex, I couldn't seem to control how I felt about her.

"I don't want it to be like that Tonya...I'm sorry baby if I offended you I just ... I'm confused I guess." I replied feeling my pride and ego perish.

"It's normal to be confused baby...it's not easy making it through all the bullshit like we have. Who knew that we would have gotten this far together as a couple that so many people envy? What happened to us Austin?"

"I don't know..."

"Remember our first date?"

"At the ice cream parlor?"

"Yeah... you remember what type of ice cream you bought me?"

"I had chocolate and you had vanilla right?"

"Yup... Watching you lick your ice cream turned me on so much I swear I wanted to have you right there in the ice cream parlor..."

"Digg that." I chuckled all of the sudden finding myself holding her and rubbing my fingers through her hair...

What the hell was going on? I found myself waking up next morning scrambling to get back to my place and ready for work. I left Tonya with a passionate kiss and a I can't wait to see you later attitude as if we were really back together again. Matter of fact I think we were back together. Honestly I'm not sure what the hell I went over there and got myself into. One minute it was operation Exvantage and the next it was operation lets act like nothing ever happend. Just that fast I went from a man with a plan to a man who couldn't follow through. It was like she knew my plan and created a counter plan of her own. One of the easiest ways to rekindle the love and fire with anybody was by bringing up the good times that were shared. We spent the whole night sharing good times and memories. It's crazy because when we were together we couldn't do anything but talk about how bad things were but now that we weren't together, we couldn't seem but talk about how good things were. Why the hell were things so backwards?

I don't know why it was but it was clearly confusing me and for her it was a good tactic that was clearly throwing me off my game and making me forget my original plan. What threw me off from the beginning was when she said how happy she was that we were back together. Then, when I asked her when we got back together she said the moment that we had sex or something like that.

Did every female think like that? Or at least try to make it seem that way so they didn't seem so animalistic like us males? I wonder because it wasn't the first time that a woman had said that they had felt a similar way after sex. Certain women felt that because she was giving me sex that in return I was giving them my commitment. There was power in pussy but damn let's not exaggerate its ability please. It may have had that type of influence on some men that may have lacked a lot of attention from the sacred fruit but for a man like myself who had the ability to find and devour fruit sections at will; it just wasn't a factor.

I think it's a shame for any woman to think that her way to a man's heart was coercion and trickery sex or any type of sex. The reality was that the only one that was being fooled was the one who had initiated the foolish idea. But since the women out numbered guys it has been accepted by many people that the women no matter her intentions especially in cases like these, were victims; when the whole time it was nobody's fault but their own. The secret to getting to a man's heart has nothing to do with how clever and strategic you are but more so to do with how genuine you can be. Having patience and giving the man the time to decide on what he may want to do is critical in most cases. If it doesn't sound fair then don't go around giving up the butt foolishly until you both have an understanding on where you stand and have a plan on how not to fall for anything. Treat yourself by allowing yourself to know what's reality and what is fantasy don't cheat yourself by forcing yourself into believing that the fantasy idea is your actual truth. The truth of the matter is you can't force anybody especially a man to be a man if he doesn't want to be nor has no idea on how to be one in the first place.

....

I stood in the hot Atlanta sun outside of the bank trying to recuperate from Tonya's beautiful encounter of operation Exvantage. As far as I knew we were back together and I was stuck looking like a sucker because I couldn't say no to her undeniable deterrent. I was clearly going to have to give Camry a call so that I could regroup. Besides this was all his fault in the first place because he was the one that gave me this idea but no real manual on how to work my way through the obstacles that may come my way. I don't even know why I was even listening to him. He was the one in the perfect relationship and with the least experience with women. Where the hell was he getting all this playeristic information from in the first place? As of right now he had me more fucked up in life about women then I had ever been in all my fuckedupness of circumstances.

"Who the hell told the sun that it could make Atlanta so damn hot?" I said out loud to myself as I looked off into the distance at the ripples that became visible from the heat. When heat started to become visible like this that's when you know it was too damn hot outside. Anytime you begin to see something that you usually don't see and are not supposed to see it's a damn problem. Just think about it; we aren't supposed to see ghost right so the moment you do start seeing one you are automatically scared as hell or confused about what you're seeing right? That is because we aren't supposed to see no shit like that; it's no different with heat; anytime you see heat when there isn't no fire around it's a problem.

Another thing that was bothering me in all my sweat was that there wasn't a cloud in sight. The sky was as blue as a Colts jersey minus the white. I'm standing here in all my musk wishing that I would have had time to have taken a shower or something. I don't care how clean your girl is, sex is one of those activities that is going to make the freshest of people a little funky. I could smell Tonya all over me. I smelled like peach Victoria secret lotion, sweat, and ass. But what was more irritating than that was the constant joining of my balls and my thigh which was probably from the heat and left over fluids from the sex to blame; I called this a case of "sticky balls". I had to take extra-long steps when I paced in front of the bank to try and not make it too obvious that I was having ball to thigh malfunctions without constantly digging my hand down there and separating them. It had gotten so bad that it had looked like

I had been doing walking lunges; you know the exercise people do when they are at the gym trying to work their legs and behind. I found it less handy for an actual workout and more helpful for unsticking my balls from my thighs. I should rename the exercise from lunges to "unsticking my balls." It's crazy because this was the only real time that anybody let alone myself would catch me doing any type of leg exercises.

"So have you decided whether or not if you were going to do me?"

"What?" I replied raising my eyebrow and turning to the voice of Mrs. Jenkins behind me." What did you say?" I said clearing my throat hoping that she would repeat what I thought that she had said.

"I said are you going to do the fund raiser or not? Because if you're not I need to find another person to do it." She said standing in front of me in a red business suit that was more on the sexy side of things. Of course she had a skirt on but the suit jacket was cut low and so was her V-neck blouse that showed the right amount of cleavage to drive any man crazy.

"Why are you doing this to me?" I blurted out accidently.

"Doing what?" She replied with a question mark on her face.

"I don't know..." I replied caught up in my words.

"If you can't do it Mr. Wells you don't have to go to the ends of the world and try to satisfy me. I'm very easy to satisfy and all it takes is a straight answer."

"Oh... no ... I'll do it I just hadn't got a chance to get back with you that's all and I apologize for that, please forgive me for my unprofessionalism." I replied trying to pull my mind out of the gutter.

"Great its next weekend at 4pm to 10pm, ok? Don't wear your uniform wear a suit and try to come about two hours early, alright? The sooner I have you there the better."

"Cool."

"Alright, well I'm done for the day, I'll see you later." She replied walking to her car.

"All that body...what I would do for just a piece of it." I said out loud to myself secretly hoping that she heard every word.

I guess that Mrs. Jenkins was my fantasy freak. You know that one person that you would love to have sex with for one night all over everywhere for as long as you wanted. There was something about her that made her more attractive than what she really was. It's crazy because I could see a person that looked just like her and think nothing of it but the moment she pops up, I pop up, if you know what I mean. She was fine like a grain of gold but I think that I was more attracted to her for her intimidating aura. Maybe it was because of the fact that I knew that I couldn't have her, was the reason that I wanted her so bad. I wasn't truly sure but for whatever the case was the temptation behind being around her was beginning to be unbearable. Now because of her I was not only having a sticky ball problem but also a hard time keeping my hard times not so obvious.

....

"So do you love her?" Camry said smiling as he reclined his self on my couch and kicked up his feet.

"What? I mean I love her but I'm not in love with her if that's what you're asking?"

"Man, stop it. Of course you're still in love with her. Love just doesn't go away overnight. It hangs around just like the stink after you flush the shit down the toilet. If you don't give yourself time to detach your feelings then you're going to find yourself right back in the same relationship and susceptible to the same hurt that you felt before. You're going to fall head over heels for her and find yourself putting that ring that you already bought her right back on her finger. Then once you're back with her you're going to give the next man the satisfaction of saying he fucked your girl in front of you. Did you forget that you walked in on her riding gods second creation also known as the black incredible hulk?"

"Man." I replied rubbing my right hand across my face.

"There isn't no coming back from that bro. It's one thing to know or have a feeling that someone is cheating but to see it with your own eyes is a totally different type of hurt."

"You're right man that shit did hurt but how am I supposed to make all this work if I'm not able to control my emotions?" I asked scratching the top of my head. I wasn't scratching the top of my head because I couldn't figure this out on my own. I was scratching my head because I wasn't sure how the hell he knew all this vital information. Where the hell was he getting all this player wisdom? Camry did read a lot so maybe that was where it was coming from but I wasn't sure yet. I meant to ask him but every time I get around him to do it, it slips my mind a second later.

"You have to dig deep inside and say Tonya fuck you! All I want to do is fuck you and after I fuck you I don't want to fuck with you! You have to say that and mean it, or you could do what I said the first time and give yourself time to recover. You feel me? Instead of going back and messing around with her go try it out with some of your other exes until you've had enough time to detach a little more from Tonya. Tap into your inner player and start playing the game Austin! Tell them what they want to hear and you'll get what you want every time. Lie... Deceive... Manipulate."

"Who are you the devil?" I replied stunned by his advice.

"The devil...? Look man, you're an ex and that means that you are single with an advantage over the next man when it comes to dealing with your exes. That means that you can tell them all type of bullshit that a new guy they meet would tell them but because you already have a rapport with them you are more likely to be accepted faster and they will feel more comfortable doing so with you then with the next man ; as long as you weren't known as a liar or deceiver to her and even if you were its still possible to work in your favorite over the next man."

"Well what about my exes that I'm not cool with? You know the bad break up ones? Like Shayla?"

"Shayla...?"

"Yeah the one who shot my car up back in high school?"

"Oh you might want to leave her alone. Some exes you just have to let be. You want to try and do this as safe as possible without becoming a victim of you your own actions. That's the glory of having freedom of choice. You do what's best for you and live life. Don't make any bad choices or you could end up paying dearly for them."

"So what should I do? Which one of my exes would you choose?"

"I wouldn't choose any of your exes."

"I'm saying if you were me?"

"I wouldn't."

"What?"

"Don't get mad at me bro but you know every girl that you've wifed up has been "Ms. Queen Get around" with the exception of one girl and I'm not even sure if you made her your lady."

"Stop it ... ok maybe... ok your right but you're only saying that because you didn't really know them."

"I didn't and don't want to know the girl who didn't or doesn't understand that having sex with the whole neighborhood or half the football team wasn't a bad thing."

"Stop exaggerating I've never been with anyone like that."

"Yeah ok let you tell it."

"Whatever bro."

"If you really want my advice I suggest you make some new exes because the ones you already have should be on somebodies corner selling ass."

"Wow! That's low bro...But what do you mean make some new exes?"

"Did I stutter? Makes some new exes."

"Who does that? So what are you saying get with some people just to dump them just so she can be my ex?"

"Yup." He replied in a nonchalant tone as if nothing bothered him.

"What did you smoke before you came over here? Meth or crack...?"

"What?'

"You have to be high on something to be telling me some bullshit like that and thinking I'm just going to be your puppet and do it."

"Hear me out first. You go out and find you some woman then get cool with her and are the perfect boyfriend then dump her for some reason that's solely her fault but on good terms so you can still have a good vibe with her. That way you will have more variety when it comes to your choice in women because the ones that you have to choose from aren't the best of choices in any neighborhood. You are going to have to put a lot of work towards the average women you have so I figured that you might as well take all that energy and put it towards getting some new women."

"Ok, wait one minute. I need to know this before we go any further. How do you know all of this shit?" I asked scratching my head.

"Dude I graduated the top of my class in one of the best colleges in Atlanta. I could have triple majored if I wanted to. I just decided to do something different with my life because Sally Mae debt was getting too steep and school was becoming too boring for me. I don't know about you but I need challenges in my life. I challenge myself that's why I have been so successful now."

"You still didn't answer my question."

"Look man ... you remember seeing any movies where there was always one person whose sole role in the movie was to explain to the main character how to do everything and provide explanations on why certain things were happening?"

"Yeah like a narrator or umm Vivica Fox in Two Can Play That Game?"

Camry paused and looked at me with disgust on his face.

"What?'

"Out of all the movies and people that created roles like that you wanted to compare me to a woman?"

"What? She is a very successful one and it was a good movie."

"Ok ... you're right but if we were in a movie that person would be me. I know what I know because I know it. I'm just one of those people that know things for no apparent reason or explanation on how I know anything."

Instead of replying I just shook my head and smiled because senseless replies made so much sense to me you would think he said things with the intent for them to make perfect sense even though they made no sense when they came out of his mouth.

"So you're basically saying get married to get a divorce?" I replied.

"Hell no, you're thinking about all of this this way too hard Austin and it's really simple."

"But that's it basically."

"That is nothing like I said. We are talking about dating and practice marriage. Practice marriage is basically the whole boyfriend girlfriend thing nowadays especially once you shack up; it's all the same but no ring. It really doesn't count, like Allen Iverson said 'We're talking about practice? Practice... Practice... not the game but practice." Marriage is a bundle of commitment, dedication, and lifestyle. Dating compared to marriage is like previews before the movie starts. What it all boils down to is that marriage is the big picture. It's the reason for the previews in the first place. You get me?"

"It makes no sense at all bro but since you said it the way that you did it's starting to make all the sense in the world" I replied shaking my head.

"So what's the plan? Camry asked standing up and pulling his keys out of his pocket, preparing to leave.

"I guess to take a break from Tonya until I can get my feelings under control and find some other girls and more exes to work on."

"Good." He replied as he walked to the front door.

"Wait man... What about you and the wife? How has she been?

"She's good."

"Everything is running smooth?"

"We are still getting used to being married but for the most part we are good. You know how it is."

"What?"

"Nothing man, we are good bro... I'll get at you later." Camry replied leaving out of my place.

As soon as he shut the door my phone lit up with a text from Tonya.

-When are you coming over? I need you. -

Now I know Cam and I had just had this long talk about being strong and taking a break from Tonya but he didn't really say when this break was supposed to take place and by the looks of things between my legs, suddenly it was harder to cope with the idea of staying away from the one person I knew could fix my big problem. I would have liked to think that I was a stronger person than what I was displaying, but who was really hurting when I was being deprived from a well needed draining? A couple more times wasn't going to hurt nobody right? It was just sex right? All I had to do was have a little more control over everything that has been said so I won't find myself getting caught in the moment. If I did that then I was sure that everything was going to turn out ok.

Maybe Cam's words of wisdom was correct and taking a little time to detach my feelings might actually make things a lot less complicated but that meant I was going to have to come up with some type of excuse on why the time apart was called for without her thinking that she did something wrong or her feeling like I was trying to avoid her. I knew this was going to be complicated but not this complicated.

10

"Laura this is really a nice house and the jewelry was beautiful. It's not hard to believe that you just raised all that money." I said looking at the blue light water fountain centered in the middle of the pool.

"Yes twenty thousand dollars is enough to donate anywhere. I'm pretty sure that my foundation will be pretty happy with my donation." Laura replied taking a sip of her champagne out of her fat bottom wine glass.

Laura Jenkins was a longtime friend of mines that I had met oddly enough at one of Terrence's games. Her husband and Terrence were close and because of that we both just ended up getting cool and now we are like the best of friends.

"I'm telling you Crystal you're going to love it here in Atlanta. Its growing and becoming such a business oriented city. Just to see how far it has grown is amazing. This city has grown from a strippers refuge to a land of black stars and thriving new businesses; a mini Hollywood."

"Yeah... I should be settled in, in a month or so."

"You've already found a house?"

"Yeah girl you know that I don't play around. I'm so ready to get out of Texas, it's almost like I'm already gone."

"I know that it must have been hard for you to keep staying there after all of this mess has plagued you."

"Yes... the death threats, his family, and the harassment from the media... it's all just too much."

"Well ... hopefully you can have a new beginning here in the land of milk and honey."

"It looks like my job is done here Mrs. Jenkins would you like me to do anything else for you? A tall hard built man interrupted.

"No. Mr. Wells that will be all thank you so much for coming I don't know what I would have done without you."

"Imagine that. Anytime you need me you know all you have to do is call." He replied.

"Did I introduce you to my friend? This is Crystal Wilks, a longtime friend of mines." Laura said looking at him raising her eyebrow.

"Crystal? Austin...Nice to meet you. Are you from Atlanta?" He asked extending his huge hand towards me.

"No I'm originally from Detroit but I'm coming from Texas." I replied as my hand seemed to have gotten swallowed by his hard large catcher mitten type hand.

"Detroit?" He replied with a smirk on his face.

"Why the face?"

"I've had a lot of run-ins with Detroiters lately."

"Yeah I hear a lot of people from there are migrating down here so get used to it."

I must admit that I wasn't ready to meet anyone but at the same time if I had to make any exceptions this guy would be it. The fact that he was a security guard didn't bother me one bit because I had no interest in a life partner but his physical stature seemed like it would have definitely been the answer to some of my physical needs if I ever needed some attention. There was nothing like a tall well-built man who was a little rough around the edges and could put in a hard day's work to help me meet my needs.

"Before today I was feeling like that was more of a burden then a blessing but now I'm starting to believe otherwise." Austin replied with a big white smile.

"Laura you didn't tell me he was a charmer?" I said looking over at her slightly biting her lip and raising her eye brow. She turned away from him towards me and whispered in my ear.

"Girl please hit that for me ... don't let him get away without getting his number." She replied as she looked back at him and walked away."

"Is everything alright?" He asked as he watched Laura walk away. I had a habit of following eyes and I couldn't help but follow his directly towards her ass.

What was it about asses that men gave so much of their attention to. I understand most men are dominating sexually and less intellectually but they still didn't have to look at every ass that passed their sight. Laura did have a nice ass but her ass didn't look better than my face.

"Hugh um!" I falsely cleared my throat to get his attention back on what should have been the main attraction... me.

"How long have you known Laura?" I asked him.

"She has been my boss for some time now at the bank."

"Oh you have worked for her at the bank also?"

"Yes." He replied looking a little discouraged when he answered.

"How do you know her?" He went on to ask.

"Hmm.." I hesitated so I could give myself the time to come up with some lie to tell him because I didn't want to scare him away by telling him who my boyfriend was. "We have mutual friends." I went on to say carefully.

His phone violently vibrated in his pocket so loud that I could hear it.

"Excuse me." He said grabbing his phone and reading the text message to himself.

"I know that this a little unprofessional but do you think that we can hook up a little later outside of the fundraiser?" He blurted out after he read his text as if he was being instructed on what to do.

Normally it wasn't my thing to give out my number to regular folks like security guards but he was so confident and attractive that I didn't feel like I was doing anything outside of the norm. He kind of made stepping out of my normal go for guy alright. Plus Laura had already given him a good recommendation so I was feeling like he was good for the go. I gave him my number and watched him gallop away on the horse he seemed to ride in on in my life. Well really he walked away but for some reason I had pictured him as a stallion of some type. Soon as he left, Laura came up to me with the biggest smile I had ever seen her with anxiously waiting on me to tell her what we talked about.

"See? I told you Atlanta was going to be a good place for you." Laura exclaimed tapping her champagne glass into mines.

"I hardly define a security guard as the tone setter for me finding a good place. Why are you so geeked about him anyway?"

"He is fine."

"So are a lot of other men that have great careers and 401 K's... and?"

"Don't be fooled by a man's uniform baby. He's very educated. Just before he started working for me he was working for some high tech computer company. The place laid him off and it's been hard for him to recover I guess."

"Really?"

"Hell yeah, he's a good guy Crystal. I swear if I wasn't so loyal I would have him spreading my legs every day. The man should be a damn model or something."

"He is fine but Laura we are talking about a security guard."

"So, that's what's good about him."

"How is that?"

"Because you have a man that you can build and mold into something better than what he is used to being; kind of introduce him into a new life. He is not going to be used to the nice cars and big houses so when you introduce him to this type of life style and give him a taste of it he is going to be eating out of the palm of your hand or wherever else that you want him to eat out of. But you know how the men are that are already rich and use to this type of life. Most of them are spoiled, stubborn, and been around the block several times and when I say that I mean they have been around the block with Becky, Judi, Melissa and whoever else that has a name, an ass, and a pussy that stays around here. Men like Austin are much better to have because he has morals. One thing that I can admit is the more money that comes into people lives the less moral value they have to get it; it's like it becomes a drug or something. Men like Austin are like puppies on a leash out in public but beast in the bed room. If he is not good for anything else it's going to be a booty call for sure."

"Booty calls...?"

"Girl don't act like you're too good, everybody needs to let go a little."

"I'm just saying that I have toys for that."

"There is nothing like the real deal and trust me girl I've been staring at that bulge in the front of his pants for months now. He's the real deal."

"You are crazy!" I replied bursting out in laughter.

I couldn't believe Laura was talking the way the she was about Austin. She was happily married supposedly but if you heard her talking like she was tonight you would swear that she was already testing the water. I was tempted to ask if she had already done so with Austin. I needed to know because I hated messing with someone's sloppy seconds, especially a close friend's leftovers. Laura was offering Austin up on a platter right now but let some time go by and she find out her eye candy is something meaningful to me and her smiles will quickly turn to squinted eyes filled with envy.

11

"You really can do so much better; no man should be treating you like that. I'm so glad that we found each other Sharon. I missed you." I said to one of my long time ex girl friends that I had found on face book. She was having a hard time in her relationship with her baby daddy who had been locked up for a couple of months and during this time she had really just wanted somebody to talk to.

"I'm just sick of doing all of this all alone. Then he has the nerve to have me running his errands like I'm his bitch or something. He wants me to send him money every damn day and write him and send his homeboys money like they can send a dime back. Then he expects me to drive four hours to go see him as if I have gas money for all of that shit. It's just hard Austin." She exclaimed rubbing a single tear that rolled down her left cheek.

"Don't cry Sharon, you're too cute to be doing all of that crying. Any man who doesn't understand who he has and that what you're doing is amazing isn't worth your time."

I had already been at her place longer than expected and was trying to be patient but all she wanted to do was kiss for a couple of minutes every other hour then tell me more about her baby daddy. She had pictures of him everywhere in the house so I could tell that she missed him a lot but to me it really didn't mean anything because I was here.

As much credit as she deserved for being there for him the reality still stood that he was gone and I was here which meant it was only a matter of time before I showed her how

99

strong she wasn't and how much she didn't miss him but more so a touch of a man.

"I'm so tired. You know how strong I am? I'm doing this on my own! Do you know how much I miss him? You just don't understand!" She shouted leaning her head on my shoulder.

"Go ahead and vent baby ... I understand. You're one of the strongest women I've ever met and known that's why I got with you in the first place and I'm sure you miss him but don't stress yourself out Sharon it's only going to get better just hang in there. You're amazing." I replied getting irritated by her constant whining about her baby daddy. I couldn't help but look at my watch as I wondered how much more of this mess I was going to have to deal with.

"You really feel that way?"

"What way?"

"That I am one of the strongest girls that you know?" She asked lifting up her head and looking into my eyes. A light bulb seemed to have popped up on my head once I saw that my efforts weren't going in vain. It seemed like she was really listening to me and that it would really pay off if I fed her enough of this bullshit.

"Yeah...?! Why wouldn't I? You're a single mother maintaining a house hold and still holding down a man in prison. It's hard out here for single mothers I understand that Sharon. You're special because a lot of women can't do that. You're a jewel." I replied hoping that I didn't overdue it. Her eyes glistened as she looked up at me as if she was staring at a star.

"You ok?"

She smiled.

"I'm just relieved and happy to know that somebody actually understands and cares where I am coming from and what I have been feeling. Wait right here. I need to go check on Amari." She said getting up off her couch and walking back to her son's bedroom to go check on him as he slept.

Amari was just eight months but he was already a hand full from what I had seen. His dad had been locked up the same amount of time that he had been born se he didn't know his daddy at all in his early life. Sharon didn't want me around him because the possibility lingered that he could start perceiving that I was his father. It was cool with me because I wasn't here to be any body's replacement dad any way. I was here to rebuild a good rapport with his mom and hopefully pop a couple potential brother and sisters of his on her belly or in a condom wrapper compliments of his moms big fat lips or grade A pussy that I hoped she still had. I liked Sharon but the fact of the matter was that we had broken up for a reason. The sad thing was it was for the exact thing that she was doing right now. She wasn't strong enough. She could get smooth talked out of her panties quicker than it takes butter to melt on a hot summer day. She was one of them loyal women in her man's presence but after about twenty four hours of him not being around, her behavior was suspect. I was surprised that she had claimed to be waiting this long for her man. I think that it had to do less with her love for him and more with the time it took to recover after having the baby.

A piece of me didn't want to take advantage of her for the sake of her man. I had a soft heart for those guys locked up because they were basically defenseless but at the same time if

I wasn't over here benefiting from her man's mistakes and misfortunes then someone else would be who might have been ten times worse. Better me than someone else right? At least for myself I knew that she was going to be in good hands. Besides I didn't want much but a little bit of comfort and satisfaction just like her for a couple of hours out the day. Technically she was still his once I was done doing what I had intended to happen. I guess it wouldn't be possible if she didn't succumb to so much temptation and make it happen for the both of us.

I wanted to dig a little deeper into Sharon's mind and really try to understand where she thought she was this super woman. She probably was a superwoman but a poor excuse for a partner. Sharon was part of the statistic, a black single mother whose man was locked up and wanting her to stay down. Of course she would agree like most women were encouraged to do by elder women because if they loved the man it was the right thing to do. But Sharon just like so many other women had no idea what commitment and dedication meant until time and hardships showed them first hand. Sharon probably had friends in one ear telling her how stupid she was then in another ear his family and friends applauding her ability to keep supporting him and going after what she loved and wanted not only because it was honorable but because it took the pressure off them as far as needs from money to attention. The negative coming from one side and the positive coming from the other doesn't do anything but make things more confusing than what they already are. Most women start with good intentions until they find out that their determination was a cry out to the universe to challenge their goal. Nothing in this world that is desired comes without a challenge or a struggle, it's the way that the energy of the world determines how much you really want what you desire. Pain for muscles or no pain, no gain is what helps me better understand things. That's just how life works; once you declare you want something that benefits you there is something in this world that has a job to simply prove you wrong just to see if you're serious but to also make you appreciate what you have earned. If you succeed, another agent of this world if not the very same one that was trying to test you or hold you back aids you to your goals; if you fail then that same agent has the glory of saying that it told you so.

I can't do anything but respect a woman who can prove the world wrong by going against the odds, that is considered a strong woman. If you are declaring you're going to be committed and loyal to anything let alone a man then why not do just that? I understand it was hard but nothing seemed to be easy from the day of birth. Just thinking about it, walking takes up to nine to fifteen months and talking clearly takes much longer and so does basics like counting money. Nothing is or ever will be so easy that it doesn't take time to understand its principle. The main thing was that whatever you set out to do, you did it in this case or any other it shouldn't be any different. If Sharon could have done that then I would have married her.

Sharon came back into the living room smiling with nothing on but a long t-shirt that was probably her baby's daddies. She had a smile on her face that I loved because it brought her dimples out. Sharon was a pretty girl; long hair and long frame with a huge chest and a descent behind. She used to try and model because she was so tall but she never made it too far into the industry because she ended up getting side tracked by school and obviously her baby daddy. She was so goal driven but much more of a dreamer and less of a make it happen type of person. It kind of surprised me that I saw her standing in front of me with nothing but a t-shirt on but at the same time it saddened me because I really hoped she could have been stronger for the both of us. I could have been the bigger person and left but the whole reason I started the whole Exvantage thing in the first place was because I was horny and too lazy to start over by going through all the same old challenges most men went through to get to find themselves in bed with someone new. My plan was working too well but I wasn't sure I was as ruthless as I set out to be.

"Are you going to stare at me or are you going to make me feel better about myself? Can you make me feel good?" She said pulling the long t-shirt over her head and throwing it on the floor. Just when I thought that I had been feeling bad my sudden erection had reminded me why I was here in the first place as I stared up at her perfectly tear dropped formed double D breasts.

"You already know what I'm going to do!" I exclaimed unbuckling my pants and kicking them off onto the floor."

Just that fast it went from Sharon and I catching up and talking about life, to us having wild jungle sex around the living room furniture and floor. Butt naked sex was the best sex to me and she knew it. Despite how good the sex felt I couldn't help but look over at her baby daddy in the numerous pictures that were in the room. She didn't even have the courtesy to cover the pictures up or place them face down so he wouldn't be staring down at us. Then I couldn't help but thank God her child couldn't walk yet because if he could nothing would be stopping him from walking right in on our naked asses. Sharon's actions said one of two things to me. Either she was very desperate to finally have a man's touch or how selfish she was when it came to her loyalty to her man. She had none if you ask me. Maybe I was being a little insensitive in a time like this? Who was going to be doing all this analyzing about someone's character and decisions? I was doing so much thinking I was totally missing out on how her body felt.

"Do you miss.....me?" Sharon moaned out as she rode me like a horse on her couch.

I wanted to say not really but telling the truth wasn't part of the plan right now.

"Hell yeah....Awe...Damn I....missed you." I moaned back trying my hardest to ignore my harsh opinion on her actions and enjoy the moment.

I left Sharon's house satisfied with my success with operation Exvantage because I was accomplishing exactly what I had set out to do. It amazed me how easy it was for me to get what I wanted. I had talked to Sharon a couple of times before I had met with her today and look at what happened. It would have been ten times more complicated if I was trying to do this with someone new. The best thing about us hooking up is I was able to keep my feelings locked away and tell her what she wanted to hear so I could seal the deal. I was able to express my feelings with Sharon but not all that successfully with Tonya. Matter of fact things had gotten so complicated with her, I'm not sure if we were a couple again or not. I would be telling her one thing then the next another. I was telling her so much stuff that I was forgetting exactly what I was saying and losing track of my lies. It's crazy because last time I checked I was the one who had got hurt in this relationship so it seemed that she needed to do whatever she had to do to please me not the other way around. The last time that I had seen her was the night of the fundraiser a couple of nights ago. We had sex and dinner then cuddled the rest of the night. As much as I wanted to sit here and act like I was some player; I know when it had come to Tonya that I was clearly a sucker for love. I would go over to her place with the intentions of a man on a mission and end up telling her how much I loved her. I didn't know if it was her pussy doing that to me or if that was just me. It seemed like every time we had sex I couldn't help but start feeling all these lovey dovey feelings afterwards. Being with Sharon today was definitely going to help me learn how to better deal with Tonya as time goes on.

....

The fundraiser was cool. I got a chance to make some extra money and meet a lot of different people. Mrs. Jenkins was looking real eatable at the fundraiser too. I know her booty had called my name several times and she winked at me at least three times. I know she was married but if she gave me the chance I'm not going to lie to myself and act like I wouldn't hop on the opportunity to pound that ass to sleep. She introduced me to her friend Crystal who was very attractive and articulate but she shocked me when she gave me her information. I know I am an attractive young man and irresistible to some women but I had never attracted a woman of the caliber that she appeared to be. I intended on calling her I just haven't gotten around to it yet. She seemed a little guarded so I was feeling like I was going to have to take a different approach with her. I was worried about all the effort I may have to put in just to get in the bed with her. I wasn't sure what I was going to do about Crystal but once I built up the courage I was going to give her a try.

It had been a while since I had heard from Camry so I was definitely planning on calling him to inform him of my progress. It usually wasn't like him to not keep in touch with me for this long so he was either incredibly busy or trying to take his relationship to another level with his wife. I'm not sure what it was but sooner or later I was going to find out.

12

"No I'm not sleeping on the damn couch! You sleep on the damn couch!" I yelled drying myself off with a towel and getting myself ready for bed.

"I'm so sick of you not listening to me Camry... I'm crying out to you and pleading with you to listen to me Camry please, I'm just..."

"Blah, Blah, Blah...I'm crying and pleading with you Camry please...Linda stop! What are we arguing about here? I thought we had solved the problem already. We were arguing about the same thing weeks ago... What is the problem?"

"The problem is nothing has changed! You think because you took a day off or two that was going to fix everything? This isn't what I signed up for Camry."

"Signed up for? What is this a charity event? What you mean what you signed up for? This is a marriage. You vowed before a man of God that this is what you wanted and here it is before you, flesh and blood."

"Is it? Is it really Camry? Lately it's been feeling no different than a fling all we're really doing is shacking up and having random sex every now and then that hasn't been all that great as of lately might I add."

"You're right it hasn't, but maybe it would be better if you did more than lay on your back all day and let out your little fake ass moan... oh...oh ...my God! Stop it with that fake ass shit. If you don't like it then you don't like it but find another way to make it better. Try throwing that ass back at me or putting my dick in your mouth without me having to initiate contact with your bedroom boring ass. It doesn't make any sense that you have all that body and no moves. What happened to you?" I exclaimed flopping down on the side of the bed.

"Oh so it's me? I'm faking and boring? So why the hell did you marry me Cam? You weren't complaining before…"

"Because before you had all the right moves; You were a beast in the bedroom but now that we are married and your locked in its like your saying fuck it. I feel like I'm having sex with my grandma and the problem is she may be more of a freak then you in real life at eighty-two."

"Bitch…"She shouted sending a right hook right across my jaw.

"What the hell!" I yelled tucking and rolling out the way.

"You know what Camry I'm sick of this shit…did you just say Grandma! I'll tell you what; since it was only good when we were dating and you will never get that back how about you go get Jacky and Palmetta and get better acquainted since my grandma ass can't please you." Linda replied grabbing her pillow and blanket.

"Where you think you going?"

"Fuck you! " She exclaimed turning for the door.

"No fuck you!" I yelled jumping out of the bed and charging towards her. I grabbed her by the arms and threw her onto the bed.

"Stop Camry...Let me have my space!" She yelled bouncing back up to her feet and charging to the door.

"Hell no!" I yelled grabbing her night gown and ripping it off her body down to the floor."

"What are you doing to my gown...Stop!" She yelled as I threw her naked body back to the bed.

"Shut up!" I yelled dropping my boxers revealing my fairly large erection and climbing on top of her.

"Camry no!"

"Shut up." I demanded as I forced open her legs and pushed my way inside of her.

"Cam... no..." Her yell smoothed out to a moan.

I ignored her request and began to thrust repeatedly inside of her. It seemed like every inch I went into her it seemed to ease my mind and her mood.

"I hate...you... I... hate...Cam...!" She moaned out as I kept up a steady pace.

Linda and I were at a breaking point but as much as I didn't want to admit it we were really falling apart as a couple but also as friends. We couldn't talk to each other like we use to or even find the time to do as we pleased with each other. She was becoming more demanding and I was becoming more distant but I didn't know exactly what to do to fix it. All I wanted to do was make more money so financially we could be more stable. We would have all our bills taken care of and our debt paid off with some lead way to enjoy life but she didn't seem to understand that. The time apart was a standing issue but there were much more problems that we both had to complain about. With me she was just too damn needy. It's seemed like she complained about everything even about how I wore my clothes. She even said something the other day about how I brushed my teeth. I swear I wanted to punch her just to see if I could knock some compliments out of her mouth. Not only did she want more time but she wanted a baby like yesterday. I wanted a baby too but who has time and money for one of those things right now. Plus she isn't fit to be no mother. The last time she had her baby niece over our house she dropped the child on her head twice and blamed it on the baby. The baby was only eight months! What the hell can a baby so small do to control a person so much that you end up dropping her on her head? The child had lumps so big in her head you would swear she was growing horns. I'll be damned if we were to have a baby only so she could drop it on the floor. Until I feel she is ready I'm going to have to stick to my guns and say no for my sanity and the unborn child safety. I love Linda but she isn't much of a long term thinker she is more of an impulse type of person that I would say doesn't make the best decisions simply because of that reason. Then finally there is the number one issue, sex.

I don't know where everything went wrong but it couldn't have gone any worse. The sex was so boring. The only reason I say it isn't horrible is because I enjoy sex so much I could look forward to having it in my sleep. I'm not a person that is hard to please which says even more about how the sex has been. I feel like I'm fucking a dead body. Some days she just stares up at me like she is somewhere else on the planet then when she finally gets started it's like she is auditioning for remake of Star Whores or a remake of Deep Throat Down. I can tell she is acting and I hate it; she is so damn phony. Then the fact that I was always the one initiating the sex bothered me because it made it seem like I was the only one that wanted it. I like to be pursued every now and then too. Sometimes I like to lay back and watch the beauty of a woman's body work. But I guess with her it's too much to ask for. Then she had the nerve to bring up me using Palmetta and Jacky to get the job done; well big deal, it's not like I haven't done it before. I have jacked off with her lying next to me before. To be honest I masturbate daily to keep myself from cheating on her. I found myself having to get one off while driving down Peach Street one time. I came up with a catchy little phrase for it and everything "JWD" jacking while driving isn't that slick? But that's just a testament to how bad things had been. I am a married man but I'm so desperate for a nut that I have to try to fulfill the urge anyway I can by risking my life, risking my dignity and other people's lives all while jacking off at the wheel. If it wasn't for Vaseline and free porn on the internet I would have cheated on Linda a long time ago. Sometimes I feel like I am cheating on her with these porn sites. It's addictive if you ask me, something like a drug. There is something about cybersex that turns me on beyond explanation. Maybe it's the fact that it's safe or I don't have to worry about impressing anyone or pleasing no one but myself but all I know is when I am enjoying porn my erection is so full long and hard like I had popped a Viagra or something. Linda would have to put in some real work to get it like that. The fact that I could have this type of attention anywhere didn't help anything. It helped a lot when I was waiting on clients in my car. I had been parked in the driveway and waiting for ten minutes surfing the web on my laptop; I went to type in boots and booty popped up.

One thing led to another and I was dry stroking in the driveway. I was one zip and a button away from getting caught. If it wasn't for my rearview mirror and a quick reaction I would have been caught dick handed and probably would have lost what turned out to be a home owner that day. My little problem had gotten so bad that it had actually taken up all my free time. So much so that I wasn't returning peoples texts like I was supposed to unless it was business; not even when it was Austin he would call and text me a couple of times throughout the day but if I wasn't at work or at home fighting with Linda I was having a threesome with Jacky and Palmetta.

I knew that I needed to see Austin soon because he needed me to help him with the whole Exvantage thing. He was probably done with the whole project and hugged up in bed with Tonya telling her how much he was done trying to be a player or something. They were probably hugged up telling each other how glad they were that things worked out for the best. I had faith in my boy but at the same time I knew exactly what pussy could do to a man's mind. It was like a remote control if you weren't careful of its power. His life seemed to be better than mines regardless if he was doing well with the project Exvantage or whether he was back with Tonya. He wasn't married which by law meant that he could do whatever he wanted to do without any legal consequence. I was screwed on the other hand. In times like these I regretted my marriage because it makes me think like we had rushed things after all this time. Over the years both our agendas changed, I guess we were both supposed to be proud parents right now and madly in love but obviously that was far from the case. Our relationship had stopped being about family and more about finance like most relationships nowadays. Most likely it was my fault but I think that we're both to blame for the status in our relationship. Plus the country was hanging on by a thread right now so a baby would be less like a good move and more like a desperate one to get more money back on our taxes if you asked me.

God I'm so tired...

Where was he in this whole marriage thing anyway? I could have sworn God was the whole reason why a pastor was included in marriage in the first place. Wasn't he supposed to be a supporting cast in the whole marriage? Then why were my wife and I in so much trouble with our marriage like so many other married couples? Why had so many people got a divorce over the years?

Nowadays it seemed like people were getting divorced just as fast as they got married. Was that because people were getting married for the wrong reasons or the huge influence that the media had on couples breaking up? There were shows out on T.V now that supported the idea of women breaking away from men and demanding them to be a certain way or else. But was that really helping us or making things worse? Marriage seemed to be more like a fad and less like forever like it was intended to be. I knew we were subject to this but at the same time I was hoping that we could be the couple that slipped through the cracks. I was tempted numerous times to cheat on my wife. I can't count how many times I was hit on by a single mother moving into a new home who wanted me to help her with the price of the house or even by gay couples (women of course) who offered me the night of my life. I had to catch myself several times because I didn't want to risk my marriage but it was incredibly hard.

I needed to vent...

13

"I'm telling you man things couldn't get any worse between Linda and I. She has been nagging and complaining like clock-work. I don't know how much more I can take." Camry said.

"That's too bad... deal with it, your married to a good one." I replied hunching my shoulders.

"Really?" He replied as if he didn't know... "Wait a minute... That's all you have to say is deal with it? Are you serious? You're supposed to be my boy and all you can say is deal with it? Whose side are you on?" Cam said grabbing an old football from off of the ground.

We were at a park not far from my place that sat off the lake throwing the football around trying to catch up on all we had missed with each other. The leaves were changing colors and fall was making its presence known but the heat from summer was more intense than ever. No matter how hot it was there was no stopping the activity of kids being present. Parents were high in attendance as their kids played with a ball on the huge playground. Beautiful women were walking around in there summer dresses and short shorts and guys were trying their best to impress them riding around in their souped up cars; Which did nothing but make it another typical day in Atlanta.

"What do you mean whose side am I on? You're my boy and because you're my boy I feel that it's my duty to inform you that you are tripping."

"How am I tripping?"

"You're a married man… That's what married men do. They argue and then they make up. The whole challenge of being married is to appeal to the idea of problem solving. That's what people who are married are supposed to be or become experts in solving problems and we know the key to solving problems is compromising."

"I've been doing that man. But she is just tripping like she's on her period all the time."

"Wait, on her period all the time bro? So that's what's this is about? She hasn't been giving you the booty?"

"Yeah she has been giving up the booty but it's been boring… I have a better time … never mind."

"No finish your sentence man, better time doing what?" I replied throwing the football hard into his chest.

"Nothing man." He replied throwing it back just as hard.

"Don't tell me you're cheating on Linda? Bad ass, sexy ass, big booty ass Linda?"

"Watch it man that's my wife and no I haven't been cheating on her."

"Yeah right!"

"I haven't but sometimes it feels like I am without actually doing it."

"How? What are you going out on dates? Seeing other women? What?"

"It don't matter man just change the subject."

"Hell no! We have to get to the bottom of this." I said walking up closer to him… "Don't tell me you're gay."

"What? Hell no!"

"Then why don't you answer the question?"

"Because I don't want to."

"Damn that's for us bro? We keep secrets now? Ok…cool. After all this time I thought we were boys." I replied shaking my head.

"Man, stop acting so sensitive… I'll tell you but let's go sit on the bench. I'm tired of throwing this damn ball around." He replied leading me to an empty park bench that sat in front of the large lake like pond.

"What's up man? It's that deep?"

"Not really I just don't want all these random people in my business that's all."

The bench wasn't all that big so we had to sit kind of close so the both of us could fit on it. It was a bench that was made for only two people I guess.

"What's up bro?"

"I'm saying man all Linda and I do is fight… I'm so tempted to go mess around with somebody else it's ridiculous. I mean it shouldn't be like this bro… I'm struggling badly and I never thought I would be feeling like this…"

"But what is she doing other than bitching? It sounds like you're nitpicking."

"No, she wants kids."

"And?"

"We can't afford any damn kids!"

"How? You're the most successful person I know at your age."

"So? That don't mean were ready for any kids! In a couple of years maybe but right now she's not responsible enough to have no damn kids. You know my niece is still a little messed up from when she dropped her on her head."

"Damn... I forgot about that... You're right she isn't ready for any kids."

"Now you feel me."

"So that's what this is all about? It can't be." I replied picking up a small rock and throwing it into the water.

"Man..." He replied saying nothing else but shaking his head.

"Tell me how you feel like you're cheating on her bro; that's why we came over here in the first place. You got me sitting all close to you on this couples bench like we lovers or something. Hurry up and tell me before I get an Indian burn from constantly bumping elbows with you on this small ass bench!" I exclaimed.

"Well, like I said I'm not cheating on her but I get offers all the time from clients and old friends about hooking up. Sometimes I have to think hard because I sometimes consider going through with it."

"What? So thinking about it got you feeling like your cheating?"

"Yeah…"

"You're leaving something out. I've known you for too long to think otherwise. Who else are you fucking?'

"I'm not doing anyone else."

"Then what is it?"

He shook his head and looked down at the ground between his legs and then off into the pond.

"Ok, but don't laugh man."

"I won't…" I replied cracking a smile.

"You swear?"

"Yeah man damn!"

"Alright… I'm married but I have to masturbate daily to keep from cheating on her."

"Whoa TMI…"

"Come on man, damn you ask me to talk to you and now I'm talking and you talking about some TMI… forget it!"

"Alright man, chill damn… I see this is a sensitive subject. So what you jack off; you're doing what you have to do right?"

"Yeah but it's like I have to do it every where all the time because things have gotten so bad. It has got to the point where I'm making up terms and getting creative with it."

"What? You're telling me too much now. I don't want to hear about your jacking off escapades."

"Bro you just begged me to tell you and now I'm telling you damn! You're going to listen to this shit. It has gotten so bad that I find myself jacking off at the wheel while I'm driving. I call it "JWD" Jacking while driving."

I cut my eyes at him and looked at him in his eyes.

"Fucked up I know... crazy isn't it?" He asked.

Instead of replying I started thinking about how ironic it was that I was going through the exact same thing and even came up with the exact term. I knew exactly how he was feeling but the only difference was that I wasn't about to tell anyone how bad things had got and how desperate I was to bust a nut. For some reason I felt I had guilt written all over my face so I quickly began thinking of ways I could separate my mess from his.

"JWD? Who comes up with phrases for times when they are masturbating?" I exclaimed in a laughter maybe a little too loud but failed to realize until two females who were passing by stopped and looked at the both of us with a look of disappointment.

"You know what they say about the cute ones." One of them said as they passed by.

"Could you put my business out on the streets any clearer? Damn you might as well announce it on a microphone at a Jay Z concert." Camry exclaimed embarrassed by the females reactions.

"Man forget about them, you will probably never see those chicks again in your life. Who cares what they think. What we need; I mean, what you need to be concerned about is your marriage, nothing else really matters bro. You have a good one that a lot of dudes would fight to have man…Don't take your good fortune for granted." I replied with a smirk on my face.

"What the hell is that look for?"

"Nothing I just wish your life could be going as good as mines right now." I replied smiling.

"What? What are you talking about? Don't tell me you and Tonya got back together?"

"Man to be honest I don't know what's going on between us. I just came from her place now that you brought it up."

"Please don't tell me you're back with her."

"I don't know man… its complicated. I think she thinks we are back together but nothing has been set in stone."

"You better be careful man it's starting to look like one of you are going to get hurt."

"I'm good man she is the least of my worries. But let me tell you about Sharon and Tiffany."

"Are you talking about Sharon from High School and Tiffany from middle school? Big booty and fat lips Tiffany? I didn't even know she still stayed down here. I had heard she had moved to California or something."

"Yeah she is still around and thank God she is still around for me when I need her."

"How did you find them? I thought Tonya made you get rid of all of your old contacts when you two were together?"

"Facebook is the number one find a missing person site. I have met so many old friends on there it is ridiculous."

"Really? So what about her?"

"Ok so let me tell you about Tiffany. You know she is a stripper now. They call her tail feather. You should see the tricks she can do in the bed."

"She's a stripper now? Why doesn't that surprise me? Why does every big booty fat lipped girl in the city end up stripping when times get hard?"

"I don't know but she says she is doing it to get by in school and put food on the table for her three kids."

"Three kids? Damn! Any of them call you daddy yet?"

"Actually her daughter did but you know that shit went in one ear and out the other."

"Wow."

"What?"

"Nothing man, just tell me about Sharon."

"She still has a nice body but she has a six or 8 month old son now."

"Where is her man?"

"He's locked up for a while."

"Damn when does he get out?"

"I forgot. Why?"

"Because you don't want to run into him by surprise when he gets out. You're doing this for some ass not for your ass to get handed to you."

"Yeah you're right"

"Well it sounds like everything is going good with you but why do you keep getting back with the least desirable exes? Whatever happened to Marie Lovejoy? She was perfect, have you tried finding her?"

"Damn why did you have to bring her up? I thought about looking for her but I haven't yet. I'm still a little mad at her. I'm still messed up about how she just left. We would have been married by now and everything. A piece of me just wants to get back with her so she can fall in love with me and then that's when I'm going to be the one that just ups and leaves. I want her to see how I feel."

"Stop; let's not forget why you're doing this in the first place. You're only doing this for a less complicated way to get some ass remember? Remember the whole thing about being an ex makes it easier to hook up with past lovers? Put all those feelings back in the closet and keep it moving. When you're doing shit like this you have to think little head first, big head second and heart dead last!" Camry said putting emphasis on his words.

"Yeah you're right."

"I know I'm right."

"But answer this since you have all the damn answers so why aren't you doing it yourself? I know you're married but I need a pro to show me how it's done. Linda is fine as hell but she will never know. Besides it will fix that reflex problem you have now when you sit down and put your hand in your lap."

"What?" Camry replied looking down at his hand that was still unconsciously running back and forth across his zipper in the high thigh area? "Oh shit!" He exclaimed folding his arms.

"Bro I get pussy everyday now and I'm just getting started. I have plenty of more exes I plan to see before the month is over. I'm in heaven."

"No, man, despite all the mess me and Linda are in, I love her too much to cheat on her. That's why I haven't yet. It's one thing to be tempted but it's another to actually indulge in that temptation. I'm good." He replied looking off into the pond.

"Well let me know how all the dates with your hands go... Meanwhile I'm going to be diving in so many asses they're going to have to name a swimming style after me. How about the ass stroke?" I said getting up and chuckling.

"You are a trip man... the ass stroke?" Camry replied as we made our way through the park and back to our cars.

14

Austin Wells

"WHY DON'T YOU WANT TO GO OUT WITH ME? All we do is have sex and hang around my place. What the hell is that? I'm just an overnight booty call? I'm getting sick of that mess." Tonya exclaimed in disdain.

"Are you really trying to complain right now? Let me get a couple of hours of sleep before you start complaining like this." I replied rolling over on my side looking over at the big red lit alarm clock. It was 2:30 in the morning and I had to go to work in about five hours.

Tonya and I had just got done doing what she was complaining about but she swore up and down on God's green earth that she loved it and couldn't get enough of it. I hadn't talked to her about how she felt or may have thought about us yet but judging by her actions I was definitely going to have to say something before it got too far out of hand. I knew I needed to say something because earlier in the day she had mentioned kids during sex. She was trying to get me not to wear a condom and once she convinced me she tried to keep me inside of her when it was time for me to climax. If I didn't have any self-control I probably would have done something I regretted. She was trying to get too serious with me too fast. It had only been a couple of months since she had sent that big black Negro of hers packing back to Detroit and now she is acting like she had never done anything wrong. I could understand her urgency to want to move on from the past because she was the one who messed up but I was still hurt by her and in my zone. I was having fun with her and everybody else I reunited with. The whole commitment thing now that I look at it seemed like a waste of time if you weren't married. I wasn't getting married no time soon so there was no sense in me acting like I was married to some woman I could only see myself sleeping with. Marriage was for guys like Camry; But the sad news was that even Camry was doubting his purpose. Talk about scary ...

"Yeah whatever Austin, you think your ass is slick or some kind of player but I'm on to your little game. I'm not about to play with you anymore. Go ahead and go to sleep but once you wake up get your shit, go to your place and don't come back here until you figure out what you want to do." She said pulling most of the cover off of me as she turned her back from me and buried herself in her pillow and covers.

"I'm trying to sleep." I replied.

"Yeah ok ... you heard what I said boy! Don't have your stuff out and you will see some bum wearing it."

By the time she got done nagging I had lost another hour of sleep. I was so irritated with her trying to act like nothing was wrong. It seemed like she wanted me to think that she had never did anything wrong. Well at least that is how she was acting. But I guess that way of thinking was typical especially when the suspect was trying to make amends. I loved Tonya but now that more women were coming into my life I was beginning to care less about who she was and what she could do for me. As a matter of fact I was supposed to be seeing not an ex but an old friend that I use to mess with after I got off of work today. I had found her off Facebook like I did Sharon and Tiffany. Her name was Alicia Jones. She used to be the quiet book worm type back in high school but freakier than what anybody would expect. I was looking forward to seeing her again after all this time and I was hoping that very little had changed about her.

For that hour of sleep that I had lost I was up thinking about Tonya trying to understand what could possibly make her think that everything was alright and we could pick up where we left off. She should still be kissing my ass right now for what she had done. It was kind of tripping me out that she just wanted to act like nothing happened. To be honest every time she rode me I couldn't help but picture her riding Mr. Porter like some damn horse. There was nothing like trying to act like you weren't traumatized from an event. I know it sounded odd but that's exactly how I felt. In certain positions I just felt like I was him.

Was that normal?

Most people would say that it isn't healthy and to leave it alone but I believe I was more into making her regret her actions over my own dignity. With my other exes it was about sex but with Tonya it was about more than that. It was about making her miss what she messed up and drooling to get me back. She was close to that point but not fully, so to get that effect maybe I needed to back off a little more but also treat her ten times better when we did see each other. So then she would want more.

Another hot day at work was the least of my worries. It was finally raining cats and dogs but it was still hotter than an oven in hell. I was exhausted from my late night with Tonya and honestly needed a break but I couldn't afford to take any days off especially with how much I was driving. I was going from house to house so much, gas had become another bill I had to add to my monthly budget. Camry hadn't told me that this lifestyle could get expensive. The good thing was that I was able to avoid dates and make nothing but house calls which helped me keep a decent amount of money in my pocket. Most girls would have wanted to be taken out and spoiled but I didn't have the funds for that. That was the best thing about already having a relationship with someone from the past; I no longer had to go through the courting stage most women required men to do when they first met them. I had passed that test a long time ago so it was no need to go through that mess again. Tiffany did bring up us going out a couple of times with her kids some places but I would always find a way to spin her so we didn't have to go out. I had her convinced that my time was limited so all we ever had time to do was have sex.

Standing in the moist heat I couldn't help but think about what mess Camry was in with his wife. Linda was a keeper and he was on the brink of giving his gold to someone else. You know they say one man's trash is the next man's treasure; well Linda was nothing but treasure, there was nothing trashy about her and he knew it. He couldn't even begin to treat her like trash if he wanted to because she was one of the most beautiful women in Atlanta. Camry is my boy and all but there is a piece of me that envies him so much that sometimes it's hard to hide it. I would love to have Linda on my arm, to me it wouldn't matter how sorry she was in the bedroom. At least she isn't out fucking Khyel or God knows who. I wonder if she is going through the same thing sexually as he is. What if she was using a vibrator when he wasn't around ... what if she was "VWD?" Vibrating While Driving? I wonder if it was really that bad for the both of them and if it was what do you do at that point?

How do you fix something that's broken as serious as the motion in the bedroom? Now that I think about it I'm glad that I am not the one married because I would have cheated a long time ago. Camry and I were going through the same thing and we were in totally different circumstances. Since I was single I could see how I could fall into a little drought concerning sex but he was married. The only struggles he was supposed to be having were in any other area except the bedroom. One thing I understood about marriage was that sex was supposed to be unlimited, if it wasn't then what the hell was the point. If there were still going to be restrictions then they might as well be dating right? The whole thing didn't make sense to me but I guess that it wasn't for me to figure out.

....

An erection rose in my black khaki work pants as I watched Mrs. Jenkins pull up in her brand new Ford Focus. Rain was still coming down pretty hard so she sat in the car for a second until she built the courage to come out and face the fact that she was about to get wet for me I would like to think.

"Good lord I can't believe that it is raining out here like this; I'm all wet now. I don't know why I didn't bring my umbrella. I usually have one sitting in the car but since it's new I forgot to put it in there. How are you today Mr. Wells?" Mrs. Jenkins asked after she ran into the waiting area where I was standing looking out into the parking lot through the large glass doors.

Two things had caught my attention; how wet she was and how visible her nipples were poking through her red silk blouse.

"Mr. Wells?" She said popping her shirt to get the standing water off of it. Her blouse was already low cut and she had the nerve to bend over a little bit as she popped the water off which did nothing but expose more of her chest.

"Mr. Wells? "She repeated this time looking up at me and catching my eyes locked on her breasts. I noticed her noticing so I quickly tried to regain my composure and answer her question.

"Umm, yes...I'm good Mrs. Wells... I mean Mrs. Jenkins. Just enjoying this beautiful day." I replied now finding it hard to make eye contact with her.

"Don't tell me you're one of those no matter what type of day it is; it's a beautiful one, type of person are you?" She asked straightening her posture.

"Not really... An ugly day is an ugly day but what makes an ugly day like this beautiful are the things it produces..."

"Like what flowers, trees and germination?" She replied smacking her lips trying to indicate how lame I sounded.

"No ... I mean those are good things too but it doesn't compare to how the water makes the prettiest women more beautiful as it runs down their skin or how the water makes their clothes stick to their body revealing a true roller coaster with all its impressive curves that normally no man but their man would be able to see." I blurted out. By the time I realized what I was saying to my boss it was too late because I was done saying it. Surprisingly she looked up at me and smiled.

"Come to my office... I just remembered there were a few things I needed to discuss with you..." She replied walking away.

"Right now?"

"Yes Mr. Wells."

I was hesitant to follow her because I had been in her office before but that was only when I got the job. The only other reason I could imagine that she wanted to see me in there was to fire me. All because I couldn't keep my big mouth shut I was about to get fired and probably arrested for some feministic reason that she felt was violated at this moment. What ever happened to freedom of speech?

Nowadays nothing was to be said out loud and if it was then you had to be prepared to face the sure enough to come consequences. To me it kind of defeated the whole purpose of declaring that law. To me it really wasn't an amendment it was just a statement stating the obvious. The only reason it was a law was to make people aware of how much the country wanted to be in control of everything all the way down to your speech. They knew from the beginning that they couldn't control any bodies tongue but they didn't want anyone to realize that because then that wouldn't work in their favor right? They made it a law to make it seem like the only reason we can say what we want is because they allow it. But even that has a limit because if we say the wrong thing to the wrong person then your ass will be thrown in jail, prison or possibly beat in the back of an alley by the police department who are supposed to be here to serve the people but what people? I'm not sure that they are referring to all people.

"Shut the door behind you." She said as she walked behind her desk and sat down. "Have a seat Austin..." She demanded suddenly using my first name.

"O...k..." I replied recognizing her I'm about to fire your ass tone gathering in her throat. I sat down in one of the two leather chairs that she had placed in the front of her desk. She logged in to her flat screen computer as she sat down and clicked a couple of buttons while I waited in silence. On her wall behind her she had a picture of a woman taking a bull down by the horns. I had never seen anything like that but it said a lot to me about how she felt within.

"You are a college grad right?" She asked still looking at her computer.

"Yes... I graduated and got my degree in computer engineering."

"You use to work at copy print but you were one of the many they laid off because they were downsizing?"

"Correct."

"So why are you working as a security guard? Do you want to do this forever?"

"Huh? No... I'm only working this job because I need a constant flow of money to pay the bills. It's not my passion or anything."

"Have you tried to find another job that has placement for engineers?"

"Of course... I've submitted my resume to over twenty companies not only in Atlanta but Georgia alone. I've even submitted in numerous companies out of state. They're just not getting back to me."

She stood up and walked over to her window and closed her blinds that looked out onto the main parking lot. Then she walked past me to her door and closed the blinds that were on it and windows.

"So have you talked to my friend Crystal?"

"Crystal?" I replied puzzled on where she was going with this. "Umm… No not yet but I intend to … It kind of slipped my mind."

"Really? She's a very attractive woman; how could you forget about her?"

"I've just been busy that's all."

"Do you have a girlfriend? Are you married?"

"Excuse me?"

"You heard me Austin… Answer the question." She replied sitting down in the chair next to mine but turning it so she could face me.

"Umm… No I don't have a girl and no I'm not married but what does that mean…"

"Are you gay? They always say the cute ones are gay." She blurted out sliding her skirt up her thigh. She didn't have on any stockings and I couldn't help but glance at her perfectly built legs. A horse would be jealous if they had seen how well they were put together.

"No, nothing even close to it…" I replied having a hard time concentrating on her questions.

I never felt that I would find any discomfort being out in this position I was in. I couldn't count how many times I had fantasized about moments like this one with Mrs. Jenkins. I was so desperate for moments like this I had even prayed for them a couple times. But now that it was happening instead of thanking the lord I was more nervous than a black man in a court room with an all-white jury.

"Then what's the problem?" She asked rubbing her finger down her thigh.

"Nothing I've just been busy..."

"You know that you have worked for me for a while now...I see you every day looking at me. We flirt back and forth all the time and I was wondering when is he going to get the balls to say what he wants?"

"Wow."

"Do you know what you want Austin?' She asked lightly biting her lip.

I was almost in shock... This had come totally out of left field... I wasn't prepared.

"Do you think I'm attractive Austin?"

"Hell yeah."

"Then stop staring at me and take this ass..." She demanded getting up and turning her back towards me and bending down over her desk. I was over whelmed by the sudden adrenaline rush that came over me.

"Mrs. Jenkins are you..."

"Boy shut the hell up and go to work!" She yelled as she lifted up her skirt.

"Oh…Lord…" I blurted out as she exposed her bare behind to my virgin eyes. Well not virgin but that's how she made me feel. Her behind was perfectly placed; each cheek filling its rightful place outside the single red line that ran down the two.

There wasn't too much more convincing that I had to tell myself and there wasn't too much more things she had to say for me to catch the hint. I did exactly what she told me to do and that was go to work. I couldn't help but look up at her large picture that was directly in front of me, you know the one with a woman taking the bull by horns. I was learning that she lived by that strong and straight forward type of lifestyle. You couldn't get any more blunt then how she was right now. I guess today was one of those days or something because her actions were totally out of nowhere. Maybe it was the rain or something from home but whatever it was I couldn't help but thank Jesus that I was benefitting from it. I tried not to look at her big ass wedding ring on her finger or the surprise of her husband's name tattooed on her behind. I tried to keep my hand gripping the part of her ass where his name was tattooed so it would be covered up and out of my view.

"Harder!" she demanded.

It had to have been a while for her because she didn't feel like she had been having frequent sex. She felt so good I had to stop several times to keep from cumming so fast. I couldn't believe that Mrs. Jenkins was giving me the butt. As happy and excited as I was you would think that it was all any man ever wanted and thought about but not me. For some reason I thought about Linda, Cams wife. Mrs. Jenkins was one of the most professional and polished women I had ever seen. She usually was very disciplined and flashy with her wedding ring and boastful about whom her husband was but yet and still she had thrown herself at me like she was desperate for something more than sex. Why?

I knew her husband was very successful and very busy. I didn't see much of him at her fundraiser or ever for that matter. Matter of fact the only reason I knew anything about him was because he was in the cities weekly magazine as one of the city's most influential men. But yet and still his wife was here with me explaining to me how to fuck her. I hadn't been more confused in my life about women at this point. What the hell did women want? She had it all so what the hell could be the problem?

Earlier in the day I was trying to side against my homeboy and defend Linda but this was telling me that maybe there wasn't any satisfying women. I said it before; a lot of women aren't satisfied with a good man for too long. After a while it seems like they want something entirely different. It didn't matter if it was all around better or worse just as long as it was something different. I say it didn't matter, solely off the fact that she had a man who was beyond the American dream and here she was throwing it back at a security guard? No doubt I looked better than her husband so kudos to me and probably packing more meat in my pants but she wouldn't have known that until now.

What if Linda was doing the same thing to my best friend all because things were a little shaky? He said that he was a little sexually frustrated which meant that she was too. He also said that he was considering stepping out on her so that meant that she could be thinking about the same thing. But what did he say she was making such a big fuss about?

Oh!

Working too much right? So the problem was the lack of attention. She wasn't getting enough of the right attention from him. I couldn't help but think that Mrs. Jenkins was facing a similar problem with her marriage and finally reached her breaking point.

So I wonder if Linda was acting this way with Camry because she was on her way of reaching her limit or had already done so. I would hate to see my boy get hurt like I did. He would probably be less reserved about his feelings unlike me. I caught my girl in the act and only hit the guy. With Cams temper, I could see him killing the guy and his wife. But I can't help but wonder if Linda was cheating on Cam. Who was she giving that big ole ass too?

The dog in me wished it was me. I would love to be pounding her ass like a dog in heat but at the same time I would never do that to my best friend. But it wouldn't hurt to imagine it for a second. I looked down at Mrs. Jenkins ass as I hit it and imagined it was Linda for a second.

"AWE! Yes! That's it!" She moaned out.

"AWE!!" I let out a lip biting moan as I exploded inside of her. "Damn Linda!" I blurted out clearly not fully out of my fantasy of being with my best friend's wife. I literally fell to my knees and back into one of the leather chairs behind me out of breath and energy.

"Are you ok?" Mrs. Jenkins asked me looking back at me as she pulled down her skirt and stood straight up.

"Yeah ... I'm... Good, just give me a second." I replied a little embarrassed.

"Well hurry up and pull yourself together before one of my assistants barge in here." She replied walking back behind her desk and taking a seat.

I hurried up and pulled it together; pulling up my pants and buckling them back up as I stood up and took a seat.

"So... I'm going to have to let you go Austin." She said sternly staring into my eyes.

"Huh? I was that bad?"

"No... but I don't have sex with my employees. Don't you want me again?"

"Not if it's going to cost me a paycheck."

"Good answer but it's not. I'm going to help you get a good paying job in your field. Have you ever heard of a place called Control Alt Delete?"

"Yes I have applied there numerous times but they never gave me a call back."

"Well I know the owner and with a phone call I could have you in there in no time... sounds good?"

"Wow... Hell yeah" I exclaimed.

"I only have a couple of request. You comply and you will have a career building job but the minute you don't I will make it my personal goal to ruin your life."

"Wow… what is there to comply with?"

"It's simple, don't tell anybody about our little thing and it will continue to be a good one. If you're going to continue to fuck these hood rats out here then please use a condom because if and when I want you I don't want any STD's coming with you to me and don't ever come back here unless I call you. Out of sight out of mind."

"Wow that's a lot."

"But is it too much to ask for? Considering how quickly your life is going to change for the better? You're about to have your career back and one of the most attractive women you have ever met most importantly." She declared raising her eyebrow.

"Have you… What about Mr. Jenkins?" I replied looking at her wedding ring.

Her arrogant look turned into an irritated one. One of the biggest mistakes any man can make is bringing up another woman's man I just quickly learned.

"That's another thing don't ever bring up my husband unless I bring him up. When will you men ever learn that?"

"Ok."

"That's all Mr. Wells… I'll see you around… good luck at your new job, expect a phone call from them very soon, like this week."

"Alright … have a good day and thank you." I replied getting up and heading toward the door.

"Oh and get rid of Crystal's number; I don't sleep with sloppy seconds from friends."

"Sure..." I replied as I opened the door and walked out.....
Thinking to myself: Is this what it feels like to sell your soul?

15

Crystal Wilks

"You know Mrs. Wilks, this is a pretty big home for just two people."

"No, it's just for me."

"Oh…I thought you had a husband or something."

"Yes, I had a husband…."

"Oh…You're divorced?"

"No…he passed last year…."

"Wow…I'm sorry to hear that."

"Don't be. It's a part of life, isn't it?"

"Oh…you're right."

"Am I? I don't really think it's an issue of me being right or not but more so about how we all handle things differently."

"What? Right…?"

"Confused?"

"Sort of…"

"If I had more time to explain it to you then I would but maybe some other time. I'll take the house."

"Really? Ok well I'll go get with the homeowners and keep in touch with you. If you have any questions don't be scared to call, alright?"

"I will do…Let me make sure I'm getting your name right…Camry Carter?"

"Yes…"

"Alright, well next time I see you hopefully it's good news?"

"Absolutely, this sale shouldn't take long at all so go ahead and get the movers ready."

"Really?! Well alright! Get it done!" I replied.

Camry Carter? He was a sight most women wouldn't mind hanging up on their wall and fantasizing about. His tall and muscular frame seemed unreal. Walking around the house looking like a model out of Ebony magazine. If I hadn't noticed that ring on his finger I probably would have been all over him. Not sexually but I at least would have hinted at it or something. I usually let men do the honors but Atlanta was a big city and some nights got lonely if you know what I'm saying. Temptation sure did know how to present its self when we were at our weakest didn't it?

I was going to have to go back to Texas and get a couple things packed up and boxed so on signing day I would be ready to go. By the way he was talking it was like he could have me in the house tomorrow. I was looking forward to making Atlanta my new home. I had a couple of friends here and possibly a new start. Atlanta seemed to be a city of opportunity that I was planning on taking full advantage of without any remorse.

I stood at my rented Range Rover truck and looked up at the large two story mini mansion. The large piece of land it sat on, and new brick look it had was just my type. The only thing it may have been missing was a wooden fence around the property limits. I loved everything about this house because everything about it said new. I think Camry said it was built a year or so ago and I was going to be its first owner. How lucky was I? The house had five bedrooms, three in a half baths and over three thousand square feet. Camry was right; this was a big house for just one person.

It kind of depressed me a little because it didn't make any sense that I was alone. I should have had some kids or something to share my wealth with. Damn near thirty and I have no extension of myself but what I possess but then again the material things aren't mine either because technically my name isn't on any of these products I own. Even though I bought and paid for my things in a sense it still feels like they are borrowed goods. Does that make any sense? Maybe I'm over thinking because I have nothing better to do right now. I have three more days in the city until then what am I going to do? I could call my friend Laura and have her show me around town. Or better yet I could call that guy she was so enthused about and have him show me around town and possibly show me some other things if you know what I mean. It just felt odd to me that he hadn't texted or called me yet. I'm pretty sure that I was the best looking woman there but probably not the only one he was interested in. Wait a minute. What am I talking about? He was a security guard. I was probably one of few that would lower their standards to even allow him to approach me. There were other black women there but it was more old white women than anything. They were walking around tooting their noses up in the air and throwing their money around to the jewelers to over compensate for the lack of attention they got from their man. I just knew that half the women there could only get their man's attention by the change of zero's in their man's bank account. The more I thought about it, the more upset I got.

Who was he not to call me? Security guard working, trey songs looking, broke nigga. I'm a millionaire, what more needs to be said? He's probably intimidated or something like most men are. I was hoping he would be different but apparently all men think the same.

What was I thinking about this so hard for? I could get attention from any man. I did not need the recognition or permission of a security guard to make me feel good about myself and show me around town. There were fine men everywhere in this city that would love to take me out. But, then again, a third of them didn't like women and the rest I probably had to search for or take the time to get to know them.

Who am I kidding? I just didn't feel like looking for anybody I just wanted to have a good time. I guess once again my desperate ass was going to have to make the first move. Why am I acting like it's such a big deal for the woman to make the first move anyway? That's what the world was about nowadays anyway, right? Going head first after what you want? Truth be told the longer I sit around the higher the risk is for me to be missing out on my opportunity of getting the man I had my eyes set on. I guess that was another downfall in a way. We were taught to wait for the man to come and pursue us but nowadays we risk losing them if we wait. Men are so sensitive and insecure now a days that instead of realizing what they need to do to get the woman they get discouraged and go after another desperate girl who doesn't understand the art of being pursued. It's a lost art I guess but it lets us know a lot about the man we had our eyes set on. I guess that's what they mean when they refer to the good old days. It couldn't have been the economy or the status of living because "us" black folks never had it easy, so they must have been referring to the dating scene. Back then I can see a guy courting a woman or pursuing one like they are supposed to but times have changed I guess. As soon as I finished my thought I grabbed my phone out my purse and called Austin.

Ring! Ring!

"Hello?"

"Hi? Umm....I was thinking that we should hookup today. Are you free?" I said getting straight to the point.

"Who is this?" He replied sounding confused.

"Wow...! You've lost my number already?" I replied in disdain.

"Wait a minute...Is this Crystal?

"Yes!"

"Sweetie, do you know that I'm married? I mean I'm flattered but..."

"Married? You didn't say that at the fundraiser. Why did you come over to talk to me then and waste my time if you were married? Oh.... I get it; you're one of those player type guys. You wanted me to be your little one nighter? Freak in the sheets? Undercover lover? Good thing?" I interrupted.

"Fundraiser? I didn't go to no...Wait a minute...Crystal? Do you know who you're talking to?"

"Austin Wells! I'm not stupid boy...Don't start with this whole forgetful act. I've been there and done that, so save it for someone who doesn't know what you're doing!"

"Crystal.... Mrs. Wilks! This is Camry Carter, the real estate agent who just left you a couple of minutes ago?"

My heart went from one hundred beats a minute to two.

"Oh my God... Camry I am so sorry... I must... I...." Instead of finishing my sentence I just hung up.

"How embarrassing!" I shouted out loud to myself. Now I knew the next time that I spoke or seen him it was going to be awkward. He's probably not even going to show up on signing day. He's probably going to send an associate or somebody to do the signing. Why was this happening to me?!

Right after I finished my sentence my phone began to vibrate violently in my lap. It was Camry. At first I wasn't going to answer it but that seemed so eighth gradish so I had to.

"I'm so sorry Mr. Carter. I..."

"It's ok Crystal. You know you don't have to call me Mr. Carter either; it's alright to call me by my first name...

"Oh... Ok..."

"Well look, I'm about to go to lunch would you like to join me? I'm not that far from you. I could swing back around and you could follow me there.

"I don't know..."

"What don't you know? If you're hungry? I saw the way you were looking at the imitation fruit in the bowl on the dining room table. You damn near bit that apple from across the room." He replied chuckling.

"Wow…." I replied chuckling along with him.

"So what do you say? We can go somewhere fancy like McDonald's or Burger King if it makes you feel a little more comfortable."

Where did all this charm come from? I thought to myself.

"Um…. Aren't you married?"

"Happily, but what's that have to do with you? This isn't a date. It's lunch…. I know you don't know Atlanta like that and you were saying that you needed to see more of the city so I figured why not invite you?"

He replied in a harmless tone.

My stomach took a second to remind me that he was on point about how hungry I was and a little bit of eagerness inside of me reminded me how bad I wanted to see the city.

"Ok… I'll go with you… but don't try any funny stuff."

"Funny stuff… Girl you're not even cute to me." He said hanging up before I could get another word in.

I almost felt like I shouldn't go after he said that but I had to check myself for a minute. He was married so I didn't want him to look at me like that anyway. I had no reason to be upset with his comment simply because of those reasons and also because I knew he was playing.

"Loosen up Crystal, everybody doesn't want to hook up with you." I said to myself as he pulled up and beeped the horn twice.

Lunch mistakenly turned into catching an afternoon movie. We were having such a good time that it didn't seem like it was harming anybody or any lines were being crossed. Camry had a very confident presence and knew exactly what to say and when to say it. He just made me feel so comfortable, it was odd.

I went back to my hotel room no longer thinking about Austin Wells and wondering more about Mr. Camry Carter. I know he was married but I could tell it wasn't a happy marriage like he would like me to believe. He had this look of vulnerability on his face that he gave off anytime we found ourselves finishing each other's sentences, saying words at the same time, or momentarily looking into each other's eyes. In a sense I was glad that Austin didn't answer the phone because I'm not sure that he would have treated me better than what Camry treated me.

Until signing day I probably wasn't going to see him again but I sure wouldn't mind spending some more time with him. Camry had given me a feeling I hadn't felt in a long time. Matter of fact, the last time I had felt the way he made me feel was when I had first met Terrence almost ten years ago. I hadn't had time to sit and register what I was feeling but for the moment I didn't want to. I was just glad that I was feeling something again. Was that selfish?

Maybe it was, but in this case, who else should I be looking out for?

15 pt. 2

Camry Carter

"I keep begging you Camry and you're not listening to me. You skipped out on our lunch date today and won't tell me where you were. I just can't take this anymore... I can't!" Linda yelled as she threw some of her clothes in her Louis Vuitton duffle bag.

"I told you I was with a client trying to sell this house. It's a big sale and I was just trying to get it done; what is your problem?"

"You're the problem Camry! Your job is the problem! You put it before everybody and everything especially me! I just can't take it Camry! I have to go!"

"Go where?! Where the hell are you going Linda?!" I replied trying to grab her luggage bag out of her hand.

"Stop please! Just let me have my space until I can get my thoughts together." She yelled clinching her bag to her hips and trying to haul it with her out the room.

"No! I'm your husband and I'm not letting you leave this house until you tell me where you're going and I know for sure that's where you're going." I yelled.

Her eyes filled with tears as if I said something so painfully damaging to her feelings.

"See what I mean Camry... We are falling apart and we are obviously growing apart too!"

"What are you crying for? What did I do now?" I said out of frustration.

She took a minute to gather her tears and catch her breath.

"You're supposed to stop me... But you won't because you don't even care anymore... You want me to leave. You just want to be alone! Camry please just let me go get some air for the sake of our marriage. I'm going to my mother's house for the night so I can let you think about some things and maybe it's time I get to thinking too...."

"Thinking about what?"

"You'll figure it out Camry....I got to go... Goodbye, ok? See you tomorrow..." she said as I finally let go of her bag and she walked out the bedroom.

I sat there on the edge of the bed feeling drained and discouraged about what was happening with us. Just like so many other marriages of my era, ours was heading down the divorce line and making its way to the front of the judge. It was only a matter of time before it was all over.

I remember at one time everybody was calling us the power couple of the decade and here we were not even a year later barely holding it together. The look on Austin's face was almost heart breaking when I told him what Linda and I were going through it. I understand why he looked that way. He modeled what he wanted his marriage to be like after ours. It was because of our marriage that he decided to go and propose to Tonya.

Speaking on Austin, I decided not to ask Crystal how she knew him; I knew whatever answer she gave me wasn't going to be the truth to me unless I got confirmation from Austin. So to avoid her lying to me I decided to go straight to the source and ask Austin first hand. I know half the time any woman that he's interested in was some super freak or just some random hot mess. I grabbed my phone and called him.

"What's up bro?!" He said all overly enthused as if he was having the best time of his life.

"What are you so happy about?"

"I just got fired!" He exclaimed.

"So why the hell are you happy?"

"I'm happy because, I just hooked up with my boss!"

"What? Who? The dude?"

"Man I was so excited I probably would have hit anybody if they were in the office but no one else, so sorry to disappoint you bro but it was just me and Laura."

"Who the hell are you talking about?"

"Mrs. Jenkins man! I just popped her cherry!"

"Hell no, she is 100 years old her cherry has been popped a hundred years ago!"

"Hell yeah and she asked me to keep my mouth shut so we could keep it going."

"Wait a minute, you just fucked Mark Jenkins's wife? I thought their marriage was going good?"

"I don't know too much about him other than he is rich as hell. He wasn't there so I couldn't ask him anything about his and her marriage. Besides, I don't think she would have answered the questions clearly with all this pipe I had laid in her kitchen."

"Wow... Are you serious?"

"Man, I'm more serious than Iran displaying nuclear weapons and threatening to bomb the U.S! I was so deep inside that woman I could tell you her thoughts before she even realized she thought them." He said chuckling at his own joke.

"This is crazy."

"Tell me about it bro... I was so surprised and excited that it was going on that I almost climaxed as soon as I got inside of her."

"Oh ... Lord...Ok man, that's enough. I don't want to hear all of that."

"What? Why not what's wrong bro? You usually want to hear about my experiences."

'Well, I don't want to hear about this one. You know I know them fairly well and it... Never mind man... I was calling you to ask you about Crystal Wilks.... Did you do anything with her?"

"Crystal Wilks? I don't know who she is...."

"Well she knew you... She said something about meeting you at a fundraiser."

"Oh! Yeah that's the pretty rich redbone I had met at Mrs. Jenkins's fundraiser the other day. Remember the one I did security for?"

"Oh yeah..."

"What about her?"

"I had sold her a house here in Atlanta the other day." I replied biting my tongue.

"That's it. How did you know she knew me? When did my name come up in all of this?"

"Oh... she just had...Well I had told her that... I... um... had told her about you because she was looking for a nice guy to help her see the city. When I said your name she had said how small the world is because she had met you already."

"Oh...What are you a matchmaker now?"

"No, I had just brought up your name. That's all. We'll, are you going to take her out?"

"Sorry bro.... As fine as she is....I can't. She's a no go."

"What? She seems like a good woman... She might be the right one for you bro and judging by the house she's about to buy she seems to have plenty of money."

"She probably is filthy rich... Damn...But I can't."

"Why not? Why every time a good woman comes your way you brush them off and chase after the sluts?"

"That's not true!"

"Come on man...stop being in denial!"

"I'm not in denial, especially when there is no proof behind what you're saying."

"No proof? Man get serious. Tonya, Sharon, Tiffany... You want me to name more?"

"What about them?"

"They're all sluts and super freaks that you decided to chase after instead of the real deal."

"Real deal? Who?"

"Marie Lovejoy!"

He got silent for a minute then I heard some glass in the background break.

"Austin? Austin!" I exclaimed.

"Yeah?"

"What was that?"

"Oh...umm nothing. My lamp threw itself on the floor."

"It threw itself? Wow... It bothers you that much that you let her get away that you're breaking stuff?"

"I didn't break anything... It fell!" He shouted.

"Yeah... Ok... So why won't you hook up with Crystal again?"

"Because I can't! Laura doesn't want me messing with any of her friends."

"Wow! So after one day of sex she owns you now? That must be some powerful pussy."

"Man hell no... She's getting me a new job and everything to show her appreciation for me. It's an computer engineering job. Matter of fact, I have an interview this week for your information. The job already contacted me."

"Wow!"

"Will you stop saying that?! I feel like I'm talking to somebody related to Flavor Flav."

"Ok… well at least you're getting something for selling your soul to the devil."

"The devil? Man you can miss me with all that shit. All I know is I'm living the life baby! You're just jealous! Just let me do me and you focus on straightening up your life."

"My life?"

"Yeah man… Work on you and Linda and let me do my thing. After all, you're the one that started all this player-tude that I'm laying down…Get with the program bro…The teacher is never supposed to envy the student but then again isn't that how it usually turns out?"

"Man you tripping! I'll talk to you later." I replied in disdain.

"I'm pretty sure you will." He replied right before he hung up.

I could feel him smirking on the other end of the phone right now. I hated Austin when he was right. I was jealous, but it made no sense for me to be. He was a scavenger, looking for a home while I never had to worry about finding a home because I already had one right here with Linda….or did I?

I was losing Linda and for the first time in life I wasn't sure if I wanted to keep her. Things were so out of whack between us two that it didn't make any sense. What really didn't make any sense were Austin and Laura Jenkins. I wouldn't have saw that coming if I was psychic. I mean her marriage with

Mark was in magazines and papers on how to be married and happy; power couples of the century, and true love and what not. What the hell was going on? It made me feel like if it was happening with them, then Linda and I just didn't have a chance in hell. Why even try and fix my marriage if theirs was failing? It just seemed that nowadays things were so messed up it wasn't exactly the smart thing to do. It seemed like people had much less respect for married couples than they use to and it only made things so much harder. Not to mention, every time I turned on the TV, another celebrity is getting divorced. It just seemed like maybe the whole "together forever" thing has ran its course.

I kicked my shoes off and flopped back on my bed and starred at the ceiling. I grabbed the remote and cut on the TV and right on cue it seemed, the television was showing another Hollywood couple getting a divorce.

"This shit is ridiculous..." I said out loud to myself.

I did have an incredibly good time with Crystal and I couldn't help but think about her. I'm not exactly sure what made me call her back and invite her to lunch. Lunch went much better than I expected and there just so happened to be a movie theater next to the restaurant we went to so it all just kind of fell into place. Not once did I stop and wonder what was going on with Linda or what I would do if she had caught Crystal and me out on a date. It had totally slipped my mind that I was supposed to be meeting my wife for lunch.

What was happening to me? Truth be told I had rather been with Crystal that day. It had just felt better. The way people were looking at us and complimented us when we were out...it just felt right.

A couple of times we locked eyes and I wanted to kiss her lips just to see how it felt but I wasn't going to be the one to force the issue. Even though my marriage was in trouble I still felt like I should act accordingly. But if you asked me now, I'm not sure that I would have made the same decision.

I grabbed my phone and stared at it for a while. I thought about calling Crystal. I was just very bored and curious about what she may have been doing right now.

"I can't call her!" I said out loud to myself throwing the phone back down by my side.

But then again; what if she was just waiting up for me in the bed just like I was? What if she was waiting for me to call her?

I looked over at my laptop and then back at my phone. It was either I get on the phone with Crystal or I fight the urge to not masturbate to some damn porn on the internet. I hated how much I've grown to contradict myself. I found myself doing so many of the things I hated to do. But oddly enough I found myself finding comfort in it.

"Fuck it! I said as I grabbed the phone and decided to text Crystal instead of calling her.

-Thanks for the good time out... I really enjoyed myself.-

I waited for a minute to receive a response then looked at the clock after a couple of minutes went by. 11:49 displayed in bright red numbers. She's probably sleep or looking at the phone wondering what the hell I was doing texting her so late. Just that fast I was regretting my actions.

-No problem. I had a good time also...Your wife is a lucky woman... I'm jealous.-

She texted back just when I had gave up hope. I looked at her response and shook my head.

-I wish she knew that-

-How couldn't she? It's hard to miss and painfully obvious. You kind of make what they say about married men true.-

-What's that?-

-That all the good ones are taken.-

-Digg that.-

-I can't dig it. Lol.-

-LMAO-

One text turned into countless ones. I couldn't believe how well we were getting along or even worse how bad I wanted her lying next to me right now. Flirting back and forth went on for hours and because of it I was finding it hard to restrain myself from saying certain things. I didn't want to come off like a player or anything but I definitely was feeling like one. She didn't seem to mind though. Her allowing this only fueled my desire to want to flirt more and text longer. And with her it seemed like she felt the same way. I looked over at the clock and before I knew it, it was glowing red numbers that said 1:00 am....

16

"I might call you later on and have you come by my place tonight. I have a feeling I'm not going to want to sleep alone." Mrs. Jenkins said as she fixed herself back up.

I hadn't even caught my breath yet and she was already talking about what she was going to have me do next. We were at my apartment in my bedroom getting a little better acquainted with one another for the third time. She was like an energizer bunny in the bedroom which told me that she wasn't doing too much at home. It was clear to me that I was filling a void but as wrong as it felt she couldn't have made me feel any better about doing it. Mrs. Jenkins was built like a race horse and in better shape than most girls my age. I couldn't really complain if I wanted to. Her body was every man's dream.

"What do you mean sleep with you? I'm not sleeping with you... What about your husband?" I replied looking up at her from the bed as she put her clothes back on.

"Boy you're going to either get with the program or get the hell on. If I want you to sleep with me because I want to feel a man's body against mine at night then that's what I'm going to get. Is there a problem?!" She replied suddenly releasing all this ghetto-tude out of her body with a combination of neck roles and hand waving.

"Awe look at the hood come out of you... Looking like Jody's momma from the movie Baby Boy." I replied making her laugh to try and lighten the mood.

"Boy stop!" She exclaimed bursting in laughter.

"But seriously… Sleep where?"

"At my house…"

"No… We can do the sleeping thing but I'm not sleeping at your place in your man's bed. That's like asking for trouble."

"My husband is in Italy right now on business. He's trying to open up a business there, some restaurant, fast food of course with an Italian twist."

"I don't care if the man was in Africa wrestling lions. It's never smart to be sleep in someone else's home where I don't belong. Do you know that man can kill me and not even get charged with anything? All he has to say is that he thought I was raping you or burglarizing the place. I like being with you and all but how dumb do I look? You're fine but you're not dying for you fine. How about you sleep here?"

"You want me to sleep here, on this fuck bed?"

"Fuck bed?"

"Yeah! That's all its good for is fucking. I can't sleep on this queen size three hundred dollar mattress. My body is used to a certain level of comfort that only a king sized Tempurpedic mattress can provide. I just can't sleep on anything." She replied with her nose up in the air.

"A Tempurpedic all alone or a queen sized bed with a man holding you while you sleep? Which one because I'm not sleeping in your house? We can keep it low-key right here at my place." I replied sternly holding my ground.

"I'll tell you what; I'm going to have a new bed and mattress set delivered to you this afternoon. So after your job interview you need to be here to get this bed. The movers should call you when they're on their way."

"Wait a minute, I like my bed. I have a lot of memories on this old thing."

"Yeah, that's the problem…. You're going to start with me. I'll see you later on." She replied getting up and leaving out my bedroom.

I sat on my bed and waited until I heard the front door open and shut before I got up to go wash up and get ready for my job interview.

I really didn't feel like getting up because I felt so worn out from Mrs. Jenkins relentless sexual appetite. Not to mention, trying to balance her with the other girls. I had totally stopped searching for any more of my ex-girlfriends. Honestly, I think I was biting off more than I could chew. To think that not that long ago it was a desert in my pants and now it's a growing sea. If I added anymore women then I would probably be drowning in pussy. Was this what I signed up for?

Now that I was getting a plethora of satisfaction I was kind of questioning how satisfied I was. Don't get me wrong I'm happy but how much longer can I go house hopping before I get sick of being the fill- in or replacement guy. This whole Exvantage thing started off as an experiment or gimmick because I was hurt and horny. I wanted a lot of sex and get it as easy as possible but also do it with people that I already developed a connection with. I mean I also had some egotistical, self-satisfying reasons but now that I was knee deep in it I was starting to have my likes and dislikes appear and disappear daily. There were alot more emotions involved than I had intended it to be. Some nights I found myself saying that I don't love these girls and that the past is the past. Some nights I felt like maybe I was just better off staying at home and masturbating like I use to because then I wouldn't have to be worried about the next persons emotions. I don't ever hear the chicks I masturbate to making any demands or getting all my thoughts all tied up but I guess all this extra emotional crap came with the territory.

I had no idea what my life was going to be like now that Mrs. Jenkins was in my life. She was so demanding it was almost impossible to have anyone else in my life without being a little fatigued. She wanted me to be her on call boy toy pretty much and if I got this job then I definitely wasn't going to have a problem being just that. I already could tell that dealing with her little requests was only going to be a small hurdle in order for me to enjoy the perks of messing with her.

....

Control Alt Delete was a company that had been down in Atlanta for a while now. They fixed broken computers or phones or anything electronic that came their way. They had a huge contract with most of the mega stores and major businesses so getting business was never the problem but more so getting the right people for the right job was. They had a huge warehouse that from the outside it looked like a large office space but in the inside it looked like a technology sweat shop. Hundreds of cubicles row after row filled a large area of the floor space while further back it seemed like several mechanical stations were put together for bigger jobs. In every cubical there was one or two people working on a laptop, either taking it apart and putting it back together or doing some type of programming to it. Standing at the door I was overwhelmed as I waited for the interviewer to come and see me. I don't know why I was nervous. I am a computer whiz and I can't wait to show everyone my expertise. I could see myself going from a lower level worker to an executive of operations in no time.

I was surprised to see so many people of color in the warehouse working. At my last job there were maybe only one or two people other than myself able to work on computers and run things accordingly like the way things were ran here. I had to say maybe one-third of the people in the workplace were black. One black receptionist sat next to a white receptionist while an Asian person brought them coffee. The place just seemed to be full of color. I was in awe.

"Nice to meet you again Mr. Wells, I am Ms. Lovejoy and I will be interviewing you today." I heard a familiar voice say from the left of me.

"Marie Lovejoy?" I said out loud to myself not even acknowledging her hand that was extended in my face.

"Mr. Wells? Are you ok?" I heard the familiar voice say.

I looked down at her black patent leather stilettos and slowly worked my way up her legs. She had stockings on but I couldn't help but zoom in on her creamed coffee complexion and a small blemish that was hardly noticeable to the naked eye. Her black skirt began to spread wider at the hips and then slimmed back down as I made my way up her body to her waist line. Her black skirt was met by a white button up shirt that squeezed on to her flat stomach and protruded outward as my eyes met her breast.

"Damn…" I blurted out… I knew those breasts and that small blemish on her knee from when she had the chicken pox and scratched it so it had left a permanent little square shaped scar. I was afraid to look up any further but I didn't want to keep my eyes on her breast and mess around and get charges pressed against me for reckless breast eye balling.

"Mr. Wells? Do you want a job?" I heard her voice say in a much more stern tone.

"What?"

"Mr. Wells, my face is up here! Thank you." She said as I looked up and into her eyes.

I quickly stood up and shook her hand.

"I'm sorry; I was lost for a second."

She still looked the same after all this time. I couldn't believe it. Her beautiful brown eyes and small red freckles on her cheeks always made me melt. Her cheekbones were perfect and her dimple in her chin always made her look unique from others. She had her long shiny black hair pulled back into a hair clip and folded up like a tail of some exotic animal deep in the jungles of South America. But what stood out more than her tempting body and beautiful face was a white gold necklace with an emerald stone hanging around her neck. I looked down at her hand and noticed she had a matching ring to go with it also…

I had bought her that jewelry. She was the only woman that I had ever bought any jewelry for. Her favorite gem was the emerald because it was her birthstone and it had an "alluring glow to it" as she put it. I could never forget the look on her face when I surprised her with it, she was so happy. I know because she literally kept saying "I'm so happy! I'm so happy!" as tears rolled down her eyes.

"Follow me Mr. Wells" She said breaking eye contact with me and pulling me out of my good times daze.

I followed her into the actual workspace of the warehouse where the cubicles were and hundreds of people were looking hard at work on numerous devices and gadgets.

"This is the laboratory. Here we receive broken goods and repair them as quickly and efficiently as possible. Follow me."

She walked quickly down the middle aisle of the warehouse and made a sharp turn and headed straight into a doorway that had the symbol of stairs on it indicating that it was the stairwell. "Up here is where you will be, working with the rest of the mid-level workers. Here they create numerous programs, websites, and software for the company. Of course you will be trialed to see exactly how skilled you are but for the most part this is where you will be; if you will continue to follow me." She said again not even really giving me the chance to take everything in before leading me up the stairs.

Up here was much different than down stairs. There were cubicles but nowhere near as many. There was much more space for every person to sit comfortable and have some sort of privacy. I followed her through the cubical space into an office in the corner of the building.

"Shut the door behind you Mr. Wells" She said firmly as she took her place behind her desk in this huge office chair.

An odd silence filled the room as I sat down in the small black leather chair in front of her desk.

"So how have you been Marie?" I said breaking the silence.

"Excuse me? My name is Miss Lovejoy and I'm going to need for you to start calling me that from now on until the day you die Mr. Wells."

"Wow….So this is how you want to play it? You really want to act like you don't know me…Alright cool, well let's just get on with the interview." I replied in disdain.

"Before we start lets clear something up. Whoever you think I am, I'm not that girl and whatever you think that that girl had with you never existed. If you want to work here peacefully and have easy work days then I suggest you get that through your head really fast before you find yourself getting fired." She declared in a stern voice.

"Ok, but let me ask you one more question and then I'm done. Where did you get that necklace and matching ring from?"

"It was a gift."

"From who?"

"That's personal, a little too personal Mr. Wells. Now, can we continue the interview? Actually it's an orientation. Interviews are for people who don't yet have the job already."

"I have the job? What am I going to be doing exactly?"

"Graphic designs, layouts, programming, etc...Whatever I tell you to do. I'm going to team you up with a floor leader just to make sure you're able to get the hang of things fairly well. You're on a ninety day probationary period so try not to mess up... You don't, and you will have a promising career, you do and good luck finding a job somewhere else."

"So when can I meet the boss?"

"I am your boss along with Mark, the tall white guy standing up waving right now."

I looked through the office windows onto the main floor at a tall white guy with glasses and a white button up shirt and black tie. He looked like the typical nerd with a basketball player's height.

"O.....K...." I replied trying to hold in my laugh. "Well at least I will have one person that looks good enough to drool over."

Marie almost cracked a smile but quickly caught herself and hardened her look.

"Let me let you in on a little secret Mr. Wells. I'm not sure who your friend is in the very high place that got you this job but if I were you I would tread lightly around here. Favors don't last too long in this place."

"What?"

"So Mr. Wells if all is fine with you then you can close my door when you leave and go to Mark for further instruction." She said in a totally different tone than the one she used to warn me about my actions.

What the hell was that? I had spent the remainder of my day listening to Mark tell me stuff about computers that I already knew. I was finding myself concentrating less on what he was trying to show me and more on holding my laugh in from his stereotypical nerd ways. This man had the nerve to snort when he laughed and he took pride in wearing ball throbbing pants that he should have gave back to the third grader he had stolen them from. Whenever he took long strides I could see the man's ankles for God's sake. But throughout the whole day this man had said one thing and one thing only that caught my attention. He said Marie was his girlfriend for almost eight months now. When he said it I wanted to punch him in his mouth for lying but why would he tell a random lie like that? I hadn't said anything about Marie the whole time and he just came out and said this bullshit all on his own. It made me think that maybe Marie had told him who I was beforehand and he was just bringing it up to mark his territory. If that was the case then his actions made all the sense in the world but what didn't make sense was them being together.

Mark and I were total opposites for one. I was black he was white. I was average height and he was a malnourished giant. He was a clumsy nerd and I am a brilliant speciment of a man. He snorted when he laughed and I commanded funny.

How the hell could she go from me, a Ferrari, to him a damn school bus? Maybe she wanted a huge... Fuck that, I'm not even going to reason for her actions because none of this made any sense. Marie was a freak in the bedroom so I know that she wasn't satisfied by him in there. I taught her mostly everything she knows in there after all, I did take her virginity. There was no way in hell this guy could be fitting the bill. I could imagine him snorting every time Marie did something to blow his mind. Then again it was bothering me to even think of her with another guy let alone him. He was pathetic in physical stature but impressive in his thinking ability but not quite like me.

For the rest of the day he had me programming computers but in the process I was thinking about Marie. It bothered me a little bit that she was acting like she never met me. Who was I kidding? It was a little heart breaking to be honest. Most of my exes were happy to see me after some time but it was like she was still holding on to a grudge.

Marie and I went way back. We dated in high school and we became the most envied couple in school. Everybody just knew that we were going to end up together for the rest of our lives. I had plans on proposing to her at our graduation and everything but I froze up. I didn't get cold feet because I didn't want to be with her but more because I didn't have a ring. I was a high school student at a fast food restaurant. I couldn't afford a damn wedding ring. We lasted maybe a year into college and then we just started to fall apart. She just kept giving me guidelines and time limits on how and when to do things and it just began to be too much pressure on me. She kept complaining about us not being married and becoming more and more negative about our future because at the time things were a little tough trying to adjust to college life. As time went on and I hadn't put a ring on her finger she began to grow insecurities and feel that I was messing with other women. Every other day we were fighting about something and the relationship started to become more of an irritant than a stimulant. Some say that we were growing apart but after the low in our relationship she didn't stick around long enough for us to fix the problem. She transferred to UCLA without a word and until today that was the last I had seen her. I had to go to her parent's house to find out that she had left school let alone the state of Georgia. Heartbroken and confused weren't even the words to describe the hurt I felt. I just didn't understand why she had just given up on me like that. For a long time I regretted not giving her more attention and using my refund check to get her that wedding ring that she always wanted. If I had known that she was going to leave like that then I would have followed her stupid guidelines and secured her insecurities but she never gave me a chance to.

There were a couple times I had got the urge to just go and find her out there but I just couldn't leave school. It didn't make too much sense for me to just take off to a foreign land and look for one girl who was probably going to be clustered among a million others. I wouldn't have had enough time, school was too demanding. Camry offered to come with me to California to find her but all I could keep thinking about was us getting there and seeing her hugged up with some other guy. I just didn't see any sense in flying all that way just to confirm a broken heart.

After a while my regret of not doing enough turned into resentment. I grew to hate women for a while then once my hormones kicked in after a month or six, I got back on the hunt and started dating again. For a long time I just chose to get with girls that I knew were more on the free spirited side because I wasn't looking for anything real anymore. I just wanted to enjoy life. I stopped looking for love and started enjoying lust, after all lust had never contributed to being hurt. Now that I think about it, lust had only brought me pleasure and a whole lot of it, so maybe that was the right path in my case. I thought like that for a while until I got sick of the meaningless sex. After so long I began to miss being in love....It was that feeling that had me upgrade Tonya from one of my most frequent sex partners to my girlfriend. With her I tried to do everything I refused to do with Marie. I allowed my heart to roam free again with Tonya to prove to myself that I could not only be the man that every woman dreamed of but most of all I wanted to be the one that Marie had wanted. Deep down inside I was hoping that she felt what I was doing on this side of the country.

I regret doing that now more than ever....You see how far that got me; watching a homemade or should I say hoe-made, in your face porno featuring the girl I was going to propose to. How lucky was I?

I had asked myself for years if Marie was the one that got away or the one that wasn't meant to be. With her sudden reappearance in my life I was beginning to feel like fate was beginning to run its course. God was playing some kind of sick game on me. How the hell did Marie go from some runaway lover to my boss?

It had been almost four years since I had last seen or heard from Marie and now all of a sudden she was here giving me orders on what to do. I was thinking about quitting the job and having Mrs. Jenkins give me back my old one as a security guard. But then again we all know that this is what I really wanted to be doing. This job was much safer and paid three times more almost. Plus this is what I went to school for in the first place so it only made sense to start getting paid for it again. I wasn't about to let something as little as an emotion, mess with something as big as my career. If I stuck with this job for a while maybe I could get a house and start paying back all these damn student loans. Staying with this job was a major career move and a show of my appreciation towards Mrs. Jenkins. Marie had nothing to do with me deciding to stay here. After all she was the one that ruined my life so there was no reason that I should be so in awe to see her in the first place, Right?

17

"So wait...You went to Gailey Academy Elementary?"

"Yes, for one year.... It was my second grade year I believe because my mom and dad were going through a thing. I was only down here for one year before going back to Detroit. It was so long ago, I hardly remember being down here." Crystal replied taking another sip of her apple martini.

We were at a local bar listening to some poetry and getting drinks since it was her last day in town. She was leaving for Texas tomorrow so I decided to give her one last night of Atlanta hospitality before she left to go get her things. It was just the day before that we had met up at the park and jogged around the whole place like we were training for a marathon. I couldn't remember when was the last time Linda and I had worked out together so to be able to finally do it with someone was refreshing. After our little workout we went to the subway for a bite to eat and ended up not seeing each other again till later that night after I had got off work. I don't know what made me agree with her but she kept talking about wanting to go to Cascades, a fairly large skating rink that she had seen in music videos and movies. Without thinking I agreed and we ended up having a great time. I felt like a teenager again out there on the floor trying not to fall and to impress Crystal at the same time. When it was time to go home I truly didn't want the night to end and I don't think she did either but reality always seemed to set itself back in once I got to my car and she left in hers.

"You said you were down here your second grade year, in Mrs. Thomas class?" I asked anxiously.

"Yeah, how did you know?"

"Wow! Wow! Crystal you don't remember me? You were the first girl I ever kissed, my first girlfriend!" I exclaimed.

"Get the hell out of here!" She exclaimed taking a harder look into my eyes to see if she saw anything that rang a bell.

"Damn! How many dudes did you kiss? How many boyfriends did you have back in second grade?" I asked a little disappointed that she couldn't remember.

"I told you I hardly remember Atlanta... Wait just give me a second.... Camry Carter... Camry, no wait they called you Summer?" She exclaimed making her eyes wide with excitement as if she had hit the jackpot.

"Wow! I haven't heard that name since way back then...Yeah that's me." I replied chuckling.

"They called you that because of your complexion right? You were the only mixed kid in the class." She replied laughing a little harder than I felt was necessary as if she were reliving the traumatizing moments I went through as a kid. "Sum of this, sum of that!" She blurted out with another huge laugh. "Remember? Anytime somebody asked what was your race Bruce would shout 'Summa this, summa that' Wow." She exclaimed taking her gasping laugh down to a chuckle after seeing that I wasn't enjoying this as much as she clearly was.

"Yeah... Yeah...Good old Bruce... You know he's dead now right?" I replied in a serious tone.

"Oh no! Really?"

"Yup, all that bullying he did finally caught up to his ass."

"Wow! That's sad because he was hilarious!" She exclaimed with another chuckle.

"You know for somebody who doesn't remember much, you sure do remember a lot about Bruce!" I said in disdain.

"Awe…. Did the baby get his feelings hurt? Did I bring back some sad times….I'm sorry baby… Do you want me to get you a rattle so you can feel better?" She said in a baby voice reaching for my cheeks.

"I hope you choke on your martini." I replied jokingly.

"Awe… Don't be like that Camry… Look at you now right? Fine as a luxury car and successful too… Bruce is dead…In the long run you won right?" She replied smiling.

"Don't offer me sympathy now…." I replied smiling and taking another sip of my cranberry juice.

"You know this is a small world and it's just funny how things play out sometimes. I'm sitting here with my real estate agent who just so happens to be my ex-boyfriend all the way from the second grade. How ironic is that?" She said finishing off her second glass of apple martini.

"It's pretty crazy…"

It was 11:30 when Crystal and I had finally left the bar and decided to head home. She was so tipsy I had to help her in the door of her place which was suite 401 on the fourth floor of her luxury hotel.

"Oh don't fall now... You got it? I exclaimed helping her keep her balance as she opened the door to her suite.

"I think so... I haven't been this tipsy since... Well it's been a while... I had a nice time here in Atlanta with you Camry. I don't know how I..."

"Don't worry about it the feeling is mutual. It's been a while since I have been able to get out the house and enjoy myself."

"I don't mean to get all in your business or anything but why don't you ever talk about your wife if you're so happily married?"

"I don't know..." I replied realizing that she was right.

I hadn't been talking about my wife at all. I guess the look on my face said more than I intended on saying because before I knew it Crystal and I were in each other's arms inhaling each other's breath and connecting tongues. I picked her up and left whatever restraint I had on the other side of the door as it slammed behind me.

Where's the bedroom?" I asked between kisses.

"Take me right here right now!" She demanded unbuckling my pants while we continued to make out.

She had on a blue dress with a bright pink belt that look good on her earlier in the day but right now I imagined it looking ten times better on the floor. The dress had a silk type feel to it so it was no surprise to me how quickly it slipped off once I unhooked her belt. The very next second I learned that Crystal didn't wear any undergarments that night as I put my hand between her legs and started massaging her clit. Her body

176

was impressive all the way from her head to her apple size breasts to her toned legs to her perfectly polished light pink toes. She moaned ever so softly as she pulled my shirt over my head and threw it over to the floor leaving us both naked and exposed with nothing more to hide from each other but plenty more to reveal.

"Do you…" she started to say but didn't finish as she dropped to her knees and engulfed all that I had to offer.

"Fuck!" I exclaimed looking for something to hold but there was nothing in sight. I grabbed on to her head stroking my fingers through her hair as my toes curled up instantly like never before. All that kept running through my mind was how much better this felt than masturbating or receiving head from Linda for that matter.

"I'm…cumin…gg!" I declared as my body tensed up. I tried to jerk away from her because I knew how women hated to have anything to do with sperm unless they were trying to make a baby. However, instead of letting me jerk away she grabbed my shaft and looked up at me as I released what seemed to be all my frustration and worries away.

"Damn!" I exclaimed finding it hard to stand on my feet.

"Come on…" She said taking a deep gulp and licking her lips while standing up and pulling me by the hand to her bedroom. I could barely walk but I dug deep to find the strength not to reveal too much of my sensitivity to her.

On the way to Crystal's bed I thought about how bad things were at home and how Linda hadn't been home not even to get her toothbrush. She had been gone for three days now and she wouldn't answer my calls but she would text me. A thought to go to her parent's house had run across my mind but it didn't make any sense for me to keep crowding her. She wanted her space so I was giving it to her. But I couldn't help but be mad at how selfish she was acting over something so essential like my work. All the nagging and complaining and bad sex only fueled my frustration but I had realized after the second night out with Crystal that when I was with her I didn't feel any of that. No worries, no anger, no nothing. It was just good times. On the second night I regretted leaving Crystal in a lonely bed and I had decided in one moment at her door that I didn't want her to be alone tonight. I didn't want to be alone either. I just wanted to let go and feel what I had been feeling with no help from my wife…Elated.

I could tell that Crystal was feeling a similar way because she was just as responsive as I was in the bedroom. It was something we both needed for a long time and in the moment it just seemed right. Her lips were so soft and her body was so firm. I couldn't complain. The only regret I was having was not wearing a condom. Technically, she was a stranger but after we revealed our history it didn't seem like it anymore. It felt like we were already connected. There were numerous times while we were having sex that I looked down at my penis and considered putting a condom on but in a sense it was too late because I was already lost in the sauce.

Sex is one of those things you can't play around with unless you're borderline crazy or just plain old reckless. I liked to compare it to Russian roulette because when it came to unprotected sex once you started there was no erasing what came next. So from the time I decided to enter her body unprotected there was no turning back. To me it made no sense to stop and put on a condom because if she did have an STD or something it was a good possibility that I already contracted it. Putting on a condom after I already entered her was like me containing the virus so it definitely wouldn't be able to leave me for sure. The only thing I could do was hope she didn't have anything or thank God for a good doctor but that's if and only if I catch something that's curable. If that wasn't the case then I was screwed. Pregnancy was also another concern but now-a-days they had so many "undo pills" and "oops I didn't mean for that to happen" drugs it was ridiculous. If a person got pregnant in these times and didn't really want it then it was because they were living either to reckless or carefree so in all reality it was nobody's fault but their own. I was too tired to be worried about all that mess. All I wanted to feel was what I was feeling and that was pleasurable relief.

....

We woke up together in what I thought was going to be an awkward silence because we both had seemed to have bitten the forbidden fruit in the land of marriage. I was awakened by a bright light glaring through my eye and the smell of French toast and eggs. The smell was from room service bringing up breakfast and the bright light was surprisingly the light from the sun reflecting off my wedding ring and into my eye.

The day sure did know how to make me feel guilty and regret all the fun the night had brought. I probably would have felt better at this point if I was drunk last night. But I was perfectly sober last night and remembered every detail today. Crystal, on the other hand, was a little drunk so she kind of had an excuse on why what happened was allowed in her eyes to

179

alleviate her from any regret. She looked over at me then back at the clock... 7:30...

"Are you going to eat breakfast?" She asked.

"Sure." I replied trying to prepare myself for her "This wasn't supposed to happen" speech. I sat up in the bed and began looking around for my boxers with no luck.

"All our clothes are in the hallway." She said chuckling.

"Wow... Ok... Let me get up and go get them."

"Why? Just get the food and come back to bed... Enjoy these last couple of hours with me. My flight is at 12, there is no rush." She said surprisingly.

"Are you sure?"

"After last night... Hell yes. I hadn't been fucked like that ever. I didn't want it to end."

My dick instantly grew rock hard from her clear stroke at my ego.

"You remember last night?"

"I'll never forget it. You were amazing. Why wouldn't I remember it? The whole night was amazing."

"Oh yeah, it was fun... I just thought you were too wasted to remember anything"

"I was a little tipsy but not drunk. I can tell you exactly what happened minute by minute last night. For instance, this is how it all started." She replied pulling the sheets from over my body and grabbing my erection.

"Fuck!" I blurted out as she made it clear that she proved her point with more than words but with the exact act that made a small flame explode.

....

I didn't get home until noon and to my surprise Linda was there waiting on me. I had missed three phone calls and a bunch of texts from her last night and this morning. I still had yet to respond to them but now I had no choice. I pulled into my drive way and took a deep breath trying to prepare myself for what was to come.

What was I going to say? I hadn't known how long she had been here and the last thing I wanted was to get caught up in a lie. It would make me look even more like a cheater.

"If she asks, I'll just tell her I was at Austin's place…." I said to myself grabbing my phone and texting Austin.

-Did Linda call you last night or this morning?

-Nope… Why?-

-TTYL-

I hurried and texted back relieved that I would be able to get away with my lie just in case it got to that point. I looked down and made sure my clothes were neatly placed on my body and went into the house.

"Damn I wish I would have taken a shower..." I said to myself as a hint of Crystal's perfume hit my nose. There's no way I'm going to be able to hide this from Linda.

My nerves almost took me back to my car so I could drive off but I was moving too fast I quickly learned as I tripped on the way there. I fell face first into the grass and was quickly reminded how over powering mother nature's scent was. I quickly started rubbing my body around in the moist lawn hoping to capture the scent of the dirt and grass over the scent of Crystal's perfume. I looked like a dog the way I rubbed and rolled across the grass like I had no sense.

"Are you high? What are you doing on my lawn?" Linda asked standing in the front doorway with a very confused look on her face.

I stopped rolling around and looked up at her as if I was totally busted. "What?" I said guiltily.

"You heard me. Why are you rolling around on the lawn like you're a damn dog?"

"The grass just smells really good to me..." I replied with a straight face. When did you get here?"

"Boy get up and get in the house. You're embarrassing me." She replied turning around to go back into the living room. I got up with the hopes that she wasn't going to bust my chops about being out and hoping she kept a distance from me once I got in the house because I wasn't sure if the grass had totally got rid of the perfume smell.

"Don't sit on none of my furniture… go straight to the shower and I'll talk to you later" she demanded as soon as I walked in the door.

Did she just say take a shower? Hell yeah! God must be looking out for me today. I thought to myself as I walked past her in the living room to bedroom to get a change of clothes. Without a word from her I gladly went to the bathroom and stripped down and hopped in the shower. This was too damn easy. I had never cheated on any of my girlfriends before but I knew I could if I wanted to but now that I had I could see how it was addictive. Linda had damn near granted me a cheaters cover up ordering me to the shower as if she had knew that I was out all night doing the nasty with what she would call a random woman. I think that every woman helped their man one way or another cover their tracks because of the benefit of a doubt. Because there was trust in our relationship that meant that I could use it to my advantage at any moment and time to my advantage. Linda had no choice but to trust my every word if she didn't have any proof contradicting my lies. Using the trust factor was like a get out of jail free card because she had to roll with whatever I told her. Like the lie earlier about the lawn. As bogus as that sounded and looked she couldn't tell me that I was lying because I was out cheating last night, she had to accept my answer. It was like she was giving me a pass because I had been a good boy all this time; I earned her trust and up until this day never used it to my advantage so why or how could she feel I was doing anything but telling the truth now?

I was glad that Crystal had left because now I could go back to working on my marriage and start living my normal life but at the same time a piece of me couldn't wait to see her again.

18

Crystal Wilks

I did mean it when I said that that was the best sex that I had ever had. There was something about the timing, the moment and I can't disregard his body that really had set me on fire. I was honestly looking for reasons not to like him or the sex but I couldn't find any; everything he was doing was right. The way he touched me to the way he said my name was right... He was perfect.

Were all men like this? Is this what I had been missing after all this time? I knew all men from Atlanta weren't this good in bed but how lucky was I to find the right one so soon. He was the right one in bed but totally the wrong one pertaining to the life that he already had right? I couldn't help but question myself on the flight back to Texas about what I had done and what I couldn't stop feeling. I knew that man was married but my body didn't care and it seemed like neither did his. I was just going with the vibe that he had given me. I even tried to remind him of his wife and he almost shutdown. I was guessing that his marriage was no better than mines and my husband was dead. Nobody is perfect and everybody needs some type of relief when it came to stress; in this case I was his and he was mines. But as much as I was trying to sit up here and justify my actions I couldn't ignore the fact that I had just became the same woman that I had hated Terrence for cheating on me with. His infidelity was the very reason why we had got into the fight that led up to me killing him in the first place and here I was playing pop that pussy Crystal for some married man that I had barely even knew.

"What was going on Crystal? "I said to myself starring down at my laptop screen that had pulled up a picture of Camry from off his business site. I couldn't ignore his divine looks. Just looking at him made me wet. I just knew if I had made one false move that my pants would slip right off me with panties and all. That man was something special but that still didn't justify my actions. I should have just sent him home and went to bed pleasing myself imagining his muscular frame on top of me. Would that had been different then actually laying with him?

The attraction was there from the beginning so it was only a matter of time before one of us gave in or he gave in to somebody other than me; it was clear he needed some relief. You could tell things weren't right at home because he was too good at his job. Any time a man was too good at this job it meant one of two things either things at home were perfect or he didn't have much of a home to call home so he spent most of his time working. At least with me he wasn't going to have to worry about tearing whatever marriage he had apart. I was going to try my hardest to never let that happen again but if it did I couldn't see myself trying to turn it into anything more than just sex. He was honestly a good lay but clearly a bad choice to try and be with. He was no different than the player who slept with all the girls on the block. The only shame was in this instance we were one in the same.

I starred at his picture most of the flight and went back and forth with myself and the thoughts in my head. Now that I had found myself on the other side of the fence I was finding myself trying to justify reasons on why what I did with a married man was ok just like so many that I had confronted when I was with Terrence. I had always felt that there was no excuse for their reckless behavior and always wondered if they saw any fault in their actions. Back then to me it seemed inhumane to do anything like that but now that it was me in their shoes I wasn't totally feeling like that anymore. I was feeling like it was the married man's fault more than the single women's because it was his responsibility to make sure he was on his best behavior when he was away from his wife not mines. Especially if he kept hot pursuit on you like he was single. Looking the way that he did a woman could only resist so much. He was supposed to be strong enough to say "I'm flattered but maybe in another life time when I'm not involved". I was just looking for a good time and a different feel and he volunteered to give it to me. Maybe if he had never texted me that night none of this would have ever happened. He initiated everything so if a man is like that I could understand why any woman in my shoes would feel like she wasn't at fault. I knew the reality was it was both our faults but I now understand why it is more so the man's wrong doing more than anyone else's. It kind of made me regret all those times I went after all those females that ended up with my husband. I would fight, fuss and have all these enemies because of him. I was chasing these girls away and only giving him a little bit of mouth as if he wasn't at fault at all. I should have been killed his cheating ass. I don't care how anyone puts it no woman is going to go after or follow after a man if she is not led or lured by him unless she is plain crazy. Was I making any sense or was I coping with being the other woman?

Camry didn't seem like the player type. It was obvious to me that he wasn't used to being touched by any other woman than his wife by his dramatic reactions to my kisses and his hesitation to engage in anything other than conversation with me. I believe that Camry was a good man who just so happened to fall victim of circumstances. A combination of his feelings and stress from his marriage was probably too much for him. I doubt if he even called or texted me again for anything other than business because he was feeling so guilty. He was probably at home right now washing off my perfume regretting every moment of his infidelity but then again I know that he enjoyed it just as much as I did and I hoped that he was wondering when it was going to happen again.

I couldn't believe that he was my little play boyfriend back in elementary school. I found that to be so cute and interesting. Almost twenty one years later here we were successful and finding out that what we were attracted to back then was still attractive today. Some things just never change I guess.

I have to admit that while we were having sex last night there was one thing that I was doing to cope with the fact that I was sleeping with a married man. Of course I could not help but notice his diamond studded wedding ring but instead I pretended that he was my husband and that large ring I had on my hand was from him. Yes, all last night and this morning I had imagined that he was my husband to make me feel better. I didn't imagine he was Terrence but that he was exactly who he already is but mines. I wouldn't mind having him being mines right now honestly.

The flight didn't seem like it was long at all. I was so lost in my thoughts that I had lost track of time thinking of him and trying to rationalize with my already convoluted decisions and thoughts.

The ride home was pretty much the same as the flight a lot of rationalizing and a lot of thinking. I hadn't totally finished packing nor decided what I was going to do with most of Terrence's things. I was thinking about giving them to his family since they were trying to hold on to him so much. Maybe then I could stop getting random death threats from his brother. I don't know how they were going to get it. I didn't want to be around when they picked his stuff up so maybe I could tell them to come get his stuff after I moved out. I'll just leave his stuff there so they could come pick it up.

Walking around the house and seeing all the photos of us; then seeing other ones of him on the field made me miss him so much. I missed going to the games and cheering him on. Going to the after parties and hopping on a jet in the middle of the night to whatever city he was in because I needed to feel his touch. Don't get it twisted Terrence was a sweet guy when he wanted to be but once he got some alcohol in his system he was a totally different person. Plus, his reckless behavior when I wasn't around was totally contradictory to what we built our marriage around.

Why can't I talk about him without mentioning two negatives with every positive? Oddly enough those two negatives were pretty much the ones that I had a problem with but I couldn't seem to try and move on from then because he would do things in public like date other women like it wasn't going to get back to me through the media or something. I hated that side of him but it seemed like it was a side that was common with every man; not the inability to keep his dirt under the rug but his inability to be a monogamist. I came to the reality that it was one of those things that majority of men just wasn't wired genetically to do. After all they do produce billions of eggs to our one a month so maybe it was something naturally that made them feel they needed as many women as they needed sperm. Maybe being a monogamist had less to do with a natural feeling for a man and more so a learned ability that they picked up on as they matured. I wasn't making excuses for their dirty dog ways but think about it. For us women, things just came natural like caring and nurturing and so on just like for a male it was natural for them to be total opposite, rough, messy and so on. One would think that for a man to do the things we do they would have to be taught and given time to understand. So with most women being prone to being a monogamist naturally then naturally they would have a little harder time getting wired to be a way that contradicted their reproductive system. Think about it; they make billions of sperm a month, some a day and you mean to tell me it was only meant to be shared with one woman? If that didn't make any sense or wasn't contradictory to nature I wasn't sure what was.

Wait, what am I saying?

All men are dogs and if they can't keep their dicks in their pants then it needed to be cut off. I must be tired or something, either that or that man just put something on me that had me changing how I viewed life. Don't you hate it when you have this made up mind on what u not gone do and wouldn't do but then this Mandingo warrior come along and introduce you to a side of yourself you didn't know you had and just that fast everything you wouldn't do your doing without one feeling of letdown by yourself... for example I said I would never take any naked pics of myself and send it to no man but I already have it on my mind to go and take a couple of flicks just to remind him on what he is going to miss while I'm gone. just that fast my morals went out the window

19

I was so tired I could hardly move my legs. I was so happy that the weekend had finally come. Trying to concentrate on work and juggle all the needs of Mrs. Jenkins, Tonya, Tiffany and Shondra brought me to my knees. This whole Exvantage thing was becoming to be too much. There had to be something else I could do to make this less stressful on my body and tiring on my brain. I was in a daze with my feet kicked up with a bag of ice in my lap because my penis was so sore. Camry was sitting next to me with his head down telling me about his troubles he was having with fine ass Linda. He was saying something about not being able to take it anymore and that he didn't mean to cheat on Linda.

Wait a minute ... Cheat on Linda?

"Wait bro... what did you just say?" I said snapping out of my slumbering daze and cutting my eyes towards him.

"I know man, I messed up you don't have to tell me." He replied in this low and shameful tone.

" I know that but say what you said again so I can make sure the dumbness I just heard was coming from a dumb ass."

"Go ahead and rub it in why don't you."

"Just give me a second and I will, now what did you do?" I asked again.

"I cheated on Linda ok! Why do you have to make me keep saying it bro!" he yelled clearly frustrated.

"Don't get mad at me but you're telling me like I'm the one who made you put your balls all on that woman."

"You might as well have…"

"What?"

"Hell yeah… All this player shit you had been asking me and bringing up lately. Making me give you advice and player material; then starting up this whole Exvantage experiment and creating an actual term for your rolling stone ass. This is your fault entirely! If it wasn't for you having me to think like this for you in the beginning then I would be good." He exclaimed in a condescending tone.

"What? Are you serious bro? I didn't ask you for any advice you just up and gave it to me like you had a hand guide on pussy hopping. Then you made it sound all smart by breaking it down like there was a science to it; Talking about the ex-girlfriends are the easiest ones to hook up with and old sex equals good memories and good memories equal recidivism when old faces attached to those good memories start to show up in the same room. So all that familiarity equals new sex over great sex because of the old connection" I exclaimed chuckling.

Even Camry had to let out a little chuckle after that one.

"Man you are crazy… but you know I didn't say half that stuff you were talking about. All I said was you should try hooking up with your exes in so many words because you were looking a little desperate for something wet in that desert you had been in ever since Tonya had cheated on your ass with an imitation of Tyrese, 50 cent and Michael Jai White all balled up in one. I could imagine him fucking her one minute singing then the next him rapping and the next him showing her why he was the first black super hero."

"That's supposed to be funny?"

"That's damn funny! Wouldn't none of this be happening if you hadn't been thinking all fucked up in the first place. I'm married and you had me thinking all messed up. I'm married and I'm out here thinking I wrote the movie how to be a player."

"I asked for help and you offered it. At least you know that it works so maybe you should write a book on it. You should write a book called Exvantage, it would probably do real numbers and change a lot of lives."

"Write a book? Called Exvantage?" Man as good as that sounds I have a feeling some fool is doing that right now somewhere else as we speak. I replied looking off into the ceiling to wonder the possibilities if I did.

"Yeah, you're probably right; we all know all the good ideas are already taken most of the time. But you should at least try."

"Try writing a book and being an author? I should do something crazy too like change my name to P.K Perkins and make a career out of changing people's lives through urban novels and children books?" He exclaimed still looking up at the ceiling as if he was visualizing his words.

"Who the hell is P.K Perkins?" He replied shaking his head side to side quickly to snap out his sudden daze. "Anyways what's been good with you?"

"No bro! Don't change the subject like you never said you cheated on your wife. You have yet to tell me who you bit the apple with."

"Oh… she said something about you… I think she knows you or something."

"Knows me?" My heart fluttered a couple extra times when he said that because most of the girls who know me were freaks and I just didn't want Camry to get caught up with those type of girls because once they had you… you were gone. What's her name?" I asked cautiously.

"Crystal Wilk's I think…? Ring a bell?" He said looking at me through the corner of his eye.

"Who?" I replied rubbing my chin.

"Crystal Wilk's."

"Who?"

"Crystal!" he yelled.

"Say her name again and maybe you will understand that I still don't know who she is, the name isn't ringing a bell genius, try to refresh my memory some other way." I exclaimed.

"Oh." He replied with a smile…. "She said that she met you at some fundraiser."

"Oh! That fine red bone with all that money! She was all on me too. How did that happen?"

"So you remember her?"

"Hell yeah. I can't forget a woman like that." I exclaimed.

"But you just did."

"What?" he replied looking puzzled?

"Anyway... I was selling a house to her and afterwards I guess she was trying to call you but ended up dialing my number talking to me thinking I was you. To make a long story short we went out for lunch and a couple days of seeing each other we had sex... five times."

"What?"

"It was one night through the next morning, that's all. It wasn't like it was on different days or anything."

"Fuck the different days and sex... You stole some ass from me? All this instructive booty, player talk you was giving me and all this time you had been booty snatching? Where's the loyalty?"

"Booty snatching? Bro she..."

"You're married for God sakes! To a woman that is fine as 24 karat gold. She is obligated to have her legs open whenever wherever. But instead of you doing what you're supposed to do you go and still some ass from me."

"Will you stop? You didn't even remember the chick ten minutes ago."

"Well I remember her pretty ass now. I'm starting to wish you wouldn't have brought her up. You old booty snatching Camry. Exvantage idealist, real estate extraordinaire, one half of a power couple, but at night in the shadows he is P.K.Perkins the number one booty snatcher." I exclaimed shaking my head.

"Booty snatching P.K.Perkins ? Who the hell is that?"

"I don't know! You said that name first!" I yelled about to get up but was quickly reminded how sore I was from the slightest movement that required putting my leg down.

"Anyway… so what should I do now?" Camry asked for the second time looking confused.

"Nothing… it was a shot in the dark right? Leave it at that. Things start to get much more complicated when you start thinking too much into them especially when sex is involved. It was just a smash and dash… so my advice to you is stay a track star but leave those quick ones alone."

"What?"

"A smash and dash? A hit and quit? A one night done night? A random tandem? A dip and slip?"

"Ok damn, I get it! That's what it's supposed to be but…"

"What? We don't do those… don't tell me you like this chick bro … the pussy was that good?"

"It's deeper than that… not only do I really like her but she is my ex."

"How…? I thought she said she was from Detroit?"

"She is but she went to our school in elementary. She was my girlfriend in the second grade."

"I don't remember her."

"That's because you didn't come to my school until the third grade. She was already gone by then."

"Wow … so if you want to count that, then that means that you have your own little Exvantage thing going on."

"I guess so… that's probably why we hit it off so well."

"Digg that so what did she say about me?"

"Nothing… after that one phone call she never mentioned you again."

"You are just a booty snatching pervert… you need to be arrested. So how is it more complicated? Explain it to me."

"Well I just got back from her place a couple of days ago."

"She already has a place here?"

"No, in Texas; she has a mansion out there. Apparently her husband was a football player for the league but she didn't say much about him."

"Wait a minute so you went to Texas to see her?"

"I had to bro… I just needed to see her. It's just hard to explain. It's like we have this undeniable connection. I just can't stop thinking about her and I find myself wanting her more and more."

"Well what about you and Linda? How are y'all?

"We are working on us, she came back home but the sex is still worthless. Sex with her feels worse than stabbing myself in the balls compared to simple four plays with Crystal."

"Damn!"

"Yeah Crystal is out cold with it."

"That's a hard one bro, literally. I need you to stop talking about sex because I'm growing a hard one thinking about it and you have no idea how much that hurts right now."

"That's a damn shame."

"So I'm guessing your feelings about Linda haven't really changed?"

"Nope not really... I mean I really love her but right now things just don't feel right. I'm really feeling Crystal right now."

"Bro, you're tripping man. Leave a booty call, a booty call away. Don't bring it home with you. You have a good thing going with Linda. Do you know how many guys are praying you two get divorced so they can have a chance with her? I even said a couple of Hail Mary's and in Jesus names a couple of times."

"Man stop."

"I'm just saying that the girl is fine as hell and she has a promising career, and no kids! Linda is everybody's dream. I don't want to just say every man's dream but hell everybody is looking for someone like her. But at the same time I am kind of glad that you took Crystal off my hands because I couldn't mess with her anyway."

"What? Why not? Wait a minute let me guess she wasn't slutty enough for you?"

"No … Mrs. Jenkins didn't want me even attempting to mess with her. I guess she doesn't want another wealthy woman to be sharing the same pleasures as her."

"Wow, so it's official? You really are her boy toy."

"You didn't have to put it like that… we have a bond and an understanding. She bought me a new bed and everything plus a new job. Oh, wait… I didn't tell you, did I?"

"What?"

"Guess who is my boss?" I exclaimed shaking my head.

"Who?"

"Man you will never guess."

"I know that's why I'm waiting on you to tell me instead of wasting my time trying to figure out."

"Marie."

"Lovejoy?" he replied with big eyes.

"Yeah man, I was shocked too."

"When did she get back here? Does she stay in Atlanta?"

"Yes and apparently she has been staying here for some time now. At least a year… She has a boyfriend who is also my boss and they have been together for eight months or so. All he does is talk about her."

"What? Is he like some arrogant black guy?"

"Hell no, he is a tall ass nerd. The boy's ankles show when he walks. He is not her type at all but he swears everything is peachy with them."

"Does he know that you and Marie were a serious couple back in the day?"

"I don't know. He hasn't mentioned it. But I don't see how he wouldn't know. If they are as close as he says they are then he should. As much as he rubs being with her in my face I would think he does know."

"Damn, so how does Marie act around you?"

"Bro, she acts like she never met me. She told me if I ever bring up the past she is going to fire me on the spot. That is the only time I have seen or heard her admit that she knows me from the past other than that I'm just another employee in the public eye."

"Wow! That is crazy. She did do you wrong by just up and leaving the way that she did. Maybe she feels guilty."

"I don't know man, it doesn't feel like that. It's more like I'm mad at you vibe that she gives me; Like I'm the one who had just got up and left. I was so torn that she left and now that she is in front of me I'm not sure what to do or what to feel and the fact that I have to look at her beautiful face every day really is making it hard for me to work."

"I couldn't imagine being in your shoes. I would just quit."

"Quit? Why because of a woman? Man please I love that job; it is what I am supposed to be doing. In a minute I'm going to have her man's jobs because I find myself showing him a thing or two every day. Besides Mrs. Jenkins doesn't want me working at an unskilled job so this is where I belong."

"Mrs. Jenkins? Will you stop bringing that woman up? She is your cougar but you're acting like she done bought you one. You better get your head in the game, its fate that you're at that job."

"What's fate?"

"That you and Marie are back around each other... Think about it as fine as she is and doesn't have any kids. She's not married and she came back home to you. I'm telling you its fate that you guys are back together. Second chances are for those who didn't get it right the first time which means chance and opportunity is on your side. Well look bro I got to go... I'll catch up with you later." He replied getting up and shaking my hand.

"So you are just going to leave me with a quote? What are you going to do about Crystal?"

He looked down and shook his head. "I don't know."

"Well just remember everybody don't get lucky twice you might have been given one chance and was smart enough to make the right decision when you married Linda. Don't ruin it bro... be careful." I said as he walked out.

I was so tired I couldn't even think after Camry left. Today was one of those days I chose to lay down and just rest up. There was no telling what the next day was going to bring but today I was ready to relax. I didn't have any plans to go see anybody and didn't want any plans. For once I was feeling like I was getting too much of a good thing needed to be left alone. It wasn't because of the sex. Seeing Marie now on a daily basis blew my mind. Seeing her with another guy only added with the pain that came with being around her. If we ever talked it was about work and anytime I brought up anything other than that she would ignore it as if she had deaf ears. She was treating me like I was the one that had done something wrong. All I did was not do what she wanted me to do fast enough. For her I was moving to slow and I guess for her that was a good enough excuse to throw our relationship down the drain. It didn't take me long to realize that I had a lot of resentment towards her more than anybody ever. A piece of me just wanted to forget and move on. After all I had enough women to tend to already. But because I had to work with her everyday it was a little hard to do that. I knew that I still had a lot of incomplete feelings and unsaid things deep inside. Every day I wanted to punch her boyfriend in the face. I hated working with his tall good for nothing ass. I would get annoyed as soon as I would see his face. I asked myself a couple time why was I feeling that way and I think that it boiled down to me still feeling like Marie was still my lady. I wasn't sure why I was feeling like that but I was. I knew everything about her probably more than her boyfriend did because it was embedded in my memory bank. To constantly see her and not be able to acknowledge that was kind of getting to me.

The other thing that was bothering me was the fact that we never broke up; she just up and left. It's obvious that we aren't together anymore but that doesn't mean that I'm satisfied with the way things ended, we never had any closure. Until now I didn't know how much that meant. My emotions were like a roller coaster when I saw her. If I could get her to come and talk to me outside of work then maybe I could release and shake some of these feelings that I had been battling with. I never felt like talking to her would amount to anything that would help me but it was obvious that after all this time I may have been fooling myself.

Camry was losing it in my book. It was all over his face and clearly in his actions. I was honestly let down when he had told me that he had cheated on Linda not only once in Atlanta but he flew to Texas to get a second helping. It kind of made me regret not calling Crystal the night I met her... she must have some good miss me when I'm gone pussy or something; in other words she had to have something special down there. I never thought that he would go to such extremes for something he had at home. Then again I guess he didn't if he had to go all the way to Texas to get it. I really didn't know what to tell him, I wanted to tell him to do the right thing but at the same time who was I to be ushering in the ways of wisdom and righteousness to a guy like him? He was my boy but a grown man first, a very smart one might I add. I'm pretty sure that he could figure out a way to put a leash on his dick and not do anything stupid enough to get caught up like invite the girl over his house or leave Linda for her. He knew just like I knew that divorce due to infidelity nowadays had less to do with going separate ways and more so with money being exchanged into whoever the victim was account. I would hate to see my boy lose everything he had worked for because he couldn't keep his dick in his pants. That seemed to be a lot of men's demise nowadays. Reckless driving might get you locked up for a day or so but reckless fucking can destroy your career and life in numerous ways. One could mess up your driving record and endanger others and the other could end your career, marriage and possibly whatever good reputation a guy may have had.

In a sense a guy stepping out on his wife probably brought men some type of excitement that most people longed for. I had never been married but if it was my guess, a person like Camry would cheat for the same reason that a regular person would cheat in a relationship. Just because he was married didn't mean that he wasn't subject to the same temptation that we was all subject to. But at the same time I looked at it like a level of achievement and because one gets married he must have reached a level of control, resistance and loyalty to past the test of time. For example I would know I was ready to get married if the Halle Berry came up to me butt booty naked and I told her no. I would know that I wasn't ready to get married if that same thought of Halle Berry mentioning that she wanted a random guy to make her feel good turned me on so much that I wanted to masturbate to the idea.

I think that every couple should put themselves through a series of loyalty and financial tests before they decided that marriage is what they wanted to do. A lot of marriages failed because they had no idea what they were getting into and truly prepared for what was to come. The harsh reality is that love isn't enough to pay the bills or keep a man's hard dick in control enough to make him want sex with just one woman. Numerous people say that if he cheats that he must not have loved the woman he cheated on but how much merit does love have on all actions? A man can still love his wife or girl if he cheats but he may be lacking other things like self-control. Love doesn't give the essentials it just gives us what we asked for, everything else comes with time and effort. Think about it, it doesn't matter your religion, does it mean that you don't love God when you sin against him? If it does then we are all doomed for hell right? The reality is that we are human and we make mistakes, bad decisions and whatever other screw up that there is to commit. Hopefully Camry will have this little bit of fun without letting any of it get out of hand but we all know that more times than none it doesn't always work out that way. I guess the good friend thing to do is to tell him to work on his marriage with a little more passion.

BRRR.BRRR.

My phone violently vibrated on my night stand next to my bed. I had been feeling a little better from earlier and relaxing watching TV in my room when I had received a call from Mrs. Jenkins. I looked at the clock in my phone "10:45pm" She never calls me this late." I said to myself answering the phone.

"Yeah…"

"Yeah? Is that the way I told you to answer the phone?" She replied in a condescending tone.

"What's up Mrs. Jenkins?"

"What did I tell you about calling me that boy?"

"What's wrong Laura?"

"I need you to come over here."

"Over where, your house? Why? I told you I'm not…"

"I don't care what you said! I don't feel like driving across town to your place so you need to make the trip over here to me!" She demanded.

"Isn't your husband home?"

"No fool! Do you think I would be calling you if he was? He is out at some event that most likely is going to go well into the morning."

"I don't know Laura, that seems to be a little risky and I don't want to get caught up in any mess."

"Austin you better get here or you can kiss that job of yours goodbye. You realize that I am the single reason you have that job? I don't know what problems you have had with your boss there but if it was up to her then you wouldn't be there so that means that you are hanging on by a single thread and guess whose that thread?" She replied in a threatening tone.

"Are you serious?"

"I'm promising you! Don't get here in an hour and find out how serious I am!" She yelled.

"You know what go ahead and take that job... I hope that it will fuck you better than I do. Oh... and by the way I hope your husband doesn't divorce you after he finds out you have been making love to another man daily... Bye!" I replied quickly hanging up.

It bothered me to hang up the phone and throw away everything that I have worked for but she was just getting out of hand. Did you hear the way she was talking to me? I had a hard enough time trying to deal with the reality that I was just her boy toy but for her to talk to me reckless was a slap in the face and I wasn't about to have it. She was letting all the stress she was having and all that power I was letting her have get to her head. If she knew any better she would readjust her attitude and talk to me in a better tone. But if she wanted to play this little game of threats then I was game for that too.

BRRR...BRRR...

My phone vibrated again but this time much more.

"You want something?" I said in disdain knowing it wasn't anybody but Mrs. Jenkins.

"So are we going to play these games all night or are you going to leave me over here dripping wet and craving for you." She said in a much more persuasive tone.

"I don't know Laura, you're getting..."

"I'm sorry ok! Is that what you want to hear? I just get a little lonely and frustrated. I don't mean to take it out on you. Now can you please come and keep me company? If it helps to let you know I'm scared in this big old house. I think I heard somebody kick in the front door."

"You better call the police then!" I replied sharply.

"Austin."

"Alright give me a minute. I'll be over there but only until twelve because I don't want to risk running into your husband and having to beat his ass."

"Well time is a wasting time then." She replied hanging up the phone.

I really didn't want to be bothered but it was kind of hard for me to say no to her. Without any real effort she was doing a lot for me. She bought me a new bed, got me a new job and every time I came around she gave me money so she was paying my bills. I guess it was her way of making me feel better about what I was doing. Little did she know that I could care less if she had got me any of those things. Laura was fine and highly wanted by not only me but, damn near every guy that she ran across. She was older but could easily compete with girls that were much younger. Not to mention she felt just as good as she looked which was unbelievable. I was beginning to question whether her husband had another woman on the side because he never touched the places I had been. If anyone would listen in on us having sex they would swear I was taking her virginity.

My nerves were getting to me and I was still in a little pain so I had popped three pain killers that I had received over a year ago because I was in a car accident. I really was hurt but I did have a couple spasms in my back so the doctor gave me some strong pain killers for all my stress. They were probably expired but I never really paid too much attention to expiration dates unless it was on dairy products or meat. What was the worst that could happen? Besides I was going to need something after a couple of rounds with her. I just knew the soreness was going to come back so I might as well try to dull the pain now.

I didn't even bother putting on any real clothes. I just threw on some gym shoes, a wife beater and some sweat pants. I should have just worn a robe because half of them were going to just end up on the floor anyway. I had never been so nervous to go please a woman in my life. It wouldn't have been a big deal if she had just come to my place but coming to her place was another type of danger. Her mansion was deep into the woods of Georgia about an hour out of Atlanta in a town not that far from College Park. Her house was sitting on like six acres or something like that. The only thing bad about it is that it had an eerie feel because it was so dark around her place. There were street lights but not as many as you would find near the city. I was hesitant to park my car at her house so I parked it at a convenient store and had her pick me up and take me back to her place. I didn't want to risk being seen so I figured that I should take as many precautions as possible. The store was nowhere from her house and she had the nerve to complain about coming to get me. Some women you just couldn't make happy in life, things made sense to them in only one way and that is their own.

....

Two hours later...

"I can't breathe! Oh my God... I'm so tired!" Laura said shaking dramatically next to me as she rolled off of me and onto her side of the bed.

"Are you ok?" I replied trying to put the spinning walls in one place. I was out of breath, sweaty and dizzier than I ever had been. I felt like I was on a rapidly spinning cloud that had no means of slowing down.

"You are trying to kill me boy? That was the longest you had ever, oh... Lord Jesus boy!" She uttered out trying to recover.

"Yeah?" I replied looking up at the ceiling and swearing I had just saw a giraffe eat a lion. I quickly shook my head because I knew I was probably tripping from those expired pills I took earlier. They were to credit for the marathon sex that we had just had. I wasn't doing too much tonight, I was so light headed I let her do all the work and it was obviously the right move to do.

"I have to get ready to go, are you going to take me to my car?"

"Call a cab. I'm not going to have enough energy." She replied struggling with her breathing.

"It's almost two in the morning and I'm in the suburbs, what cab am I going to be able to catch?!" I mumbled out.

"Then stay here."

"Hell no! Are you crazy? What are you trying to do get your husband beat up? Because I'm telling you if he runs up on me I'm going to beat the hell out of him."

"My husband isn't going to be home tonight if he isn't home by now he isn't coming. He is probably out with one of his tramps enjoying a long blow job while surfing the web on his blackberry." She replied in a carefree tone as if she permitted his behavior.

I wanted to respond but nothing was really registering for me. All I could think about was getting the hell out of there before something truly had jumped off between her and her husband. I wasn't really caring what happened I just wanted to leave.

"We have to go." I replied rolling onto the floor and grabbing my clothes.

"You're so scary... why don't you stay a little longer? Maybe we can get one more round in?" She suggested touching my back.

I almost fell over, pulling my boxers up on my waist. It seemed like the room had spun but the cloud I was on was getting ten times higher. Sweat dripped down my chest along the sides of my body as I sat there trying to gather myself to put on the rest of my clothes.

"You ok? Are you alright?" She asked sitting up behind me and reaching over into my lap." It feels like you want to go for one more round baby." She insisted wrapping her hand around my still surprisingly erect shaft.

I was so high that I hadn't even realized I was still hard. I couldn't feel anything, not even my face. This was all bad. I knew that I shouldn't have taken those pills but at the same time if I didn't I would have been in much more pain than ever before. I wish that they made pills that took away pain but didn't have the psychedelic effects. I just didn't want to feel any pain all this other shit I was feeling was really unnecessary. I just so happened to look up at her wall that faced the bed and noticed one of two things. There was a camera hanging in the corner of the room pointing directly at us and another picture of a woman wrestling a bull just like the one in her office but this one was much different. It was much more real life like and instead of her having the bull by the horns she had it by the balls. I shook my head and looked at the picture again and she was riding the bull with one arm in the air.

"What the..." I blurted out.

"What's wrong baby?"

"We need to go." I replied grabbing my pants and slipping them on and stuffing my feet in my shoes.

"You're no fun." She said clearly disappointed.

"Well maybe some other day. I just don't feel right." I replied putting on my shirt.

"I guess… Do you need any money? I know you do, so here." She said grabbing an envelope and handing it to me. I looked inside of it and noticed it was a lot more than she normally gave me.

"What's this for?"

"Your troubles and a token of my appreciation; you really do make me feel better." She replied getting out of bed and putting on a red silk house coat over her naked body. I put the money in my pocket and just so happened to look back over at the picture on the wall. I swear she was fighting with the bull again instead of riding it. She was trying to stop it from mounting her like it would a cow but her efforts fell short.

"We have to go." I said in a stern voice trying to regain my composure.

"Ok … I'm ready let's go."

I had a hard time trying to keep my balance walking through here huge hallways and wide rooms. For the first time I had noticed how many cameras they had in the place which was beginning to make me a little concerned. All her husband had to do to see what his wife was up to while he wasn't home was check the footage. Why wasn't she concerned about that? I know if I had cameras at my place and I was married I would never have anybody at my place. Her actions made no sense to me at all. It was almost as if she wanted to get caught. I didn't really mind if that is what she wanted to do but I didn't want to get caught up in some bullshit. She was fine but I didn't want to be the one who replaced her husband. I liked the sex alot but not necessarily her enough to want to replace anybody.

A little bit of relief had come over my body once we reached her car and began to leave. We got in the ford focus and were leaving her property when her husband was pulling up into the property right in front of us. I didn't know it was him at first until she panicked and pulled my head down into her lap as his car approached ours.

"Baby? Where are you going this late at night?" His lightly toned voice said.

"I'm making a run to the store... I need some girl stuff."

"It's that time of the month already? Are you serious? Well I guess my night won't be what I thought it would be."

"What you thought it would be?"

"Yes, I won the game at the event, sort of like a bet... baby I'll explain it later, just hurry back. It's too late to be out this time of night."

"You want to come with me?"

My heart skipped a beat and I bit a little into her thigh nervous and confused. What was she doing? It was obvious now that she didn't care. She wanted to get caught.

"Oh no baby... I'm so tired and I have a lot to do in a couple of hours. I'm sure you will be fine, just hurry back" he said clearly in a rush to do something.

"Fine." she replied pulling off. "It's safe now."

"What are you crazy?" I exclaimed lifting up my head and looking back at her house as we pulled off the property.

"I knew he wasn't going to say yes."

"What if he did?"

"But he didn't, he is too busy thinking about either washing the sex off of him that he just had with probably some young blonde at the party or he is in such a rush to try and get a quickie in with Vicky."

"Vicky?"

"You've seen Vicky, she is our maid; a short petite long black hair young Mexican lady. She is about your age and barely speaks English."

"I've never seen her."

"Well she stays on the east wing of the house. I took her in after seeing her stranded at a bus station in Texas. Poor thing didn't know anything. I let her work for me as a maid and offered her room and board along with minimum wage pay. She was thrilled. I called myself doing a good deed. Then after about a year, Mark and I were having some problems so I left for a second and then when I came back home after a couple of days I caught them two having wild sex all over the hall on the east wing floor.

"You saw it for yourself."

"No... I viewed it on the camera while it was happening. I wanted to kill him but I just learned to deal with it."

"Does he know you know?" I replied noticing that my daze that I was in had faded away a little bit more.

"He has to know I know and if he doesn't then he is dumber than I thought. But I would be dumb to assume that because he is one of the richest people I know and he came up from nothing just like so many other people who used their heads. He knows I know; I just haven't said anything about it. I haven't said anything because of all the advantages of being his wife."

"Advantages? So what are you saying money over your feelings?"

"Don't start! We all know that money trumps everything in this world. It's the god of granting wishes, the automatic river of power. I have my own money but it's not like his money."

"Are you serious? What about God? I thought that he was the ever flowing river of power."

"Let's get real now boy! You don't ever see God and the closest thing you do see about him is on a dollar. You can't be that naïve boy! This is the world that we live in, not some fairy tale lie that was told to our ancestors to control them without using so much force. They forced their fairy tale religion on us because they were losing so much of their investment through violence. You want to control someone give them something to believe in and they will do whatever you want. It's always one of the two its either something to believe and if that doesn't work then give them money, so they can depend on you." She replied in a stern tone as if she had written these words in a book of nonsense herself.

"Don't you have some money put away?"

"Of course I have money but nowhere near enough to maintain my lifestyle. It's just not something that you can give up after ten plus years, it's a process. That's why I bought this car, not only is it easy on gas but it's a good move for any middle class American. That's where I figured I would fit in even though without my husband I would still be worth a large amount of money."

"I was wondering why you had bought this car. One day you were in a Benz and the next it was this."

"Yeah I have been doing a lot of planning and I'm just making sure that I am prepared. But in the meantime that's why I have you."

"Yeah, you have me but what do you think? That you are going to have me forever? I have a life too."

"Well we will deal with it when it happens. Until then you're my escape from this mess I call my marriage." She replied as we pulled up to the convenient store where my car was parked.

"I'll call you the next time I need you which you know will be soon."

"Wait. Let me ask you something. Do you ever wonder what's going on in my life?"

"Austin I don't think it's my job to care because if you cared yourself and had anything working out for you in that area I don't think that you would be answering my calls at any beckoned time. You can stop this thing you have with me anytime time you want; Nobodies forcing you to be here."

"Nobody's forcing me to be here?" I replied cutting her off and looking at the time shine on her dashboard. "It's too late for this. I'll just see you later." I said getting out of her car and getting into mines. She just let me go without a fight which is what I expected but it had never felt so cold.

I couldn't find it in myself to drive home. I was extremely tired and I wasn't sure when those pills were going to kick in so I just went to sleep right there in the car. It was funny to me when Mrs. Jenkins said that I had no choice to be with her as if she gave me one. She only reminded me and threatened me that she was the reason that I had a job and she could be the reason I lose it. She knew just as well as I did that if I had just walked away now then she was going to try her hardest to make my life miserable because I was her fix and she depended on me right now and I kind of depended on her too. I hadn't really looked in the envelope since I had put it in my pocket but I was sure that it was at least three grand in it. A grand was the most she had ever given me at one time. I knew I was being used by her but I didn't really know why until tonight. I could only imagine what she was going through in that power stricken head of hers. Seeing and knowing her husband was constantly messing around with not only random women but also the maid that she had took in, must have been crushing. It was clearly eating her up inside. She was like dope fiend but instead of using a syringe she was using my dick to inject her with a high. Her drug was much more natural and in her eyes much more safe. The only problem was she wanted me to put my life on hold until she kicked her addiction or escaped her circumstance. This was fun in the beginning but now that so much has been revealed I'm not sure that I want to keep living my life like this. I went from shit to sugar but all this sugar seemed to be giving me diabetes.

I went from being a man on a mission to get married to a broken hearted man looking for relief to a student trying out an ingenious project titled Exvantage and now I am something like a gigolo. Let's call it like it is I was getting paid for sex by my boss and filling in for most of my exes missing in action boyfriends who were either locked up or just hadn't decided on what they wanted to do with their lives. I was just a fill in; but isn't this what I wanted? I mean you can't get a little without giving alot right? I think I was starting to forget why I had started messing with so many women in the first place. I just wanted to forget about love and relationships and get what I wanted without all the strings involved but now that I was getting it I don't think that I was enjoying it like I thought I would anymore. It had been only a couple of months but I was starting to feel like more of a tool and less of a man.

20

"Just remember everybody don't get lucky twice. You might have been given one good chance and was smart enough to take it when you married Linda. Don't ruin your chances. Be careful"

Those were the words that stuck with me after I left Austin the other day. It had almost been two months since then and I must admit that I was taking his advice and truly trying to work on my marriage. Because he was right I was a lucky man to have Linda and just because we had a couple of differences here and there didn't mean that it was ok for me to give up on her. I knew better but sometimes I just felt inclined to do other things to escape my reality that things were far from perfect.

....

"We haven't had fun like this in a long time. I can't wait to get back to the house and show you how much I appreciate this baby. Better yet why wait?" Linda said as we were on our way home from a night out on the town. Whole in one gulp, dinner and a movie was one of her favorite things to do and she was letting me know right now. She unzipped my pants and pulled my penis through the boxer passage way and began sucking it right there in traffic. As soon as the light turned green I began looking for a place to pull over so I wouldn't have to worry about somebody with a truck looking down on us and getting a rise out of my rise.

"Yeah that's it crystal, just like that." I blurted out biting my tongue but Linda didn't stop. I had the music on so I was hoping that she didn't hear me over the heavy bass and smooth tunes.

Regardless if she had heard me or not I couldn't believe I was slipping like that. I managed to pull over into a residential street in front of a vacant house and park so I could finish enjoying a sign of her appreciation. I reclined my seat and watched as she had done what I had been longing for her to step up and do for the longest. Ever since we started working back on our marriage the sex slowly started to get back to great like it used to be. It was like she was doing more than lying on her back. I must admit that being with two women weren't that bad from the simple fact that I was able to teach her a couple of moves that Crystal had shown me.

BRRR...BRRR...

"Oh God not now." I moaned.

"Answer it..." Linda stopped and said.

"Why?"

"Because I want you to know they need not to call around this time. I want them to realize what they are interrupting. Wait who is it?"

I looked at the number, it was Crystal.

"A client?" Linda asked.

"No it's my cousin Sholanda." I blurted out naming someone I knew and she wouldn't want me talking to with hopes that she would change her mind about wanting me to answer the phone.

"Oh yeah, answer it I hope she gets so grossed out that she never calls back I hate that bitch." She replied looking up at me with her hand around my shaft anticipating me to pick up the phone.

Damn it backfired! I thought to myself as I answered the phone. "Hello? Awe... fuck!" I blurted out as Linda stuffed my whole cock in her mouth and quickly began sucking

"Hey baby? I know that reaction...you busy? Is your wife finally doing her job?"

"Awe... yeah ..." I was barely able to reply without breaking my tone.

"You like it?"

"What? What's up? Awe... what do you want .... Can I call you back?" I uttered.

"I know you will, but I was just calling because I wanted some of what she getting right now"

"Huh?"

"Does she do it better than me daddy?"

"What?"

"Does she suck your dick better than me? Does she lick the shaft at the tip and around the sides like me? Does she make your legs shake and your eyes roll in the back of your head like my fat lips do? I want to suck your dick so bad I can taste it."

"Oh my ga!" I blurted out being excited even more from Crystals tone.

"I want to suck every ounce out of you baby. I want to feel it sliding down my throat. Come let me suck it baby! Please!" She moaned out over the phone.

I started to start the car up and take Linda home so I could go to Crystals. But something was happening in the midst of Linda giving me head and Crystal talking dirty to me. I could feel my dick fill with more blood. I was about to pop! It was like I was having a threesome but without a third person being totally present.

"Don't stop!" I moaned talking to both Linda and Crystal. Linda sped up and tightened her lips around my dick while Crystal kept on.

"I want you to put it all the way in my mouth, cum in my mouth Camry... cum!"

I couldn't take anymore.

"I'm Cuming! Awe shit!!" I loudly moaned as I began exploding in Linda's mouth she jumped backward into her seat trying to dodge every ounce of my climax.

"Awe... What happened she didn't swallow? Miss me don't you?" Crystal said as she hung up.

"Napkin... Grab me a napkin from out of the glove compartment." I said to Linda who was spitting out the window.

"Get it your damn self!"

"What's wrong with you? Get me a napkin so I can clean this up." I said grabbing myself a napkin and cleaning myself off along with the steering wheel, the dash board and the driver's side handle.

"And you wanted me to do what with that? That's how you look at me Camry?"

"What?!"

"You were just going to come in my mouth like I'm some type of hoe? Is that what you want me to be?"

"How does that make you feel like a hoe? I thought it would make you feel like you were pleasing your man?"

"Hoes do that Camry you know that. How many times must we go through this? We both know when we was growing up the one girl who had a reputation of swallowing was a hoe. Is that what I look like to you?" she yelled folding her arms

"That's the dumbest excuse I've ever heard all because you don't want to do your job. Why would I look at my wife like a hoe? I like getting my dick sucked and not having to worry about where I'm going to have to place my fruits. If I thought that you were a hoe I would have never married you."

"You married me because I have never done anything hoeish like that. I made it clear to you that you were marrying a lady." She yelled.

I threw the semen filled tissue out the window and drove off without another word.

"Are you cheating on me Camry?"

Linda shouted breaking the silence.

"Huh?" I said rather suspicially.

"Ok you want to play dumb who the hell is Crystal?"

I almost crashed the car when she said that. She must have heard me call her that when she was giving me head. I tried my hardest not to react but it's hard to do that when you're close to being busted.

There was two ways that I could play this off. I could act like I didn't know what she was talking about or I could admit to knowing who Crystal was and admit my wrong doing..... Quickly thinking about my options I didn't think that either one of those choices were good options. There had to be a better way out of this mess and then it hit me.

"Crystal is my name for you when you do all the things I like in the bedroom." I replied with a straight face almost bracing my jaw for an expected punch.

"Like an alter ego?" she replied raising her eyebrow.

"Yeah exactly like that; you know everybody has one. Tiny, the rappers wife calls herself Rider in the bedroom. I was just trying to spice things up that's all but if you don't like the name then I won't call you that anymore."

"Really; Spice things up huh? Well just let me come up with one on my own next time ok?" She replied looking suspiciously down at my phone.

"The head was great baby; I can't wait to get home so I can return the favor. I can taste it already. Matter of fact, give me that. I replied steering with my left hand and with my right fingering my way under her dress through her panties.

"Yeah you are ready!" I exclaimed feeling the moistness around her clit.

Her attention quickly went from my phone to relaxing in the now reclined passenger seat and enjoying the touching ride home.

Once we got back to the house I honestly was anxious to get to the bed room with hopes that we were going to have some electrifying sex but instead it was back to the stiff bodied boring sex that was pushing me away from home in the first place. I just couldn't wait till it was over. Everything about Linda and her selfish ass was making me a little frustrated. All I wanted was a good fuck from her and everything would get better. That's why I spent so much time at work because she gave me an excuse to stay away. This is why Crystal was right for me right now... Without her in my life I probably would be sexually depressed.

After the boring sex I laid there and thought about all the events that happened today. I couldn't believe that Linda had accepted the excuse I had gave her for calling Crystal's name out. I thought she was going to grab my phone and try and call the girl but she didn't. She kind of accepted what I told her and that was that. That goes back to the whole trust thing that I was talking about earlier, she had no other choice but to believe me. I wanted to say that I had felt ashamed for telling her so many lies lately but I know if I told her anything close to the truth she wouldn't try and understand my perspective in the whole thing. All she would see was me being the bad guy.

Then she really pissed me off in the car with the whole dodging my cum like it was bullets. Where the hell were we? Are we still in the eighth grade or something? After all this time of sex and fluids she still acts like she's a little girl. I don't understand it. She will let me cum anywhere else but not in her mouth? Don't let it get on her hand and she sees it, you would think she had got acid or something repulsive on it. Talking about swallowing is for hoes. Well damn it maybe I should have married a hoe because I want someone who's going to swallow, damn it. If anybody was supposed to be doing it for me it was supposed to be my wife right? I mean I do whatever there is to be done to her. I even lick her ass on a hot summer day with no shower if I have to, why? Because I love her and will do anything to make sure she is satisfied but you can't tell Linda to do the same for me...No, Linda has morals and she feels that certain things will demoralize her. I wonder did anybody tell her that when she got married nothing was supposed to come before it. Fuck some morals, I want a freak in the sheets not no damn dead body!

You damn right I should have married a hoe, If I was using the right head I would have but I called myself using the big brain instead of the "little one", well I hate to admit it but in this case the little one knew what the hell was the right thing to do. There were plenty of other girls willing to do whatever to be in Linda's place but I stuck it out and chose the best looking and smartest one and who I thought could satisfy me the most in the bed room but clearly that was wishful thinking. Linda was too selfish to take her ability to another level. I loved her dearly but this was far too frustrating for me to be happy with our marriage right now. There is no way in hell that I should be lying in bed with a woman as beautiful and thick as my wife and be wishing it was some other woman. As bad as I wanted to lie to myself I couldn't. I wanted Linda to be Crystal right about now because I know my body would have still been shaking right now from whatever she was doing to it.

Brrr...Brrr...

I quickly rolled out of bed and answered my loud vibrating phone. It was a text from Crystal.

-I'm wet, can you cum help me tighten up these leaky pipes.-

It was 1:30 in the morning and Linda was in the bed sound asleep. I was wide awoke and so was my second coming. I wanted to fix those pipes but what do I tell Linda?

"Hey baby I'm about to fix a client's pipes. She said they were wet and she wanted me to clog them?" I said to myself. While I was coming up with a lie I grabbed my boxers and some clothes and put them on. It was cold kind of now in Atlanta so I had to do more digging around than usual to find some warm easy to take off clothes.

"Where are you going?" Linda mumbled lightly waking up out of her sleep and peeking out of one eye.

Why did she have to wake up so soon, I wasn't ready with my lie yet?

"I'm about to shoot over to Austin's place, him and Tonya just got into a real bad fight, the police are over there."

"Oh...My God... I thought they broke up?" She replied opening the other eye.

"Yeah they did but they're like off and on...It's just a process that's taking a little longer than he expected. I have to go check on him." I replied with a convincing tone of concern.

"Ok, well be careful...You know he doesn't stay in the best place...Do you need me to go with you?"

"Hell no! I mean no baby I got it get your rest…I'll be back soon"
I replied kissing her on the cheek and walking out the bedroom
with my keys and phone in hand.

Lie after lie after lie seemed to be working for me. I had
never felt so good about lying in my life. I mean I felt bad but I
knew once I got to Crystal's place I was going to feel great so to
me it was worth it. Crystal was just trying harder to get my
attention while Linda on the other hand felt like there was
nothing else that she needed to do to keep our marriage intact.
I don't understand where she could get the nerve to feel so
comfortable after we were coming off of the worse fight we
ever had not too long ago. Matter of fact it was that fight and
her leaving that kind of opened the door for all this mischief.

Going to Texas only made me try and speed up the
process to get Crystal in Atlanta even more. After we had
hooked up that first night I was a little skeptical about how she
may handle things but once she started spending more time
with me and showed me she wasn't going to give much of a
fight with the whole marriage thing I just knew this could work.
Plus the way she was out in Texas was amazing. The woman had
a new Ferrari for God's sake. She would have let me drive it too
if I had wanted to but I was too nervous to be driving a car that
expensive.

I was only there for two days but the whole time I
enjoyed myself. The house was so big it really didn't matter if
we went anywhere because waking up in a different room in
another part of the house gave off this hotel type of feel. I
didn't really want to leave Texas and come back home to my
wife but I think that I would have been a fool to try to see if the
80-20 rule was true. I knew Linda was at home waiting on me

and Crystal only played a major role in one part of my life so the reality was I need to get my ass home.

Once I got home I felt like I wasn't giving Linda a chance. So that's why I decided that we should try and work things out. At the same time the bank had come through for Crystal's house and she was able to move into her house a little sooner than expected. To be honest I needed her to be away a little longer to shake the feeling and good thing that I was having with Crystal. Because my marriage was getting a little better and it was obvious Linda was actually making an effort to keep me satisfied and I was working forty hours instead of trying to work eighty.

But all it took was one incident to make me feel like it wasn't going to work and I found myself right back in bed with Crystal. Now that I think about it I should have delayed that sales process a little longer so I could have gave my wife and I a little bit more time to fix our broken marriage. By moving her here I wasn't doing nothing but digging a bigger grave for myself.

"Can we talk baby?" Crystal said rubbing her fingers across my belly.

"About what?"

"Everyday life...There are some things I want to know."

I already knew where this conversation was about to go. We had just got done with our second round of sex and the morning sun was maybe an hour or two from rising. I was exhausted but not sleepy enough to not entertain a conversation with her. I enjoyed talking to Crystal because she was very down to earth and easy to talk to.

"What's on your mind?"

"I want to know what's going on with you."

"What do you mean?"

"How are you and your wife?"

"I don't...Do you really want to talk about this right now Crystal?"

"We need to talk about it...You don't ever talk about what's going on in your head...Clearly I'm in there but you don't want me to know anything other than that."

"...So you want to talk about Linda?"

"That's her name?"

"Yeah...Um we are having a rough time right now and I'm having a hard time dealing with it. It just seems like she doesn't....She doesn't do..."

"She doesn't do you like me? Is that what brings you to me every other day?"

"Sex is a big deal in a relationship especially if I'm comparing you two in the bedroom is like a slice of bread to a souped up fully loaded subway sandwich. She's boring and less alluring in the bedroom while you have a whole assortment of things jumping off."

"Is that all you come to get me for is sex?"

"Actually it was at first but now it's like I have such a good time with you, I find myself wanting to be around more and more. I mean Linda and I have our good times but it's been bad for a long time. I'm battling right now with you two because I want to work on my marriage and not fall into the stereotype of a black man and the high percentages of divorce but at the same time…." I stopped because I caught myself saying way too much too soon. I wasn't supposed to be saying any of this, I was just supposed to be keeping it fun, not emotional but I was afraid no matter how much I tried to ignore it, it was far too late.

"At the same time what?" Crystal replied anxiously.

"Maybe we shouldn't be talking about this." I suggested almost in regret.

"What? So is that how it is? You can't talk to me or express anything? Oh…I get it… I'm just the side thing…The booty call right?" The red bone trophy piece you have locked up in the closet for your own pleasure. I know that Camry. And I like you so much I wasn't even tripping about that but to act like you can't even talk to me…that hurts." Crystal replied turning her back towards me and folding her arms.

"Crystal…Don't be like that please…I apologize, I just have a hard time comprehending all of this…"

"All of what!" Crystal interrupted.

"These feelings that I'm feeling, they are coming out of nowhere and I don't know what to do with them."

"Feelings? Like what?" She replied digging deeper into the issue.

"Are you really trying to make me go into this?" I replied shaking my head disappointed with my inability to just keep sex, sex.

"Yes…You need to stop being so damn selfish."

"Selfish? How?"

"Um…Hello, am I here? Am I not with you every other night? What do you think I am a robot? You think I don't feel too?" She replied turning back towards me.

"I'm not saying that…I'm saying I'm not supposed to be feeling anything for anybody but my wife but I can't stop feelings things for you."

"Like what?! Face the music Camry! Just because you're sitting here trying to hold back your emotions doesn't mean they aren't there. Tell me!" She insisted.

I took a deep breath and looked at her directly in her eye quickly questioning if I should reveal my feelings and open up that Pandora's Box. What was I getting myself too? I asked myself but nothing like an answer compiled in my head the only thing that I could do is hear myself talking to Crystal.

"When I'm away from you I can't stop thinking about you. When I'm with my wife sometimes I wish I was with you. Sexually I'm not even really turned on by my wife compared to how I am with you. I swear if you hadn't called while I was with her earlier I probably would have went soft and the cat would have been out the bag. Crystal I shouldn't be having sex with my wife and thinking of you, hoping that you were doing the same to me…This just isn't right."

"Well how do you think any of this makes me feel? So you seriously think that I enjoy having sex with a man I know has to leave me to go back to his wife. It may not seem like it now but when I was married I hated women like myself. Who made their bodies a home for my husband and now look at me."

"Don't be like that...its different."

"No it isn't, I'm just a jump off to you just like any other girl."

"Stop it...It's not like that..." I insisted.

"Then what is it?" She replied expressing her frustration.

Crystal was pushing the envelope and almost forcing me to open up for her feelings and validity. I really didn't want to say any more but at the same time I didn't want her feeling the way that she was because the way she was feeling was so far from the actuality. If I didn't say something now I may lose her but if I do I may be taking this fling we have to another level. I wasn't sure that another level was what I needed but there was a chance that she needed those next level words to make her feel better about herself.

"Crystal, I love being with you... I more than like how you are and how you treat me."

"Then what are you saying? You love me?" She replied cutting her eyes at me and staring deep into mines.

I hesitated for a minute and thought about a response.

"I love how you make me feel and what you make me feel. I love that when we are having sex we are not fucking but making love." I replied trying to use my words wisely coming as close as I could to saying I love you without really saying it.

"What does that mean Camry? You love all this stuff about me but you don't want to tell me you love me?" she replied in disdain.

"No...I'm saying...I think I love you" I blurted out. "But I don't want to."

"What the hell does that mean? I don't want you to feel or do something that you don't want to Camry." She said rolling her neck and eyes away from me.

"It's too late...You already have and I'm glad you did." I replied touching her chin and turning it back towards me and kissing her softly on the lips. "I love you." I said in between kisses.

"I love you too." She replied taking a deep gasp of air and shifting her body and climbing on top of me.

In this moment everything from the kisses to how we touched felt fulfilling. The morning sun rose and shined on us as we made love as if it was blessed by the Gods and that's exactly how I felt. In this moment, this was my home and as dangerous and deep as I knew things were getting I'm not sure I cared anymore. I just liked what I was feeling, what I needed to feel. I was feeling blessed by something that I was sure was going to prove to be a curse but until it proved to me otherwise, I was enjoying the moment.

....

Twenty one

CRYSTAL

"Acting brand new." Linda said rolling her eyes at me

"You are something do you know that?' I replied shaking my head.

"So you're not going to tell me."

"Oh my gosh... I have."

"Well who was it? Did you hook up with that security guard? Please tell me you waxed that ass for me!" She exclaimed smiling.

"You know it's funny because how I hooked up with the guy I'm about to tell you about. I was trying to call the security guy what's his name? Austin? But had dialed the wrong number and ended up talking to Camry Carter."

"The real-estate agent?" She replied raising her eyebrow.

"Yeah and I know what you're thinking but it is more complicated than just sex."

"I'm not looking or thinking anything. Yeah he is married but that man is fine. It would be hard for anybody to turn him down."

I was very surprised with her answer because she seemed to be very loyal and a great example for married women. I kind of expected her to be more disappointed in me then to be more enthused for details.

"Well we are and have been hooking up for some time now and its getting kind of serious."

"Wait are you serious? Baby having sex and fun is one thing but taking it further than that is another. Now how serious is it?" She asked staring deep into my eyes.

"He told me he loved me."

"Damn! Already! What kind of pussy do you have, one with cupid arrows and a love potion? How long has it been?

"Umm it's been about 3 or 4 months."

"Wow, do you love him back?"

"Yeah that's what I told him."

"But is that how you feel?"

"I believe I do."

"Wow."

"But it is so hard because for a long time I hated women like myself. I wanted to kill every side chick and every jump off on the planet so my man and I could have a great life together. But now I'm in the same position as those I hated and I'm so confused but because of the way that I feel about him I kind of embrace the position."

"First of all don't embrace anything that requires you to be second and if you are you better make sure he is doing things that are making you feel like you are first. Second what's going on with his marriage? Are they happily married or separating?"

"It sound like to me that they are on the verge of separating but he is holding on. He is a good guy so of course he is trying to work it out but it doesn't sound like it is going anywhere. He comes crawling to me taking out his frustration on my body daily."

"You let him hit you!" Laura exclaimed.

"Hell no! I'm talking about sex. He told me the other day how he felt about me and I did the same. I just feel right no matter how wrong society dubs our actions."

"So it's just the sex or he does other things too?"

"He does pretty much everything except pay my bills because he is with me so much."

"Well where is his wife in all this? If he is spending all this time with you that means his wife is either home alone or spending it with someone else."

" He said that she works a lot and usually so does he but I'm not going to sit up here and lie and say that he doesn't take less hours for me."

"Anytime you have men missing money it's serious. Be careful baby because you are playing a dangerous game but as long as you're happy I am too. But how is the sex? How big is his dick?"

"You don't hold anything back do you?"

"Well if I don't ask then I will be sitting here wondering. Why would I do that when I can get you to tell me?" She replied smiling.

"I guess. "I replied looking down at the large cup of lemonade that sat in front of me." It's about the same length as the cup and straw, wait let me pull this up a little more." I said pulling the straw a little further up out of the cup so it could be taller.

"You lucky bitch... You don't run across too many of them too often. I guess that when you get a man that is fine with a good job and packing like a moving van then I guess he is worth the risk. But baby let me get serious for a second and say this. If you really love him and want to be with him you need to step up and take him. Nothing worth having comes with little effort. I don't know what you should do but if you want something more with him other than being the side chick you're going to have to make him see you are the better choice and demand commitment. If you are as good as you say you are then he won't let you go especially when his wife isn't doing too well. If you got him on the hook you better reel him in before someone comes along with a net and catches him. Be a little more aggressive and a lot smarter because married couples aren't anything to just dib and dab in, often times death follows adultery."

"How do you know all of this?"

"How do you think I got my man? I took him from the stiff he was with years ago. He got a hold of this entire ass and a taste of a real black women and he left that old white stiff woman for the spoils of America." She replied laughing." I may look good but baby I'm no angel. We all make difficult decisions but the thing is not the decision itself but how you handle it. Now look at me, richer than ninety percent of the country. Let me share a secret with you and I shouldn't be telling you this because your ass might come and take my man but I met my husband when I was a waitress at a strip club. Could you ever tell? I'm shining now baby."

"I guess..."

"If you're going to mess around don't throw out the idea of just making him a good thing. It is a lot less complicated and devastating when shit hits the fan."

"Good thing?"

"A fling, a boy toy with strictly one purpose; I'm telling you this because I don't want to see any more of my sisters get hurt all because of some damn emotions. If it's just sexual keep it like that but clearly it is too late for you guys. Y'all are "in love" the most dangerous stage of love might I add. Just think about keeping your feelings aside. I love my husband but I have me a little thing on the side too."

"Really... Who..." I exclaimed.

She smiled back at me and shook her head.

"Austin..."

"No! How? Why? Why were you telling me to talk to him if you were doing him?"

"That's my point no emotions baby. My man is out doing as he pleases but most importantly bringing home that money and lots of it might I add. I have needs baby and Austin definitely fulfills them. But it's nothing more than sex." She replied now sounding like she had this whole thing down to a science.

"Wow, I would have never guessed that you and him were doing anything."

"And that's another point. No one should be able to tell. Regardless if you're the wife or you're the mistress. It's always easier to get away with your dirt when the lights are off... remember that."

Laura and I spent about another hour talking then looked at a couple more stores before going our separate ways. I couldn't believe how much she knew and how much advice she was willing to give about basically getting ahead. I was shocked to hear a lot of what she said but at the same time not too much of anything surprised me now a days. She had me thinking a lot about what to do with Camry and I agreed with a lot of the things she told me. I just wasn't too sure if I wanted to just have sex with him. I love him and don't feel he is boy toy material. He has potential to be my next husband. She did say that either I should back off or go after what I want and clearly backing off wasn't an option for me. I needed to figure out how I was going to get him to commit to me but I wasn't sure that I could be so deceitful. This is a dog eat dog world and if she doesn't want to tend to hers then I will. She is practically pushing him away so why shouldn't I take advantage of the situation?

21

Austin Wells

"So, how long are you going to act like this?"

"Act like what employee?"

Marie and I were alone in the break room for the first time in a long time. She was taking her lunch break and I had decided take my break once I saw her taking hers. As bad as I wanted to move on and forget about her, I couldn't. I worked with her for God's sake. Every time I looked at her I couldn't help but think about how we left on such a sour note before. I could tell she wasn't as happy as she was trying to make it seem with her super geek boyfriend. I believe she was thinking about me just as much as I was thinking about her.

"You're acting like you don't even know me; like we never existed. I've been working here for a couple months now and pretty soon I'm going to be running this place. You know that I know more and am much more creative than that clown you call a boyfriend."

"My clown boyfriend earned his job... You probably fucked your way into this one... You think I don't know about your sugar momma who is the only reason you have this job and more importantly the reason I can't fire your ass. It's just a matter of time before you fuck up and can no longer exist in my world."

"What did I ever do to you that was so bad?"

"If you don't know then there is no point in me reminding you little boy... Like I told you before the past is nonexistent to me... Nothing ever happened."

"You know you have to be one thick skinned bitch to keep on acting this way. I wonder how many other people have you hurt and did incredibly wrong."

"So now I'm a bitch... Wow, it's so typical for you to point the problems at me... I'm glad."

"You're glad? About what?"

"I'm... It's no purpose in even talking about this. Like I said it's the past... Just leave it alone." she replied in disdain getting up out of her seat and heading to the door.

"Yeah... do what you do best... run." I blurted out regretfully.

It took me this long to get through to her this much and I was wasting precious time arguing. What was I doing? I quickly began to think back to Tonya and what tactic I used to get back on her good side.

"Ok… Lilly Flower, act like that if you want to but you can't go on trying to act like you don't know who I am."

"Don't ever call me that again!" she replied turning around in disdain and stopping at the door.

"What? Lilly Flower? Why? Is that your favorite? What did you think I was going to forget how much you love the scent that they give or what they represent? Or that your favorite color is green and it's because of your emerald birthstone? Or that your cup size is 34 DD and you want to get a breast reduction because you feel they're too heavy. Or what about the small red stretch marks at the start of your…"

"Shut up! Just stop it!" she shouted charging towards me as if she was going to hit me but stopping right before she got close enough to do so.

It had finally seemed like I broke through to her hard shell but what do I do now? I knew that if I stopped now then I would never get a chance like this again, but if I kept digging into her I could risk bringing up harsh feelings or opening back the door to her heart.

"What are you going to do hit me Marie?" I replied standing up and facing her. "Please hit me….Because maybe then I would be able to feel again. I can't explain how your touch would make me feel… I've been missing it all this time, dreaming about it, fantasizing about it, yearning for it…. Baby please touch me." I said lightly moving in for a kiss.

Slap!

I couldn't believe she just killed my high with a hard momma slap to the face but I didn't let it move me too much. I just turned my head a little but held my ground.

"Yeah... that's it... now please do it again." I exclaimed trying my hardest to not show how much that slap hurt.

Slap! Slap! Slap! Slap!

She began to swing away hitting me from both sides and both hands. I was under attack! I grabbed her by the waist and pulled her into me and dug my face into her shoulder so she couldn't hit it anymore. "I fucking hate you! I hate you! I SWEAR I HATE YOU AUSTIN!" She exclaimed as tears began to run down her cheeks.

"Baby....I apologize....I'm sorry. I'm sorry okay...I'm sorry please..." I replied softy but squeezing her tightly so she could calm her assault.

After a full minute of being attacked she stopped hitting me and wrapped her arms around my neck as if she was embracing my hug. She cried softly on my shoulder mumbling out her emotion filled words.

"I hate you Austin... You don't know what I've been through or what you made me do. You just let me leave! You were supposed to stop me! You were supposed to be there for me Austin! You made me do this all on my own" she cried out.

"Baby... I'm sorry... I'm sorry...Please... Stop crying....I'm sorry." I pleaded.

I didn't know what else to say. All I could think to do was what I use to know would calm her down. She used to always say the touch of my lips could calm a mad lion and electrify the clouds. I guess now was the time to find out. Without hesitation I stood straight but kept my arms around her waist and kissed her softly on the lips. Quickly her crying out became silent and what was a risky kiss to calm her nerves turned into a kiss to calm my own. I had never felt anything that felt so right. The wet cheeks from her tears moistened my face as the kiss went on and our lips sent waves of emotion throughout our bodies. Our tongues intertwined as if they were dancing to the thump of our heartbeats. As much as I didn't want to stop something made me and it was good because as soon as I did her boyfriend came walking into the break room with his bagged lunch.

"Hey guys? Hey babe, what's going on?" he asked nonchalantly as he opened up the refrigerator door and started looking for something to eat.

I quickly sat back down and Marie casually walked to the exit door.

"Nothing, I'm just about to get back to work." Marie replied walking out the room.

"But your lunch isn't over for another 30 minutes!" He exclaimed as she left. He quickly shut the refrigerator and looked right at me but I refused to look back so he could see the proof of guilt written all over my face. Instead I tried to pretend like I was extremely interested in the news that was showing on the break room flat screen.

"Austin?"

"Yeah..."

"What was that about? She seemed like something was bothering her. Is there something I need to know?"

"I don't know that's your girl so that is your problem…. I don't get involved in domestic issues." I replied not even looking his way.

"Thanks for the help, Jack Ass." He replied storming out to the room leaving me there alone to try and comprehend what had just happened.

I knew Marie hadn't totally gotten over me like the way she said she had. Even though it had been a long time it was obvious that there wasn't enough time for her to totally forget what we meant to each other. In a situation like ours you could back seat the emotions but it was nearly impossible to kick them out of the car. But now that I had broken through to her I was unsure where I was going to go from here. There was no telling where she was going to go or do while she was in her office talking to her boyfriend or what was going through her head. Maybe I ruined my chances of ever getting her back but at least I know that there was something still there.

What was bothering me just as much as knowing was the blame she had been placing on me for whatever she had chosen to do in life while she was gone I'm assuming; and possibly for her choices now. But her life now didn't seem that bad with the exception of her dunce of a boyfriend. The only reason I kept on apologizing is because it was too sensitive of a matter for me to start putting up a fight. The best thing I could have done was apologize or maybe that long kiss would have been long slaps. Now that she had taken a minute out to vent and express her frustration when was it ever going to be time for me to express mines? By the looks of it, it didn't seem like she wanted to hear my truth; she just wanted to continue to be the victim. The only question I had to myself was how long was I was going to be able to tolerate it.

....

I didn't see Marie for the rest of the work day in her office or on the floor so I was assuming that she had took the rest of the day off. After all it was a Friday and on these days it wasn't unusual for her to take off early. It was a little sad to me how oblivious her boyfriend was. We worked together and he acted like he had no idea what was going on. He was being his normal self, talking about computer mainframes and internet graphics made me wonder what type of man was he for him to not know that something was wrong. Either he knew or maybe he didn't care but the fact of the matter is he didn't seem too worried about what he did or didn't see happen in the break room. I am pretty sure that we separated in time but we were still pretty close when he came in the room. The rest of the day I was keeping a sharp eye on him just in case he was putting on an act only to set me up for a blinding right hook.

As soon as I got off of work I had received a text from Tonya who I had been distant from but am glad to hear from now because I was so stressed I needed a relief. Since I had this job I didn't really seem to have too much time for anybody but Mrs. Jenkins and her sporadic requests to see me. Seeing her required a lot of work. Plus, Mrs. Jenkins continued to provide me with green incentives to keep coming to her. With the money she had given me all together I am sure that I could go and get myself a nice car but instead 15 grand sitting in the bank thanks to my new job and Mrs. Jenkins so naturally her request for my services would come first. I said services like I was a gigolo or something. Maybe I was, maybe I wasn't but I would like to think of our relationship as her being my cougar and myself being her driver.

I left work and went straight to Tonya's so I could get a sweat dropping session in and clear these confusing thoughts I had running through my head about Marie.

"Yeah that's it… That's my spot….baby! Oh…shit!" She yelled as I sped up on my assault into her body from behind. She felt great but a little unfamiliar like something had been different about her but I couldn't put my finger on it.

"Damn it… stay… right… there… Tony!" she shouted out confidently.

"Tony! I shouted in disdain stopping but not totally pulling out of her body.

"What? Why did you stop? Who is Tony?"

"What do you mean why did I stop and who the fuck is Tony? You just called me Tony! Is that who you're fucking now, some guy named Tony?!"

"No…. That's my name for your dick when it's doing what it's doing to me…. Now come on baby don't stop!" She moaned sweetly.

I wanted to give her a high five for the player excuse she just came up with but instead I slapped her on her ass and continued my assault.

"That's the name I have for you…" I thought to myself repeating in my head the excuse she had just gave me. I grew angrier thinking about it because I knew she was gaming me instead of just telling me the truth. I sped up not only to make myself explode but to also hurt her a little in the process.

"Don't call me Tony! My name… is… is… Makacumaldai… Say it, Makacumaldai."

"Awe…Don't stop… Makacumaldai…!" she moaned out.

"No! Say it! Make her cum all day… Makacumaldai" I shouted pounding harder into her body nearly knocking her over.

"Maka…. I'm Cumming! I'm Cumming…." She shouted.

"You're what?! Whose… making… you come?!" I shouted giving her my best long stroke as I watched her body release all her cream on my coffee stick.

"Oh… don't… stop… Ooh Khyel!!!"

"You dirty… bitch!" I replied pulling out of her and quickly getting my clothes.

"Shit! Tone, I mean Khyel…. Oh my God! Austin wait…!" She pleaded getting out of bed as she fumbled with my name.

"Don't worry about it baby… You don't have to worry about remembering my name anymore… I'm done!" I declared as I put on my pants and stuffed my feet into my boots without really even looking.

"What the hell!" I said realizing that I suddenly had too much space left in my boots. I looked down and realized that they weren't mine but somebody else's shoes. Matter of fact my boots that were about six sizes smaller were on the other side of the room looking like booties compared to the boots I had my feet in.

"Wow!"

"Austin… I can… explain baby!" Tonya exclaimed with big eyes once she realized I had on one of her fuck buddies shoes. "Damn!"

I kicked the boots off and shook my head." "Explain that?"

She looked at me dumbfounded.

"That's what I thought!" I replied putting on my shoes and storming through her apartment and out of the front door.

"Dirty bitch! Fuck and suck everything walking! I don't even know why I mess with her nasty ass!" I shouted out loud as I hurried to my car.

I drove home angry and wondering why I was battling with as many emotions as I was. She wasn't my girlfriend but I was kind of hurt and disappointed as if we were really still together. There wasn't any difference in the way I was feeling now and the way I was feeling the day I walked in on Tonya and Khyel. I guess this is what Camry was talking about when he was saying that this whole Exvantage thing could get complicated. I don't know why I was feeling like she was only supposed to be having sex with me. I mean she wasn't my girl but at the same time she was the one who kept mentioning that we were a little more than friends. Not too long ago she was telling me that we were back together. So if that was the case what the hell was she doing fucking Tony and Khyel? I guess that came with the territory of being an ex… I had no right to get back at her lying and sluttish ways. I had no real say so on what she did and when she did it. It was then that I realized that I did not like having that much control. I guess I was thinking I could have my fun and somehow expect nobody else to do the same. I didn't like feeling this way. This whole Exvantage thing was too convoluted for me. Now not only was I confused and disappointed but I also was still horny and stressed out from the mess I was dealing with at work. I couldn't wait to get home and take a long shower and I guess relax this weekend…. I wasn't too sure what I was going to do aside from sleeping.

Once I got to my place I thought to call Tiffany or Sondra to make some time for me but I didn't feel like driving across town to either of their places and feeling like the fill in boy that I am to them. My sudden bursts of emotions were wrecking my brain. I got to my apartment hall only to have my brain wrecked even more.

"What are you doing here?" I said as I walked closer to the front door.

"I missed you…and we need to talk." Marie said standing in front of my door with a tired look on her face as if she was exhausted.

"How did you…"

Before I could say anything else she rushed into my arms and kissed me with much needed passion. I kind of wanted to stop her so we could get in the apartment but I didn't want to mess up the moment. I swear that I had dreams like this that I just knew would never come true. We held each other tight and twisted tongues for about five minutes before we were interrupted by some kids shouting down the hall.

"Smack her ass! Get a room!"

On cue I pulled out my keys and unlocked my door but as I went in but Marie stood in the doorway as if there was a force field stopping her from coming in.

"What's wrong?" I asked puzzled as I turned to face her. She had this look of indecisiveness on her face.

"I'm not sure I should be coming in there."

"Come on… What other reason did you come here if you're not going to come in?"

"Austin I just want to talk… Can we just talk? She asked timidly.

"Let's talk…" I replied reaching out to her for her to take my hand. She took it and I lightly pulled her into my arms closing the door behind her. Our lips met again.

"I just want to talk…" she said in between kisses.

"Ok…" I replied as we continued to kiss.

She pulled off her suit blazer and let it fall to the floor as I kicked off my shoes still trying to maintain our tempo of aggressive kissing. Next came flying off were both of our button up shirts and slacks we were wearing.

"Just… Awe! Talk… Right?" She moaned out as we continued to kiss and make our way to the bedroom.

"Yeah… baby… just… talk…" I replied as we both flopped onto the huge bed.

"Damn it felt good to be kissing her." I thought to myself as I reached behind her back and popped her bra off.

"Ok… Wait… Austin, I can't do this right now." She replied in a stern voice letting me know she was serious.

I took a deep breath and shook my head.

"Ok… I know baby… Let's just talk…" I replied laying my head on my pillow and stretching out on my side of the bed.

"Can you cover that thing up?" she asked looking down at my unusually large erection poking through my boxer briefs that I wasn't sure that the fabric was going to hold.

"Cover up what? This?" I replied popping it a couple times before I threw the covers over myself. I enjoyed watching her eyes light up and her body squirm as I did so. It just made me understand how hard it was for her to keep her hands off; it basically meant the feeling was mutual.

"You're such a tease…" She replied snapping her fire red bra back.

"I don't have to be… We both can stop teasing each other right now." I replied rolling on my side towards her and resting my head on my arm as I stared into her eyes. She lay next to me in the same position gazing right back at me as if she was thinking about it.

"So what do you want to talk about?" I replied breaking the silence.

"I don't know…"

"What?"

"Oh... Um... Well I came here to tell you that what happened at work today can never happen again...." She replied in an authoritative tone.

"Do you think I'm supposed to take you serious right now? You're lying in my bed half naked talking about it never happened or will never happen again. Marie stop fighting me and be real with yourself for once."

"I am being real; earlier was a mistake." She exclaimed.

"What about now? Is this a mistake too or are you here because you want to be?"

"A mistake." She blurted out.

"Is it really? As far as I remember I never gave you my address, told you to wait outside my apartment for me, nor did I tell you to come lay in my bed half naked so we could talk."

"You're absolutely right.... I should just go. I don't know what I was thinking coming here." She replied sitting up about to get out of my big bed.

"No...wait... Let's just talk..."

"No... this is a bad idea let's just leave it at that." She replied standing to her feet and walking out the bedroom in search of the remainder of her clothes. I quickly got up and followed behind her as she made her way through my apartment picking up her scattered clothes that had made a trail from my bedroom to my living room. I couldn't let her leave now... Not without getting any answers. I still wanted to know a lot about why she had left and what she had done in California. I still wanted to know who she was and why she had come back. I know there was plenty of innovative jobs in California so why come back to Atlanta? I had all these questions but as I stood there and watched her put on her clothes I wasn't sure that I could build the courage to say what I had been longing to say for years.

"I'm sorry I ever came here Austin... I really don't mean to confuse you...." She said buttoning up her white blouse.

"Why did you come back?" I blurted out.

"What?"

"Why did you come back Marie? You left without a trace or explanation and then years later you show up out of nowhere...? Why did you come back?"

"I go where ever the money goes." She replied looking down at the floor as she dressed herself.

"Stop with the hard ass attitude and be honest. As bad as you don't want to admit it Marie, I still know you. I know when you're not being honest and masking your feelings; I've known it all this time. That's one thing about you that hasn't changed and I'll never forget. Can we just talk real? Can we just sit down and have a real conversation?" I pleaded walking up to her still in my Calvin Klein boxer briefs with both hands out ready to take hers. The look on her face had saddened and I could tell she had been through a lot but just didn't know how to tell me. I was hoping that now was the time.

"Ok..." she replied looking up at me. We walked over to the couch and sat down next to one another.

"I came back because I was home sick. I wanted to see my family and start my life over here." She simply put it.

"That's it?"

"Yeah..."

"So... I didn't have anything to do with you coming back?" I asked anxiously.

"Why would you? I hadn't seen you in years and I had already had a boyfriend. Why would I be thinking about you?"

"Damn... Sorry for asking." I replied feeling a sharp pain run through my chest which was probably an indicator that my heart was being broken. "So you're saying the whole time you were gone you didn't think of me at all?"

"Yeah... I thought about you at first but after a while I had no other choice but to move on. Thinking about you only made things harder on me. I was going through enough stress getting adjusted to my new school and learning how to be on my own."

"I see... So... I'm confused. Why did you leave the way you did?"

"What? Why do you keep acting like you didn't know I was leaving? I wrote you a letter and I told your brother that I was going to California for school. I gave him the time and date. Plus the note I had left you..."

"What are you talking about? My brother never gave me a message. You know my brother and I don't get along. We haven't got along since high school... I know nothing about this note you're talking about.... I never got any note."

"You had to of received the note because I slid it under your dorm room door the night before I had left.

I sat there and tried to think back long and hard but nothing was ringing a bell.

"Now I never got any note but if you slid it through the door then Camry probably swept it up and threw it away because you know he's a neat freak and cleaned our dorm room every other hour. He was probably thinking it was one of the many party fliers we would get and he threw it away. Wow..... This is crazy."

"I don't believe you" she replied shaking her head in disbelief.

"Marie, I swear my brother never told me anything and I never got any note this is all new to me....Why didn't you just come out and tell me?"

"You know we were on the verge of breaking up I didn't know how to tell you that I was considering leaving. I just knew you wouldn't let me go... I didn't want to leave either but I left it for you to decide."

"What? How?"

"The note told you when my flight was and where I was going. I figured if you loved me and really wanted to be with me then you would be there to stop me from leaving but if not then that was my sign from God saying that we weren't meant to be. You never showed up so that was my sign that..."

"That's the dumbest shit ever!" I interrupted. "You had a life here in the 'A' and you just decided to gamble it away like that? I didn't even get any of your attempts to test me or my love for

257

you. That was so drastic Marie…Even for you… Why couldn't you just tell me?"

"And what? Get the same results I got when I would tell you about whatever else I wanted?"

"What?"

"Don't play stupid Austin… The whole reason we were even fighting was because you had a problem with committing…"

"Hell no!" I interrupted again. "You wanted me to marry you which is a whole new level of commitment. I was committed but not how you wanted me. The problem was that I wasn't moving fast enough for you with the ring so you decided to throw everything away because you didn't have any patience!" I exclaimed unconsciously raising my voice.

"I had been with you for quite some time Austin! How much patience did you want me to have?! All you had to do was put a ring on my finger and I would have been satisfied but you couldn't even do that!" she yelled back.

"You can't force anybody to marry you! I wanted to be with you for the rest of my life but you didn't give me a chance to show you that. You just up and left me. I think this has less to do with me and more to do with you; it was all just a front because deep down inside you knew I was going to come around."

"So what are you saying? That I was scared of taking it to the next level? How could that be? I'm the one who wanted you to step up and do it in the first place?!" She replied in disdain.

"I believe you chickened out… Your talk was good but when it came down to it your walk was as good as a paralyzed man. I don't believe the whole leaving it up to fate story. Talking about you wanted me to come stop you and if I had you would have never left. Who does that? People don't do that in real life." I replied loudly as I shook my head.

She looked at me with this pissed look on her face.

"I knew this was a mistake… I'm leaving…" She said getting up and putting on the rest of her clothes.

"Yeah do what you do best… run!" I shouted fed up with fighting with her.

"Run?! Whatever little boy… I'm not about to do this with you. I have a man at home that makes me happy. I don't need to hear this mess rom you."

"That's what you call a man? All brains and no body? The man's head is bigger than the rest of his body."

"You got that right. His head is very big, both of them." She said with a smirk as she headed to the door.

"Well he must not be doing too much with it. Your ass is over here fighting with temptation and hoping you can get Mr. Makacumaldai"

She stopped and looked back at me with her hand on the front door ready to exit.

"You're still using that nickname for yourself?! I gave you that name… It should have died when I left… Don't you think you're getting a little too old for nicknames for yourself? Mr. Makacumaldai? "She replied shaking her head and walking out of my apartment.

I quickly walked to the doorway and yelled out with no regards to the couple standing in their doorway talking.

"Yeah... Mr. Make-her-cum-all-day! That's what they call me and that's what I used to make you do! Don't you ever forget it! She won't ever forget! She won't forget me or Mr. Makacumaldai will she?" I yelled as she turned the corner and was now out of my sight. The couple who was in the hall was looking at me blank faced as if I were a psycho or something.

"Yeah... Mr. Makacumaldai... Damn it... That's what they call me because I make...her...cum...all...day!" I shouted thrusting in the air with every word. "Take the name if you want but there is only one baby!" I exclaimed as I closed my door.

      I stormed through the apartment to the living room and cut the shower on in the bathroom. I just wanted to get a nice hot shower and go to sleep. Sex would have been a good thing but it's not as important as I claim it is. I wonder if I'm the only one that feels like sex is a daily essential like a vitamin the body needs to function properly. I had something like a love hate relationship with sex because when I wasn't getting it I felt I needed it and now that I was getting it on a regular basis I felt like it was no big deal. I guess I felt the same way about Marie. One minute she's giving me not enough attention and I was yearning for her to acknowledge me then once she started giving me that attention I found myself showing her and myself that her attention was no big deal by arguing with her instead of taking advantage of the moment and using it to make up with her. Now she was probably on her way back to her man wet and steamy for sex... Sex that was fueled by me but was going to be used for his pleasure... Ain't that a bitch!

I was kind of impressed with Marie a little bit because her stubbornness kind of made me want her more. Out of all my exes that I had been with she was the only one strong enough to hold out past a couple of days. I'm not sure if her man had something to do with that or our history. We had a lot of problems that needed to be addressed but every time we came close to talking about them we got nowhere but into a fight.

As soon as I stepped into the shower and the hot water began to run down my body, I heard a loud repeated knock at the door.

"Damn!" I said to myself after the tenth knock. I hopped out the shower and wrapped a towel around my waist and walked to the persistent knock at my door.

Without looking out the peephole I opened it only to see Marie standing there with tears in her eyes. I shook my head and stepped to the side so she could come back in.

"Mr. Makacumaldai!" I heard from one of the people out in the hallway as I shut the door.

"Marie... I apoli..."

Before I could finish my sentence she kissed me and wrapped her arms around me tightly.

"Wait... Are we going to have sex now because I swear if I keep getting teased like this then I'm going to get blue balls."

"You are crazy..." she replied kissing me and trying to pull off her clothes at the same time.

Just like before we struggled trying to make it to the bedroom without falling or tripping over her clothes as she peeled them of. By the time we got to my bed we were both naked reintroducing our bodies to each other and I don't think there could have been a better way to do it.

Marie took great care of her body. Her smooth skin and DKNY Delicious candy apple smell did nothing but make my mouth water. For the first time in a long time my tongue began to tingle and my lips started to electrify. I had to taste her. I craved it so bad I had an urge to bite into her skin. I didn't even waste time licking around her neck to turn her on. Instead I tore her panties off and went straight for the jackpot.

"Awe! Baby! What are you doing?" she moaned out loudly as I put my index finger inside of her and flicked her clit quickly with my tongue.

"Unh" I moaned back surprised by not only the candy apple taste but also the firm fit her pussy had around my one index finger. She couldn't have been having sex with her man feeling like this... This was it's been a long time tight. Usually oral sex wasn't my thing unless I was receiving but in this case this was something that I had wanted to do for a long time. Her body jumped to every lick I delivered to her body and I couldn't do anything but get more excited by her reaction. I worked my single finger in and out of her slowly and couldn't help but to wonder how was I going to fit in this tiny hole that my finger had a problem moving in.

I couldn't help but to wonder what type of relationship her and old boy from the job had. Marie could be very sexual and for her to feel this way I knew something wasn't right. I knew if I was in a relationship there was no way in hell it would be able to survive without some sex at a constant level. So what was making theirs survive?

I licked a trail from her sweet spot to her belly button and from there to her perfectly round breasts and from there to her neck.

"Don't leave a hickey..." she said as I sucked at her neck while adjusting myself in between her legs. I was ready for lift off and wasn't thinking anything about coming back for a landing until there was no more gas in my tank.

"Wait! Go slow..." She said as I tried to push myself inside of her. At that moment it just didn't seem possible, as if there wasn't enough room but after a little bit of adjusting and poking around, I managed to push my way in and enjoy the Lovejoy experience.

"Damn! You feel good as fuck..." I said as soon as I entered her body. "Too good." I stressed trying to get a rhythm going but before I could I found myself...Awe Shit!" I moaned as my body tensed up and my heart began to beat out my chest.

"Are you Cumming?" she asked almost in a panic tone.

"I'm.... Cumming! Oh... Awe" I kept on moaning.

She grew silent and stiff as it seemed like every ounce of energy flowed from my body to hers. That one climax only opened the door for several more as one hour turned into two and we both indulged in what I thought to be pure heaven. I wasn't too sure what was going to happen after this but I was pretty sure that in this moment I wasn't going to forget or regret anything that I was doing.

"So where do we go from here?" I asked Marie who was lying beside me half sleep.

"I don't... know... Where do you want it to go? She replied.

'I'm not sure.... But I'm down to do whatever you want to do...."

It had only been eight o' clock but my body was making me feel like it was twelve. It was beginning to look like she was going to stay the night but I think it had less to do with what she was going to do but more so do what I wanted her to do. The last thing I wanted her to do was go home but the reality was she had a man who was probably wondering where she was.

"You want to stay the night?"

"Yeah but I can't because..."

"Yeah... I know.... You don't have to say it... I missed you." I said sitting up.

"I missed you too..." she replied laying her head in my lap.

"I want the old us back..."

"The old us was good but it wasn't good enough for me, you know that." She replied.

"What if I could make it right?"

"How...?"

I got up out of the bed and went into my top dresser drawer and pulled out the red engagement ring box that I had originally bought for Tonya.

"I'm making it right... I bought you this ring and was going to ask you to be my wife but you took off. So now that I have you in front of me again, I would feel like a fool if I let you slip away again without giving you what you deserve." I said wholeheartedly.

"Are you serious? Stop playing?"

"Marie will you take this ring? Will you marry me?" I replied opening the box and showing her the ring.

Her eyes lit up and watered as if she was waiting on this for a long time but I could tell something was wrong as she shook her head and covered up her eyes to stop the tears from falling down.

"What's wrong?"

"Austin... I can't do this... It's not logical."

"How?"

"You think you can just pop back up into my life and take me away from the one I already have? "She exclaimed.

I paused and thought about it for a minute as I saw the expression on her face change from happiness to a distraught look. I didn't know what to say but with the feeling that she was going to say no, I began to lose confidence.

"I mean... I still love you Marie Lovejoy and I don't want you to slip away like before. I just want you to be happy and to be mines...."

"Stop!" She interrupted. "Just say yes Austin."

I looked at her and smiled. I forgot how much she loved my confidence. "Yes Marie... I think I can pop back up in your life and take you away."

"Well do it then..." She replied smiling. "Put it on my finger fool!" she exclaimed as tears of joy fell down her cheeks.

We sealed each other's happiness with a kiss that was nothing like any of the others. It was a kiss that felt like the start of my new life.

....

I hated to watch Marie leave my house knowing she was going back home to that clown of a man she had. I wanted to go with her but she insisted that I allow her the time and opportunity to dismiss her rinky dink boyfriend on her terms. I watched her walk out the door with the ring on her finger but I was pretty sure she was going to either put it on another finger or place it back in the box and keep it out of her boyfriend's sight until she made it clear to him what she was going to do. I was skeptical about letting her go because who knows what could happen when she went back home. The last thing that I wanted was her coming up to me with my ring telling me she couldn't do it all because I underestimated the goof of a boyfriend she had.

Honestly, I couldn't believe I had asked the girl to marry me. It just kind of felt right I guess in the moment. I wasn't sure if that's what I had wanted to do or if it was an act of desperation to keep her in my life. Either way it went I know that it was too late to turn back now. There was no sense in back paddling when the places I wanted to go with her were ahead of us. I wondered if she would ever find out that the ring was originally meant for the girl that I replaced her with. I don't see how she would but if she did then she would be devastated.

Burr... Burr.... My phone vibrated next to me on my bed. I was hoping that it was Marie telling me she was on her way back to my place but instead it was Tonya texting me to apologize for everything that she had been putting me through. I really wasn't sure what to say back to her so I didn't say anything. I just tried to forget about her loose booty ass and move forward like I said I would. Burr... Burr...Not long after that I received a text from Mrs. Jenkins.

-Come drive me home. - The text read.

I was about to text her back but I received a call as I started texting.

"Hello" I said looking at the alarm clock beside my bed that read 11:30pm.

"Yeah, come take me home." She replied sounding perfectly normal.

"What's wrong? Your car broke down? Are you drunk? What's wrong?"

"Nothing is wrong. Just bring your ass outside and take me home. Damn!" she yelled in disdain.

"Where are you?"

"Boy I'm outside your house in an all-white Cadillac waiting on you."

'What?"

"Get your ass out here!" she yelled hanging up the phone.

"Mrs..... I mean Laura..." I replied but it was too late.

"Shit!" I said to myself as I hopped out of the bed and shuffled around my drawers to find my clothes. I just grabbed my black Polo sweats and hoodie and threw on some Nikes with no socks and made my way down to Mrs. Jenkins. But on the way I couldn't help but wonder how much longer I was going to be able keep this up. I already know once Marie and I settled our issues that she wasn't going to be going for the whole leaving in the middle of the night thing. I'm sure she knew about how I got my job but not the full details so I was sure that it was something that she was going to want me to end. But if I did that I was probably going to lose my job also.

As soon as I got outside I noticed the all-white Cadillac DTS; it had to have been an up to date year because it had that up to date futuristic look that Cadillac had been going for.

I walked up to the car and Mrs. Jenkins was already sitting in the passenger seat staring me down like a lion does its prey.

"What's going on? Why do you need me to drive you home?" I asked getting in the driver's seat.

"Just drive and stop asking me questions." she demanded cutting her eyes at me.

As I got into the car I looked her up and down and noticed she had nothing on but a long red cashmere coat and some heels.

"Is your husband home?"

"No… He probably left for one of his floozies a couple hours ago. Why are we still sitting here?!" She yelled.

"You better calm your ass down before you end up driving yourself home!" I blurted out no longer caring what happens. It seemed as though the current events may have had an effect on my tolerance from other women already.

"Excuse me boy?!"

"I'm sick of you talking to me like I'm not shit….You can go find you someone else to talk to that way but it's not going to be me." I said surprising myself.

"Well look who has grown some balls!" She replied quickly reaching between my legs and grabbing mines. It easily made my legs quench and my mind to think about her paintings on the wall of her wrestling a bull.

"Mrs. Jenkins!" I said annoyed with her ridiculous antics.

"Laura!" she exclaimed cutting me off and squeezing my balls tighter.

"Laura… You're going to have to find you a new boy toy. I can't do this anymore." I found the courage to say at possibly the worst time ever.

"What do you mean you can't do this baby? You're right I could find a new boy toy but you're my boy toy and it's going to be that way for as long as I want. Understand? What are you getting sensitive on me? Do I not treat you well? I'm sorry…. Let me make it up to you baby…" she replied yanking down my sweat pants and wrapping her juicy lips around my already exhausted but "can't stop, won't stop" penis.

"Awe! Damn!" I moaned out as she began to give me the Mrs. Jenkins experience. Head was something that she never did to me too often but something I always liked receiving.

"Drive!" she shouted up at me between strokes.

"Drive?"

"Now! Or I'm going to stop." She said defiantly looking up at me.

I started up the car and tried to concentrate as I backed the car out of its space but was doing so horribly. I almost hit a car parked next to me on the way out.

I don't know why women in my life liked to do things to me like give me head while I had their lives in my hands. Despite all the hype and popularity of sex at the wheel, it was a very dangerous activity that probably outcasts like Bonnie and Clyde came up with during one of the many times they had been getting chased by the police.

"Oh… Shit!" I yelled out swerving away from a large black truck that was followed by two others as I left my apartment complex. They were coming in as I was going out and turning onto Main Street.

"Boy! Act like you got some sense and drive!" She demanded shouting up at me like this task that she was putting me through was easy and didn't require serious skill. Getting head at the wheel felt good but also felt dangerous. However, despite the risk I tried my hardest to concentrate. Thirty minutes into the drive she was still sucking and I had begun to concentrate a little better.

"Why haven't you came yet?" she asked perplexed.

"You have me trying to concentrate on too much stuff. I'm trying to but I'm afraid if I do I'm going to mess around and crash into a tree or something."

She looked up at me and stopped totally; sitting back in her seat and taking a long breath.

"I'm so hot!" she said fanning herself.

"Sorry..."

"Sorry for what? That you didn't cum? That's your loss not mines. You're the one who might get blue balls not me." She said in disdain.

"You're right..." I replied keeping it simple because I knew that I wasn't going to get any blue balls knowing I didn't cum because I was so exhausted from my recent experience with Marie. I hadn't stopped thinking about her since she had left. I was wondering why she hadn't texted me back to let me know she was alright. I wanted to text her and find out what was going on but between Mrs. Jenkins and driving, I really didn't have any room to stop and call her. Mrs. Jenkins wouldn't have liked me calling her anyway. She usually is an "all about her" type of woman. If she wasn't getting all the attention then she was going to have an attitude.

"So what's been going on with your job?" she asked changing the mood and subject as my blood began to circulate back around my body.

"Um....It's good....a perfect fit or me. She's just so amazing and I always felt like it was a place I should have always been. I love her."

"Love who?"

"What?"

"You were saying her like you were talking about some bitch..." Mrs. Jenkins replied cutting her eyes at me.

"Oh....no...that's what I refer to my job as because it's my life. So much of my time goes into it; it just feels right referring to it as a woman." I replied dragging a lie out of my closet of bullshit after realizing that I was talking about Marie.

"Oh... Well I'm glad you are adjusting to it well. I wasn't sure how good you would do seeing how just a couple of months ago you were a security guard but I see you really know your stuff."

"Yeah...I wish things could be better for you..." I blurted out.

"What?"

"I didn't mean to say that...."

"If you didn't mean to say it then why did you say it?"

"I don't know... I guess it's really been bothering me how bad your husband has been treating you."

"Yeah... Well, it's none of your fault plus it's doing nothing but benefitting you so why should you care? You should be happy." She said staring of into the distance.

"I don't like it when anybody I care about is getting hurt no matter how much I'm benefiting from it."

"Well don't let it bother you... I don't..."

"You're too beautiful to be enduring so much mess..."

"Yeah I know but this is life... Now change the subject." She demanded as we pulled up to her place.

I pulled up to the front of her place and unbuckled my seatbelt. "So how am I going to get back home? You're going to call me a cab?" I asked looking over to her.

She went in the glove compartment and pulled out a folded piece of paper. "Sign this." She said handing it to me.

"What's this?" I replied unfolding it and seeing it was a proof of purchase title.

"It's yours. Just sign it and take it to the DMV to get everything switched over."

"Have you lost your mind? I can't take this. Your husband is going to kill me." I exclaimed.

"Will you stop? I have bought purses that cost about the same on this car altogether. Take the car Austin, it's yours.

"What do you want in return?"

"Just keep doing what you've been doing to me. Keep making me feel what I've been feeling and I will bless you with even more."

"Are you serious?"

"Come here…." She replied leaning into me for the kiss. I leaned in and met her lips. Sort of hoping that kiss was all she wanted but that wish was short lived. She peeled open her coat exposing her naked body.

"Lay back…" She demanded climbing over the middle console onto my lap. I pulled my pants down and once again found myself in an uncomfortable position. Having sex was one thing but doing so while looking out the rearview mirror worried about her husband showing up was another?

"Can we just go into the house?"

"No! I want it here! Now!" She replied grabbing my re-energized penis and easing down on it.

"Yes!" she exclaimed.

I reclined the seat all the way back until it couldn't go back any further and watched her slowly bounce up and down on my lap like she was a jockey at a horse race. Something was going on with her and I think that it had to do with more than just stress. The way she was acting tonight was a different type of desperate. It was almost like a long cry for help. She said I could have the car as long as I kept having sex with her basically but that didn't make any sense because she could have sex with anybody. I'm not going to sit here and lie to myself about being unique. All I had was a penis like a billion other guys. Mrs. Jenkins relationship went from a professional crush to a fling to a gigolo thing but this car was something more than that; it was a large deposit for something much longer lasting.

"I'm Cumming baby….Cum on bay!!!" She moaned out running her hands across her breast and biting her bottom lip with her eyes constantly opening and shutting.

She was feeling incredibly good but I don't know if she noticed that I was a little too tired to do anything but sleep, let alone bust a nut. My mind just wasn't into it anymore. I couldn't stop thinking about Marie.

"Cum baby!" She demanded leaning into me and lightly biting and sucking my neck. It was something about that right there that made me crumble.

"Oh…shit… get up, I'm about to cum." I groaned.

"Oh yes baby…Come on… Give it to me…" She moaned out as she sped up on top of me faster.

"Get up….Awe! I'm cumming! Awe! Fuck…" I shouted.

"Yes…. Give me it all….Oh yes!" She moaned out as her body began to shake on top of mines.

"Thank you … Thank you… That's all I wanted." She replied after a moment while easing off of me back into her passenger's seat.

"What was all that about?" I asked catching my breath.

"Austin you know this is a brand new 2012, 60, 000 dollar car?"

"Uh yeah, that's why I don't want to take it."

"Well you know I'm on my way to forty and I don't have any kids…."

My heart jumped an extra beat.

"Kids?"

"Yeah. I want a child and my husband's cheating ass can't give me one so I thought I could get one from you."

"What? You're talking like you're asking me for something like a cigarette... We're talking about a baby! You felt you couldn't tell me...Is that what this car was? Instead of conning me to cum inside you?"

"If I would have told you that's what the car was for would you have done it?"

"No, but at least you would have asked."

"Well I'm not a woman that takes no for an answer so taking what I want seems to be my answer for everything nowadays."

"Who does shit like this? Well what about your husband? He's going to take everything away once he finds out you're having a baby by another man."

"Too late... I filed for divorce three months ago... Technically we are separated now but trust me I have more than enough evidence to make sure I get enough of his money that I will never need for a man again...except for sex."

"How did you get evidence?"

"I told you I caught him sleeping with my maid. Well I have cameras all throughout the house. I have every time they had sex recorded on tape. I showed it to my lawyer and all he saw was dollar signs."

"Three months ago? But he was here last time I was here..."

"So what? I have a mansion… There are so many rooms here that there could be people staying here that I don't even know about. He has his space and I have mines."

"But… ok… We had sex on your bed so isn't that on camera?"

"It was but I deleted it so we are fine plus that was long after I filed for divorce. I was just keeping everything under wraps until my divorce was officially set in motion."

"Well… What if I wanted to be in my baby's life? I'm not that type of guy who just has babies everywhere.

"Don't worry… You won't even know it's here…" She replied folding her legs as if she was locking my sperm inside her body.

I shook my head trying to stop myself from getting angry.

"This can't happen…"

"It's done! Now just keep your mouth shut and answer when and if I call you. I don't need any man for anything not even for a child." She replied opening the door and stepping out.

"Laura!"

"See you later Austin! Thanks!" She replied shutting the door and walking to her house.

"Bitch!" I shouted hitting the steering wheel and grabbing at the wheel.

There was nothing I could do… I just started up the car and sped off back to my place.

This wasn't like Mrs. Jenkins. She always seemed to be this professional all about her business type of person but today it was nothing like that. She was unstable and desperate for some type of place in life. She usually was upfront with her ideas and intentions so I was surprised when she used trickery to get me to do what she wanted me to do. The good thing was I had come in her before and nothing ever happened so I was hoping that it was going to be no different now. The only thing that made me doubt that it would was her confidence as if she had prepared for this moment; like she had been taking some fertility pills or shots or something. I was going to have to send a serious prayer up for this one because it was completely out of my hands. I had come in Marie several times earlier carelessly with a little bit of hope that she would get pregnant but now I wasn't the only one hoping for a miracle through desperate actions to not be alone.

By the time I got back to my place it was after 1 in the morning and my mind was in overload thinking about the crazy day that I had. Even though my mind was cloudy I couldn't help but recognize the same large black trucks like the ones I had seen earlier when Mrs. Jenkins and I were leaving. I couldn't help but notice them because they were so big and in my lot of the apartment complex. I had to park in the lot next to mines because all of the spaces were taken. I couldn't wait to get in my bed and finally get some sleep, maybe then I could better digest my thoughts.

When I got to my apartment I stuck the key in to unlock the door but I could tell by the lack of slack that the door was already unlocked. "I must not have locked it rushing out to see what Mrs. Jenkins wanted." I thought to myself as I opened the door and locked it back behind me. My apartment was always pretty dark especially at night if I didn't have any lights on. The only type of light I would get was from the parking lot lights that shined dimly through my curtains. In the corner of my eye I had seen a couple of dark shadows on my couch but I had never been the type to investigate anything out of the ordinary, so instead of cutting on the light to see what the dark shadows were I just quickly walked past them and headed straight to my bedroom so I could at least get my gun that I was afraid to shoot and then investigate. But before I could I felt a hard object hit me across the back of my head that sent me crashing to the floor.

"Look at her she is so pretty! She looks just like Austin doesn't she...? Oh look she's opening her eyes for the first time!" My mother exclaimed standing over Marie and what I was guessing to be our baby.

"Let me hold her." I said holding out my arms and taking the tiny girl in my hands.

"Awe! Look at them, they're so cute!" Marie exclaimed looking over at me clearly exhausted but still beautiful after labor.

I couldn't believe it... I was a father already... Where did the time go? It seemed like just yesterday I was just getting back with Marie, I said to myself as I looked down into my daughter's big brown eyes. She was beautiful, a perfect replica of her mother and I. I stood there quietly holding my daughter and looking into her eyes for what seemed like an eternity before suddenly Mrs. Jenkins barged in the room with a little boy holding her hand and he looked exactly like me.

"It's time for you to take care of your son! I'm tired of doing all of this on my own!" "What?!" "Who is that?" my mother asked looking at Mrs. Jenkins and the child.

"Austin... Come get your baby before I lose my mind! He needs to know his daddy!"

"Austin! How could you do this to me Austin!? How could you? I hate you!" She screamed in her bed frantically.

"You need to wake up boy! I don't know how you let this happen." My mother said.

"Wake up bitch! You need to get the fuck up!" Marie yelled repeatedly as her voice got deeper and deeper.

"Wake the fuck up bitch!" I heard a deep voice say as the room began to fade to black and a small white man appeared in front of me in an all-black suit. He had low-cut black hair and dark blue eyes. He looked familiar but I wasn't totally aware to know for sure who he was.

There were three white guys and one large black man sitting across from me on the couch glaring down at me looking mad as hell like I had just killed one of their moms.

"Wake the hell up! You think you can go around town fucking my wife like you're going to get away with it?!" The small white man yelled slapping me across the face.

"Oh!" I yelled as the sting from the slap seemed to have an after effect on my cheek.

My eyes were wide open now and I remembered clearly who was standing in front of me. It was Mr. Jenkins.

"Do you remember who I am now?! Did you really think that I wasn't going to find out you were fucking my wife on my bed? Pulling up in my house in that raggedy ass car! I have cameras you dumb ass!" He yelled this time punching me across the jaw. "What do you have to say for yourself?"

I tried to look him in his eyes but this rich white man must have had metal implanted in his hand because I couldn't focus enough to only see one of him.

"You're fucking pathetic! She cheats on me with a bum! Little apartment, little couch! Pull his pants down... I bet he has a little dick too....I want to see what hell he has been poking my wife with!"

Two of the large white men got up and grabbed my legs and tried yanking down my pants. I grabbed my sweat pants and tried my hardest to keep them up but my display of restraint got me a big fist punch in the face, sending the room spinning.

"Come on man! I'm sorry man! I'm sorry!"

"You fucking monkey! You were stuffing that in my wife!" he yelled as another punch sent the room rapidly up and down as another big fist crashed into my face.

"What's stopping me from killing your ass!" He asked sitting down across from me on my glass coffee table.

" I..."

"Pull your fucking pants up....you monkey! No man speaks to me with his pants down."

"Man…. I can't feel my face… man."

"What? Did you hear him Barry…? He says he can't feel his face. Help him out…." Mr. Jenkins said looking over at the super large black guy with a smirk on his face.

"My pleasure." He replied in a deep voice quickly walking over to me and delivering a punch square into my face that I was sure broke my face and sent my head deep into the frame of the couch.

"No, no! Don't go to sleep son…Focus! The minute you sleep I'm going to cut off your balls!" Mr. Jenkins exclaimed. I didn't need to be told that twice. As painful as my face was the sound of my balls being cut sounded like no pain that I wanted to experience. "Now answer me before I have Barry hit you again!" Mr. Jenkins roared.

"Oh… My… God…Ok…Ok! Just don't hit me anymore please Mr. J….She told me you guys were separated and you had been with your mistress… She told me everything was alright…Mr. Jenkins…I swear I wouldn't have done anything if I had known any different."

"No! You wouldn't have done anything if you knew you were going to get caught. Don't sit here and think that I'm going to believe anything you say when you were just with my wife when I pulled up…Tell me what you would do if you saw your wife giving some bum head in a car that was bought with your money?"

I didn't know what to say back besides the pain was so bad I was having a problem trying to comprehend exactly what he was saying anyway.

"You know what… You don't have to continue to speak to me and feed me all of these lies… Just stay away from my wife. I don't care what lie she made you believe, the reality is she is mine! You can keep the car and whatever else she may have given you…It doesn't make me any difference just stay away from my wife.

"Ok…Ok…Ok man… No problem… I'm sorry! I'll never come near her again."

"You damn right you won't….That's assuming you make it through the night."

"What?" I replied looking up at Mr. Jenkins who went into his pocket and pulled out some gold brass knuckles.

"You hammered my wife…Now it's my turn to return the favor." He replied sending a punch to my face that made my view go black…

All of a sudden my gigolo ways and my playeristic life hadn't seemed so cool anymore. My pursuit to happiness through my dick is what got me here. All because I was horny and put all my morals aside I was finding myself getting my ass beat to death for what seemed like more than just sex with his wife but also for my exes boyfriends and baby daddies who were locked up and whoever else I had messed with. Who knew that I could get into so much trouble just trying to satisfy my own selfish needs? Just when I was feeling like it was time to make a change. I was feeling like I wasn't going to get another chance to change it again.

22

Crystal Wilks pt.1

"I have to go baby but I will see you sometime around tomorrow alright?"

"Wait... why don't you stick around and talk anymore? I have something I was wondering about."

"Like what?" Camry replied scrambling to put his clothes back on.

"I was wondering why you don't have any children. Can your wife have any? I asked as I lay in my bed naked under my Champaign colored silk sheets watching him get his self together.

"Yeah she can have kids I think. I mean we have tried but nothing seems to be happening so I guess it's not time yet. I even went and got my sperm count checked out just to make sure that it wasn't me who was holding us up."

"So was it? You can't get it up?"

"Hell no, the doctor said I have enough sperm to populate a large continent on my own. I have so many kids in my sack I can repopulate the world if need be by myself. You can call me super juice." He replied proud of his health.

"That is nice to know."

"Why are you asking me about kids? Why you want some? Wait let me guess you're pregnant." He replied chuckling.

"Hell no" I replied convincingly.

"You know if you were, we would have to get rid of it. I can't risk losing all my belongings to my wife in a nasty divorce because that is exactly what she would do if she found out that I was sleeping around let alone getting people pregnant."

"Imagine that. I do think about kids sometimes; it crosses my mind especially when I'm sitting up in this room all alone wondering when the next time my married man is going to come to his second home and keep me company."

Camry sat down on the bed and got really serious after I said that.

"Stop bringing up my wife ok? I think that things would run a lot smoother if you didn't do that. I don't know where this whole kid thing is coming from but if you really want one why don't you go to some sperm bank or something."

Oh hell no did this fool just suggest that I go to a sperm bank? I thought to myself as I watched his selfish mouth constantly blurt out bullshit.

"Why should I go to a... never mind." I said biting my tongue.

"No what were you about to say? We are talking right?" he replied trying to engage himself in the conversation.

"Why should I have to go to a sperm bank when I have you?"

He looked deep into my eyes and got incredibly quiet.

"I just told you that nothing like that can happen though."

"Why not? You swear up and down that you love me." I said defiantly.

"You know why! I just told you why! You're not my wife! Yes Crystal I love you and I have feelings for you but I like what we have. Why change it? Don't you like it?"

I looked at him and wanted to punch him in the face but didn't see any purpose in starting a fuss about how he was acting. I'm the one that let him get away with his doggish ways, before me he had never cheated on his wife. I shouldn't have ever let him run to me after fucking his stiff wife or letting him spend time with me after he realized how much of a stiff she is. I'm the other woman but yet and still he has the nerve to try and play me like I'm the first option once he sees daily that his first option can't compare. But regardless of how I felt it was time for me to shut the hell up and just play my position in order to get my way. I learned a long time ago that bending a little didn't mean that you were breaking the rules or values but instead allowing me to be more durable to get my desired outcome.

"I love you baby and you are absolutely right. I just find myself tripping about being alone sometimes. It's no big deal." I replied trying to hide my anger and make him feel at ease about his self.

"Yeah me too; well I have to go so, like I said I'll see you later. You want to come see me out?" he asked standing up.

"I don't have the energy. You're a big boy, you can see yourself out can't you baby?" I replied puckering my lips for a kiss.

"You're right." He replied kissing me and walking out the bedroom.

I waited till I heard the front door close before I moved and made my way to the tissue filled garbage pail I had in my room that was filled with Camry's mighty sperm that he would constantly pull out and squirt wherever he saw fit on my body. Today he came three times and all of that sperm was in multiple balled-up tissues in my pale. I reached in and grabbed them all and opened them one by one.

"Sperm bank? Who needs that?" I said to myself collecting as much as I could from the moist napkin and piling it onto my index and middle finger tips. Just looking at it grossed me out a little bit but there was still a little bit out warmth to it but sticky feeling. I wasn't sure if it would still be effective but I did hear that sperm had a surface life of a couple of hours at least as long as it stayed at a certain temperature and lubricated.

"Here goes nothing" I said as I stuffed my two fingers as deep as I could go inside of my vagina and slowly pulled and pushed them in and out.

"Awe... thanks baby! You feel so good" I moaned out to myself as I fingered myself deep into sleep.

"Little Camry or Camara... welcome to the world in 9 months." I blew out as I shut my eyes and laid my head back on my pillow excited about the possibilities.

I don't know why so many men just thought that they could have all the fun in the world and not take anything seriously. There was no way in hell that Camry could be thinking that I was going to be totally ok with being his side chick forever. I tolerated our little fling mainly because he was making it seem like it wasn't going to be long before he got rid of her. Plus the connection that we discovered we had from our child hood quickly bridged the gap that we had in the beginning. Once I learned that he was my ex-boyfriend it seemed to have made me feel a lot more comfortable messing with him. It really didn't seem to matter how long ago it was or how much I had forgot and needed to be reminded; as soon as the link had been acknowledged, it became ten times easier for me to do something that I swore that I would never do.

My big mistake seemed to have been that I had made it comfortable for him to run to me whenever he felt like he wasn't happy at home with his wife. I don't know how I let things spiral out of control like this but now it was less about trying to figure out how this happened and instead start making things work for my advantage. I swear men nowadays had it too easy. Each year things were getting worse and worse for women when it came to what we had to choose from. Now it was more about swagger and sex appeal and less about morals and honor. If a woman wanted to be happy and make it in this country nowadays she was going to have to do it on her own. That's exactly what I called myself doing, looking out for me. If Camry couldn't make up his mind about what he wanted to do then I was going to make it up for him. Maybe then he would take us more seriously and focus more on me and his child.

Could you believe that he had the nerve to look at me with displeasure when I mentioned kids? He tooted his nose up in the air and made his eyes squint like he had smelled something foul. Well I'll be the first to say if he did smell something foul it would be coming from his own ass. I told him in the beginning that I wasn't comfortable being any body's side thing and maybe I am a victim of my own circumstances and decisions by letting him feel it was alright to do anything in the first place. But there should still be something in him that would make him feel like what he is doing is wrong. I guess in the beginning it was kind of cool for him because at least in the beginning he made it clear that we were just fucking but if I remember correctly he was the first one to say he was falling in love with me. His mistake was mixing feelings with fun and my mistake was letting him. As much as I regretted it the reality was there was no turning back. I was going to have to make a way for us or give up on everything that we built up to this point. It would have been a big deal in the beginning but now that a baby may have been soon involved, hopefully things would change and we could start thinking about a life together. The problem is that I know that he wasn't too geeked about the whole baby thing, so I don't think I was going to bring that up anymore unless he wanted to.

I was going to have to get to him some other way that seemed less desperate and more voluntary so he wouldn't draw to the idea that I was crazy or trying to trap him and I think I had the perfect plan to be able to kill two birds with one stone.

23

Crystal Wilks pt.2

"So what are you doing for your man for Christmas? "I asked Linda who was sitting next to me in my living room sipping on a glass of wine.

"I'm not sure, probably go to his parents' house and then my parents' house to open presents and spend some time with them."

"That sounds traditional."

"We really didn't have any big plans. Camry is more of the stay at home type of guy."

"Is he like that all the time?"

"He has been lately. If he isn't at work then most likely he is at home looking for new ways to make money. Wait, don't let me forget his best friend Austin, he does go over there and get lost sometimes."

"Really? Did you know my nickname use to be Austin? Every time I hear that name I feel like people are referring to me." I replied with a dirty smile on my face.

"Really? Austin is a long ways from Crystal. How did that nickname come about?" Linda asked totally clueless to my mischief.

"Oh, my child's father used to call me awesome and then Austin in public."

"Your child? I thought you didn't have any kids" Linda replied raising her eyebrow.

"Oh I never had a successful pregnancy but I have been pregnant before." I replied trying to clean up the verbal mess I had just made.

"Oh, I'm sorry to hear that. Hopefully God will grant you better luck whenever the right man comes along and lays it on you. Atlanta is definitely a hot spot for one of them."

"I have a feeling that you are right." I replied taking a long sip of my glass of red wine. I don't know why I was drinking wine around her; it made me feel too relaxed when it came to expressing my opinion. I was a sip away from telling her how well her man and I were doing.

"Did I ever thank you?" I asked pouring myself another glass as I finished off my first one.

"For what?"

"For being such a lousy wife to your husband and handing him over to me. Keep doing me a favor and keep ignoring his needs so I can keep giving them to him the way that he likes it. Maybe then he will come to his senses and get rid of your stiff ass."

"Crystal? Hey.....?" Linda said snapping her fingers in front of me to get my attention.

"Excuse me?"

"You were about to say something? Are you ok? You kind of went off into space in the middle of thanking me."

"I didn't say anything? I replied confused but relieved at the same time.

"No." she replied with the same confused look on her face.

"Oh thank God!" I blurted out with a drunken laugh.

"Girl you are crazy! Maybe you should put the wine down or give me a sip of that stuff. Are you sure we are drinking the same thing?" she replied laughing with me.

"No really though, I want to thank you for extending your hand to me. I have a lot of adjusting to do and over the past couple of weeks you have been making it really easy for me. It's nice to know I have a friend in you." I said looking deep into her eyes so she could feel my words.

"Girl it's no problem, as quiet as it's kept I needed somebody like you to come along. I have a lot of girlfriends but none like you. You're like the one I run to when I just want to get away and don't want to be around the normal crowd."

"Really?" I replied lost for words but at the same time noticing that she and Camry were pretty much coming to me for the same kind of relief in a way. One was coming to me for the mental and the other was for sexual reasons. Just that fast I went from feeling special to downright used. As much as I could sit around and be amused by hearing Linda tell me her life I had a plan that I needed to set in motion before I got irritated with this whole thing and went on my way.

"So are you and you husband on good terms or no? I asked after Linda finished her third glass of wine and began to look a little light in the ass.

"We are ok but not like we use to be. I'm not sure how to get it back to how it was."

"What do you think that problem is?"

"I'm not sure. I was thinking that it may have something to do with how much time we spend away from each other. It's always been my issue but he argues that we need to get as much money as possible and stick it out until we have a certain amount saved up. I feel totally opposite so I've been kind of purposely giving him the bare minimum in the bedroom."

"Really? That's a true power move right there." I replied giving her a high five knowing that her actions were hurting her more than they were helping.

"Isn't it?! There is no way in hell that I am going to get anything when he gets everything he wants all the time. If he doesn't want to see things my way some of the time then he is not going to be getting anything special out of me in the parts of our marriage that he feels is significant." She replied confidently.

"Listen to you! That's what I'm talking about girl hold your ground. But you know you're going to have to do something special for him on Christmas. You have to give him more than enough every now and then to keep him on the hook. You can't hold out and expect him not to get sick of waiting if you know what I mean. Trust me when I say that baby I had to learn the hard way."

"I have been harsh on him. But I told you why. Do you think I'm messing up too much and not doing enough?" She said worriedly.

As bad as I wanted to tell her no I knew if I wanted to get her full trust that I was going to have to make some sense about certain things and dish out the truth. She didn't seem like a total dumbass after all she did graduate from college. She had a degree and a very good job to back it up so she had to know something.

"Yes girl, you're messing up "I replied reluctantly.

"I know... I just don't know what to do. I mean I want to please him but if I give in all the time what would that say about me? I'm just trying to have some type of stance you know what I mean?"

"That's good but sometimes you have to bend a little to get a little."

"I understand but I just don't know what he wants form me. I mean I can turn it up in the bedroom if I wanted to but it's like what am I getting in return?"

"Well, why not spice it up? Lead by example and make him see you're trying, which might make him try to bend a little more for you."

"How?"

"I don't know, try something different. What has he wanted that you wanted also but neither of you have ever done?"

She looked at me and smiled. "You know every man's dream…" She replied giggling.

"What?"

"You know, another girl…"

"What?"

"A threesome, geez. Must I have to say it out loud?" She uttered out blushing.

"Girl, I swear that seems like every man's desire. I don't know what all the hype is about I mean don't get me wrong it's fun and very pleasing one would guess but more so than anything it's like a workout slash job."

"How is that?"

"Well we both know good sex is a calorie burner but when you throw another person in the mix it's like you have to make sure you do your end of the job which is making sure that everybody is happy. There should never be a dull moment; everyone should be working long and hard if you know what I mean."

"So you have done it? You don't even look like the freak type." Linda replied looking a little deeper into my eyes.

"There is a lot that you don't know about me" I replied with a smirk on my face.

Today was one of the many days that Linda and I spent together. We had been on plenty play dates and luncheons which helped us grow pretty close in a short period of time. I really didn't like her one bit but I felt I need to keep her around to find out what Camry liked about her other than her amazing physical appearance. Her personality seemed to be lacking the fire he loved from me. Linda was like a Mary Poppins compared to me; clean cut and by the book. Camry didn't care anything about that mess. I think he did what he felt was right and married the typical good girl but in the process sacrificed what he liked in other areas for an image. That was his first mistake and his second mistake was thinking he could have sex with me and ever be satisfied by his wife again. I don't care how hard he tried. I worked so hard in the bed to make every moment unforgettable. I was trying to make sure that every time Camry had sex he couldn't do anything but think of me.

Linda had no idea who she was dealing with or what she was getting into by making me a friend with her ideal way of thinking. While myself being a pragmatist, I was willing to do whatever it took to get the job done.

A piece of me felt like it was getting to the point that she trusted me whole heartedly already and it hadn't been that long. It was kind of amusing going from her to her husband then back to her. One day I had purposely went to meet her after I had been with Camry without washing up so his smell could still be on me. He wore a strong cologne that might as well been called sex because when I smelled it I would get turned on every time. I went to her after meeting with him hoping that she would still smell his scent on me but she was so naïve she said nothing about it. I wanted her to know so bad but not to break them up and leave me looking like the bad guy because then I would lose Camry but so she could either remove herself from the situation or be pushed away by him and I could have him all to myself. Linda didn't know how to treat him. I envied her so much deep down inside...I couldn't believe I was letting this get to me; but I was at the point that maybe I needed to start doing drastic things to have my way.

24

Camry Carter

"You sure you don't want me to empty out your waste basket for you?"

"Why are you so concerned about a couple pieces of tissue at the bottom of my trash bin? Crystal replied.

"Well you know the tissue could leak and stain the bin only making it really sticky and nasty smelling." I replied as I buckled up my pants and slipped on my shoes.

"Boy get out...Go see your friend, I got it." She replied in a less than grossed out tone.

"Alright baby...Bye...See you later."

"You better...Hope your friend gets better." She shouted as I left the room and walked through the large hall of the front door.

It had been a while since I had heard from Austin. I was thinking it was because I was spending so much time with Crystal but it wasn't. Sometimes he got jealous and wouldn't call but that wasn't the case this time. He had been put in the hospital by some thugs or at least that's what he told the police. Something about they had broken into his house and tried to rob him. The police ended up buying the story and I knew better than to do that. Austin didn't have anything worth value and he was never really flashy for anybody to get the idea that he had any type of money in the first place. He ended up telling me the real deal once the police left. Come to find out the cougar broad he was creeping around with hadn't been covering her tracks and had led her husband and friends right to Austin. Something about being caught on tape in mid stroke is what led them to him. I was assuming he meant that he had been caught on camera, license place to his car and all.

I was so angry to see Austin so messed up. I felt like it was my fault because I was the one who convinced him to start hoeing around town like it was nobody's business. I did tell him to be careful but that didn't matter, it was my fault regardless. Because of me he was sitting up in the hospital with some broken ribs, jaw, two loose teeth, a black eye, busted lip, bruised chest and an unexplainable twitch that would certainly occur in his eye that wasn't swollen whenever the light was on. Then the doctors had the nerve to put blue bandages around his forehead. I swear every time I looked at him I thought of Mr. Potato Head with a blue hat on because his face was so swollen.

A lot of his family would be there every time I found time to see him. But the biggest surprise of all was Marie. She was there every day by his bed side after she got off work looking so down. I would look at her and wonder if she really knew why Austin had got his ass whooped the way he did. I could tell by all the concern and sympathy on her face that she didn't. She was as clueless as a question mark with no sentence in front of it. Hopefully it stayed that way; sometimes the things best kept secret are meant to stay that way. I was glad to see them back together. She told me they had moved in together and everything or should I say since Austin been in the hospital she's moved in his apartment. I don't think she had any other choice because she was staying with her boyfriend and I guess once she broke up with him he put her out. I found it amazing how love didn't seem to have an expiration date in all cases; especially in their situation. I don't think that I would have ever forgiven Linda if she was in Marie's shoes and left me here to figure things out for myself. Then once she finally couldn't avoid facing him she acted like she didn't even know who he was? That was a cold play right there. But whatever happened from then on out must have been for a reason because here she was by his side like never before. All I knew is if he gets really serious with her and starts considering marriage he better handcuff her legs so she won't try and leave him there looking sad like before but this time at the altar.

I wanted to go after Mr. Jenkins but I kept looking at Austin and imagining myself in his place. It wasn't like Mr. Jenkins had done anything wrong. It was his wife for God's sake so it was almost expected but none of us would have imagined that it would be this bad.

It made me think about my own situation a little bit. I was married and basically in a love triangle just like the one Austin was in the only difference is I'm the one who can do some real harm in this case. I couldn't see Linda or Crystal trying to do any real harm to me but at the same time there was no predicting any woman's actions. They were so emotion driven that they were unpredictable when they allowed their actions to be dictated by such emotions. A flash of myself in Austin's hospital bed crossed my mind then another flash of Linda in Austin's place and finally Crystal. I guess the bottom line was that somebody could get hurt if any of this got out of hand. I wasn't planning on letting it go any further than it already had though. I went down to the court house the other day and asked a lawyer friend about possibly getting some representation for divorce. Things were just continuing to get worse between Linda and I and constantly improving between Crystal and myself. I knew the moment I opened my mouth and told Crystal how I felt that things would spiral out of control. I was crossing the line that I had created but it was too late for any reconstructing; the foundation had already been built for Crystal and I and torn done for my wife.

The only thing that was throwing me for a loop was Crystal's sudden talk about babies. I mean I wanted one but only when the circumstance was right. I am still married so for me to allow any gut blowing decisions like that to happen I would be a fool and might as well hand Linda over half of everything I own. Crystal would constantly remind me that she was a millionaire and that because I was with her that I could afford whatever losses I took but I haven't ever been a type of man that keeps his head all up under his ladies ass and hand all in her purse. Even though Crystal did have his beautiful Ferrari that she barely even touched sitting in her garage. She did say I could have it once I made up my mind but I am yet to do so. Being with Crystal made me feel good but I don't know for sure what to do. It seems like I have a web of thoughts and I'm tangled up in all of them. It kind of spooked me out a little bit about how perfect Crystal is despite the recent baby craze. It's like she came out of nowhere like a thief in the night and totally stole my heart from Linda. I always wonder what her husband was like and how much of a fool he must have been to die on a mind blowing beauty like Crystal. Some guys would say that I was a fool for risking Linda for Crystal but what can I say? I'm stuck between a rock and a hard place.

Speaking of Linda, I'm starting to suspect that she had been sleeping with someone else. It has to be either her old boyfriends or one of her co-workers or something because now she's gone entirely too much and when we are home together she's having all these text messages in secret. I checked her phone one day while she was in the shower and most of them were from a guy named Chris who I guess was border line gay because some of the texts I read seemed a little feminine but at the same time she did have a picture in her phone of some dark skinned guy so I was assuming that he was Chris. The guy reminded me a lot of Khyel...the one who got caught screwing Austin's ex but it wasn't him. Even though it wasn't I couldn't help but imagine him power driving my wife somewhere behind a restaurant on a garbage can. I wanted to call this guy but every time I went to copy down the number she would be coming as if she knew what I was trying to do.

The sex wasn't getting any better and when she wasn't working she was going out more with her friends supposedly for unexplained hours. All the signs were there but every time I would call myself investigating something would end up coming up.

I did have a close call one day on my way to Crystal's place. On my way to Crystal's house I had caught a glimpse of Linda's bright white 2012 300c going the opposite way and I knew for a fact that at that time she had no business in that area. Matter of fact I think that she was supposed to be at work when I saw her. I swear I couldn't stand liars or cheaters and I guess that was the day that changed everything and I started considering a future with Crystal instead of Linda. I'm still kind of tied between two trees but I was beginning to lean towards Crystal's side as long as she continued to act accordingly.

(Christmas Eve)

"Oh...My...Yes! That's it baby!" I shouted tensing up and enjoying the pleasure of oral sex from my wife.

It was Christmas Eve and she said she wanted to surprise me into the Christmas day. She also had apologized for the way she had been acting in the bedroom and promised tonight that she was going to make it all up. I would be lying through my teeth if I had said that she wasn't. She had my hands and legs tied to the bed post and a blind fold over my eyes. This was a new kinky to me that had me beyond excited. She was doing things to me that I had never felt from her. It made me feel good but at the same time pissed me off because I couldn't help but wonder were these all the sudden new moves and tricks that she had learned from the guy that she was cheating on me with? They had to be because we had never done any of this shit.

"You like that baby?" Linda said as she stuffed my dick back in her mouth.

"Awe! Yeah...!" I shouted. Now I wasn't sure if I should have been mad at the guy she had learned this from or thanking him.

"Remember I told you I had a surprise for you baby?" Linda said as I continued to feel the deep throat sensation.

"What?"

How was she giving me head and talking at me at the same time?

"Baby...Oh...What's going on?"

"Shut up and just enjoy the moment baby." Linda replied kissing me on the lips while I continued to receive amazing head from whoever the other person was. I can't believe my baby...My wonderful, wonderful wife had the courtesy to fulfill one of my long awaited fantasies. I was so elated but now I had to see it.

What good was a moment if you couldn't see what was going on?

"Baby take this blind fold off...I got to see... this...Oh...Tell your friend to slow down...She's going to make me cum!..." I warned as I felt a large build up from throughout my body.

"Shut up!" Linda replied sucking on my neck and sucking on my nipples as the build began to get more intense and the deep throating began to go into over drive.

"God...I can't...! Awe..." I moaned out as my body tensed up and the buildup began to find its way out of my body. I felt the head quickly stop and the weight of a woman quickly ease on to my erupting penis.

"Fuck!"

"Yeah...That's it baby...Give it to me...Give me all of it..."The woman said.

I couldn't help but recognize the voice as she began to speak more and I began to comprehend what was going on. But it couldn't be...I quickly grew impatient and asked Linda again to remove the blind fold.

"Come...On...OH...Take this blind fold off. I want to see." I uttered out.

"Ok..." Linda replied pulling the blind fold up off my eyes. "Surprise baby...Merry Christmas!" She said smiling as she grabbed Crystal's breast lightly with one hand and kissed her in the mouth while Crystal continued to ride me.

My reaction was a little delayed because of the unexpected revealing. My heart had to have stopped then started back beating in over drive once I realized what was really going on.

"Crystal?" I accidently blurted out.

Both of them kept on kissing and kind of looked at me at the same time as if I had called them both. Right then and there amidst all the licking, kissing, sucking, and fucking I began to wonder what type of sick trick God was allowing the devil to play on me.

So did this mean that Linda had known about Crystal? Was I being set up? How was I supposed to react? This had to be a set up...that's why they had me tied up on the bed so I couldn't escape. There probably going to get all they can out of me and then cut my balls off.

" Oh, God? Why me lord? Please forgive me this one time for my sins. I promise I will never do them again. Lord just give me this one break? Do me this one favor please?" I said in a desperate plea to God in my head.

I never thought that it was possible to be in two places at one time and also be in two different moods at once as well. I was in hell panicking in my head but my body was in heaven feeling so much pleasure it was almost unbearable.

"My turn..." Linda demanded.

"Ok..." Crystal replied getting a couple more moves in before getting off as she glared down at me with a slight smile on her face.

Linda got on top of me and eased down on me and began grinding on me while Crystal licked her way up my chest and neck then finally to my lips.

"Don't worry...She doesn't know...Just relax and go with it, enjoy yourself baby, indulge yourself in the moment." She whispered in my ear.

I looked at her as to say ok and watched her slide off the bed and untie my feet and hands. I don't know what was going on with Crystal but I guess that she was right about me trying to enjoy the moment. This was an opportunity of a life time and there was no sense of me letting it slip away especially if Linda didn't know anything. Even thought it was a little harder to pull myself out of the panicked state that I was put in once I discovered them two together.

After about 5 minutes of having my limbs back and being able to take a little control of the situation my heart began to ease and I could begin to focus on the task at hand which was releasing the beast. There was so much to do but not much space to do it on my Queen sized bed. If I was hitting Linda from the back I couldn't help but watch Linda as she tended to Crystal's body quite well with her tongue. If I was putting down the pound game on top of Crystal I had to constantly remember and accept the extra feeling that would pop in my body from Linda licking, sucking and kissing whatever parts of me that she wanted. Then I had to remember to breathe when one of them was riding me and the other was sitting on my face. I considered myself to be in shape but there was no preparing that I could do to get ready for something like this. There was never a dull moment and I couldn't stop myself from losing control while accepting the challenge of trying things I had never tried before.

Talk about a Merry Christmas? We went into Christmas morning intertwined like a dirty game of twister and I had no shame in it. I knew Christmas was supposed to be a holiday that we were supposed to celebrate our savior but on this morning I couldn't do anything but thank him. If I was sinning then I was going to need to be forgiven because right now every moment felt like a blessing. It wasn't until about 3am that we all had finally fell out because we were all so exhausted and went to sleep. Linda in one arm and Crystal in the other;It couldn't get any better than this.

I thought it couldn't get any better until I woke up to the smell of breakfast food and a tugging sensation my penis. I opened my eyes only to see Linda coming in the room with a large tray with 3 plates of food on it and Crystal sucking away at my dick like she wanted her breakfast to be an explosion of vitamin filled essentials. Who was I to deny her that privilege?

"Fuck...I'm cumming!" I couldn't say no more all I could do was grip the bed sheets and hold on to dear life as this rocket ship took off.

Breakfast in bed? Crystal waking me up with a good morning? What type of king was I? I must have been dreaming because the last time I checked stuff like this didn't happen every day. I had my wife and my mistress working together like two kings servants on his birthday.

"Good Morning baby!" Linda exclaimed as I recovered from the sudden exclamation point in my already energetic day.

"That's an understatement…" I replied as Crystal finished and came up and laid her head on my chest.

"Well I know it's a little late for an introduction… but wait you will never guess her name?" Linda exclaimed sitting down on the bed opposite from Crystal.

"What?" I replied going along with the assumption that I didn't already know who she was.

"Chrissy!!" Linda exclaimed bursting in laughter.

I looked oddly around the room as if I didn't understand what was so funny.

"Doesn't her name come real close to the name you came up for me? Think about it baby?" She replied still giggling.

"OH…Ha! Yeah it is…Digg that." I replied starting to feel a little bit uncomfortable suddenly.

"What is so funny? I want to laugh." Crystal said lifting her head up off my chest already smiling as if she knew what was so funny.

"Well…" Linda started to tell.

"So…How did this happen?" I interrupted.

"What?" Crystal replied.

"Linda…How did this whole threesome thing start? Better yet how did you two meet?" I asked grabbing my plate of hot breakfast and passing it to Crystal then sitting up and grabbing one for myself. "Let's eat and talk." I said looking down at the plate of plentiful eggs, sausage patties and waffles.

"Well…Um… We met at the gas station actually. I liked her truck and she liked your Beemer and from there we exchanged numbers and that was the start of a good friendship." Linda simply put it.

"How long ago? "

" Several months ago." Crystal blurted out glimpsing at me.

"Really?" I replied cutting my eyes at her.

"Yes…I don't know how we got so cool but we did. She is so cool and comforting. We just hit it off. I don't even spend that much time with my friends anymore; I just go over her place and kick it with her." Linda said taking a bite out of her sausage.

"Digg that." I replied quickly thinking about the day I had seen her leaving as I was going to Crystal's house and the name Chris that I was suspecting to be the man she was cheating on me with that I kept seeing in Linda's phone. The whole time it was Crystal!

"She kept telling me about wanting to spice things up for you in the bedroom so I suggested we give you one of the most desired man fantasies." Crystal said.

"And what would have been a better Christmas present than this?" Linda finished.

"This is definitely a surprise and a fantasy all at the same time but Linda when did you start liking woman?"

"Umm…I don't Camry…I'm just doing this for you and besides Crystal just makes everything seem easy for me. Like so comfortable I can do anything around her." Linda replied smiling at Crystal.

"Imagine that."

"Well, since you're ok with all of this I have another surprise for you...Umm what do you think about Chrissy spending the Christmas holiday with us?"

"Auk!" I blurted choking on a piece of sausage after Linda broke that news to me. "What? Why?"

"Baby, don't be like that...Chrissy doesn't have any real family here and I thought that it would be a good idea to have her join us this Christmas."

"But...We are going to my parent's place and your mom's place...I mean are you sure you want to..."

"Want to what? Come on Cam don't be like that...Where is your Christmas spirit?"

"No its ok...I'll just go home and spend the day alone in my house eating ice cream and crying on the couch." Crystal interrupted as if she was affected by me uninviting her.

"No! No! You're spending it with us and that's final! You're my friend and I want you to come with us so that's that" Linda replied putting her stamp of approval on her choice

I took a deep breath and shook my head.

"If you want me to go then I will...I don't want to be around if I'm not wanted." Crystal replied is disdain.

"No...It's going to be ok...He's fine he just doesn't like sudden changes in plans that's all, he will get over it." Linda said to Crystal insisting she stayed.

What the hell was going on? I couldn't help but think that maybe this sweet dream wasn't much of a blessing at all but the beginning of a nightmare. What was Crystal thinking? After all this time, she was going behind my back and spending time with my wife! Who does that...? They met at a gas station? I'll believe that when hell freezes over and the devil complains about people being cruel to each other. There was no way that I could begin to feel comfortable about this. The threesome was one thing but this hanging around and being buddy- buddy was another. I don't care how much I benefited from the whole joining together mess of my wife and mistress. Now that I knew it was Crystal that my wife had been hanging around with I couldn't help but wonder what they were doing with each other all this time alone in Crystal's big house or if anything that they were portraying to me was genuine. I asked Linda privately three more times throughout the day if they had done anything; just the two of them and every time she replied no but all day I couldn't help but think about how at ease Linda was during the threesome while she was kissing Crystal or even going as far as eating her out while I did my thing. Maybe I was over thinking or beginning to panic but clearly I was over doing it in something.

Because of the sudden change I didn't want to go to my parent's house anymore. I just knew that they were going to call it like they saw it and nine times out of ten they were going to see it for what it was because they knew me so well. Plus Crystal could not stop staring at me whenever Linda turned her head. I just knew that one of them would pick up on that immediately. I wanted to go to the hospital and see Austin. They were releasing him today so I figured that seeing him would possibly cheer up his day with the humorous situation that I was in. But at the same time he wouldn't want to be seen in the condition that he was in so I chose otherwise and went straight to Linda's parent's house where they were having a Christmas party.

I couldn't believe how well Crystal and Linda were getting along. Linda sat in the passenger seat while Crystal sat in the back directly in the middle constantly staring up in my rear view mirror at me as I drove.

"Don't worry too much about my family Chrissy, they are good people. I just know that they're going to love you. My brother especially...I think he's single." Linda said bobbing her head a little bit to the light sounds coming from my stereo.

"Really? I usually get along pretty well with people. I should be fine...How does your brother look?" She replied keeping her eyes locked on me through the rear view.

"Girl my brother looks like Morris Chestnut fine without the big vampire smile...You would like him."

"Well I can't wait to meet him maybe he can be my new buddy." She replied rolling her eyes.

I cracked a smile and shook my head.

"What's so funny Cam?" Linda asked.

"You know your brother doesn't look like Morris Chestnut he looks and is built more like Pooky from New Jack City or better yet MC Gusto from the movie CB4 on a good day."

"Uhn Huh!" Crystal replied bursting in laughter.

"Stop talking about my brother like that!" Linda replied hitting me on my arm." He just hating because he don't have all this dark skin...You know how there is an ongoing feud between the light brights and the midnight dark guys.

"I tend to have a thing for light skinned guys but my husband was dark so I guess whoever treats me right is all that matters."

"I hear that...Well once we get to my parent's house you'll see my brother and you can judge for yourself.

"Yeah and I can't wait for you to agree with me." I blurted out.

"Stop hating on my brother!"

I couldn't make up in my mind whether I was hating on her brother or if I was getting a little angry at the fact that she was trying to hook Crystal up with him. I couldn't help but feel a little possessive but I have to bite my tongue and catch myself before I make it clear to Linda that I knew Chrissy a little bit more than what she thought.

....

We were just getting back from the Christmas Party and settling in over a glass of wine and conversation at my place when I began to feel like Crystal was over staying her welcome. It was almost ten at night and she hadn't even made a move to the front door unless we were leaving with her. At the Christmas party she blended right in like she was one of them and made herself at home as if she had been there before. Everybody loved Crystal and that bothered me a little bit. She was supposed to be my little secret and here she was stuck to my wife's hip like she was a conjoined twin. I kept my distance from her at the party and hung around with Linda's dad and uncles' so no one would suspect anything. But the whole time I couldn't help but feel a little uncomfortable. Now the day was almost over and she was still here? Linda was acting like she didn't want to see her leave and now that we were back home drinking I knew she was going to insist that Crystal stay the night.

"Girl I told you my brother was cute...are you going to call him?" Linda asked gulping down her wine.

"Yeah, he was cute but I wasn't very surprised because he favors you a lot"

"You guys would be cute together."

"I'll think about it." Crystal replied downing her glass of wine.

"Well I guess that I should be going...It was fun but it's getting kind of late and I'm beginning to feel a little too comfortable if you know what I mean." Crystal replied standing up but stumbling to her feet.

"Oh...No! You can't go anywhere like that..." Linda insisted

"No...I'm fine...I just...Whoa!" Crystal blurted out flopping back down to the couch.

"Yeah...its official you shouldn't be driving...You're staying here for the night." Linda declared standing up trying to help Crystal but she was wobbly her damn self. Whoa! She shouted as she flopped down next to Crystal bursting out in laughter.

"Look at you two...Light weights drinkers. Who lets a couple of glasses of wine get to them..." I replied shaking my head and finishing off the bottle.

"Whatever Camry...Everybody can't polish off a bottle like you and still be functional a hundred percent. Anyway...I'm about to go jump in the shower...We should go jump in the shower Camry so...Come on..." Linda said getting up.

"Ok...I'll be there in a minute just let me clean up out here...Ok...Don't take all day boy. I'll be in here waiting for you." She replied as she walked out the room.

I grabbed the empty bottle of wine and all the glasses.

"You ok?"

"You know I am." Crystal replied getting up and following me to the kitchen.

"Then take your ass home! What are you trying to do! Ruin my marriage!" I yelled in a low tone.

"Is that what you think? She replied once we got in the kitchen.

"Hell yea! First you secretly hanging out with my wife and popping up in my bed with her and now you're staying the night? What the hell is wrong with you? Does she know about us?"

"I told you yesterday that she doesn't know ok. Stop being so damn paranoid everything is fine we are all just having a little bit of fun."

"This shit isn't fun to me...Your crossing the line and you know it."

"I'm crossing the line. Like you weren't when you told me you loved me? Or better yet when you slept in my bed? Or even more the first day you decided to double back and take me out! You're the one who had crossed the line. Now that I've stepped up my game you want to back off? No boy! It doesn't work like that!" She exclaimed in disdain.

"Lower your tone! Before my wife hears you"

"Your wife! You call that weak bitch your wife? I have her ass wrapped around my finger Camry. She might as well be a robot for me. She's so dumb she doesn't even see your cheating ass for the man you are?

"Shut up!"

"No...You shut the fuck up! You had the nerve to call the broad my name and she still hasn't figured out I'm the one. She probably hasn't even figured out Chrissy is short for Crystal...Damn shame...I see why you run to me every other day like a kitten in need of milk."

"What the hell is wrong with you? Where did all this come from?"

"What's wrong with me? What's wrong with you? Thinking that you could get all that you wanted but when it came to my request you just shot my shit down like I don't deserve anything from you but some lousy dick and a lonely night."

"What you are you talking about?"

"You're selfish just like every other man on this planet. You want to wine and dine then fuck in secret whatever woman you see fit but don't want to do anything outside of your comfort zone."

"Do you think I'm comfortable cheating on my wife? Having my mistress..."

"Mistress? Last time I checked I was your girl!" She declared in disdain.

"What..." I took a deep breath and bit my tongue to stop myself from saying something that would blow her over the top. "Crystal look...you can't understand how uncomfortable it makes me feel to see you with my wife? You don't see how that can be a little uncomfortable?"

"You should have thought about that long before today Camry. You don't have anything to worry about...I'm the one with my heart on the chopping block. You don't understand that I have to look out for myself now? I thought I had you in my corner but it's beginning to be clear to me that I'm nothing but a "thing" to you."

"Oh my god will you please stop with all this mess!! I told you how I feel about you Crystal but you don't see how you're crossing the line?"

"I have to do something...If I leave it up to you I would be girl number 2 forever and alone...I want to have a child Camry...I want..."

"So go get pregnant! I'm not stopping you from going out and doing you! Nobody told you to be faithful to a married man!"

"Go get pregnant? You think it's just that easy? You want me to just go fuck anybody? Insensitive bastard! I'm going to get pregnant but it isn't going to be from anybody! What do I look like to you? Doesn't it feel like yours? She said grabbing my hand and rubbing it across her belly."

"What the fuck is wrong with you? Stop acting like this...Maybe you did get one or two many drinks in you" I replied backing away

"I'm fine boy...You know...If you don't get it together and make things work...then I will! I don't have a problem with being girlfriend number 2 for right now but you better get it together soon before I do it for you."

"Are you threatening me?" I said walking a little closer to her in a more aggressive stance to try and intimidate her a little bit.

"Hell yeah I am..." She replied with a smile... You better poke that little ass chest of yours back down and step away from me. It's funny how a man always resorts back to thinking that physical harm will work. My husband thought the same thing and he was twice as big and three times as strong."

"Cam! Baby! Come on!" Linda yelled from the bathroom.

"Here I come baby...!' I shouted back "You better get your ass out of my house."

"Is that how you really want to do this baby?" she replied reaching for my crotch.

"Stop it!" I replied slapping her hand away. "You take your ass home and I'll tend to you later."

"You really think it's just that easy? You think you can just send me off and that's that?"

"Why are you tripping?"

"Because you think you King shit? You just can't go around treating people any type of way."

"Ok...Ok...I get it...It's just this situation you two have me in has me really uncomfortable. Just please let me digest this and I swear everything will pan out."

"You promise?" she replied with a calmer tone.

"Yes..."

"Now please can you let me tend to my wife and leave?"

"See there you go being selfish again...I want her just one more time...Us three again tonight and then I'll give you your space."

"Crystal..."

"Crystal noting...You better learn to compromise or you're going to find out that life isn't as pleasing as you would have thought it to be."

I just shook my head and walked away feeling defeated.

"Ok...Crystal you win" I replied as I headed to the bedroom kicked off my clothes and finally got in the shower with my wife.

My luxury was finally coming back to bite me in the ass. My wife had made Crystal a house guest and Crystal was secretly looking forward to taking her place. I knew things could get out of hand if I had let them and now I had to come to the reality that I was in too deep to just act like nothing had ever happened. Everyone was just too emotionally involved. Crystal wanted a baby and I was beginning to feel that I was going to have to make a choice pretty soon. Either stop messing around or give Crystal what she wanted which is for me to end my life if you ask me. Earlier I was debating on leaving my wife but it seemed like now I didn't have a choice because Crystal was forcing me to choose. If everybody just played there roll then it would be alright but clearly I was living too much of a dream.

When we got out the shower Crystal was in our bed waiting on us or should I say my wife because she was the first person she pulled the towel off of and began to explore. The repeat of Christmas Eve had begun again and didn't end until the next morning just like the day before. As good as she made both of us feel I couldn't wait until I got some time alone to look up Crystal on the internet or have my lawyer friend check her out for me. I may have been a little too late looking into who she was but now was as good a time as ever to find out. There was something off about Crystal that I was either missing or hadn't seen till now. She was desperate and manipulative which were two deadly combinations to add together. I had something I needed to find out before I lost everything that I called myself building.

25

Crystal Wilks

I didn't want to reveal this side of me but some men didn't understand anything but crazy. Especially when they thought they could use their hands on me for anything other than sex. For the first time I was beginning to see a man that I thought was the finest thing walking turn into a little boy. It seemed like that's all you had to do now a days if you wanted to see a man squirm was to disrupt their harmony of life. Threaten their flow or routine and it was almost a guarantee that they would begin to act right.

I wasn't even sure that I wanted Camry's pathetic ass anymore. Hopefully I had taken enough from him to get pregnant so I could have a family of my own but honestly I was beginning to like Linda more than Camry. I mean I hadn't been with a woman but one time before to try and please my husband which was a fun experience but it was something I said I would never do again because of my morals. But this time I was doing it to get closer to Camry but it was looking like it had freaked him out. Linda seemed to like it a lot though and if you asked me, it wasn't her first time either. She was handling the situation better than I was.

Maybe after all this time I was going after the wrong person. Maybe men were the wrong direction for me to go in from the very beginning? It would have only made since on why I haven't had any luck with them. I left one abusive relationship just barely to walk into another man's relationship and play the home wrecker.

Why did my life have to be like this? All I wanted to be was happy and here I was struggling to may up my mind. I hated it when people brought the worst out of me!

Terrance and Camry were no different...They were both some cheating, dick following, pussy chasing bastards that had no regards for their wives. Camry had the nerve to act like he was going to hit me after I didn't want to leave? All I wanted to do was make him happy and satisfy him through the night and he wanted me to get out? He said he loved me so why didn't he kick his wife out?

Wait a minute; I get it... He didn't love me at all he was just doing what all men did and was telling me what I wanted to hear right? He was running game on me right? I almost didn't recognize it because it had been a while since I had been single enough for a guy to do it. I almost forgot how shitty it made me feel but now that I had been reminded I think that it was only going to make me decide what I wanted to do a little easier.

....

(A week later)

"Linda...Yawl marriage still isn't getting any better? Here it is a new year and he still wanted to be out supposedly working all day?"

"Yeah...but I don't think he's working all those hours. I'm gullible but I'm no dummy." Linda replied filling her glass with some more wine and kicking her feet up on my glass coffee table.

"You think he's cheating on you?" I asked looking really interested.

"I think he is...He comes home smelling like other women and rushing to the shower...After swearing he was at his friends place...I know he's lying I just feel it." She replied beginning to tear up.

I scooted a little closer to her on my cashmere couch.

"I knew Camry...before you introduced us..."

"What?"

"He was dating my best friend. I went on a double date with them a while back and had no idea he was married. They were all hugged up and lovey dovey I just knew he was single. Camry Carter right? He's a real estate guy. His birthday is next month?"

"Yeah?"

"Yup he is planning on going down to Florida and taking my friend with him. She said he had a place down there or something?"

"Yeah...We have a time share on a condo off the beach."

"Yup that's him then. I didn't want to tell you because I didn't want to see anybody get hurt and you know I had already been down that road but me and you have grown really close and I just don't want you to go through what I went through and I don't want to see you hurt but you do need to know."

"Are you sure? I mean we haven't been on the best of terms now and I...Oh my God!"

"Girl I'm positive."

"That's probably why he didn't want me hanging around you anymore..."

"Excuse me?"

"After you went home the day after Christmas he told me to stay away from you. Something about you giving him a bad vibe or...wait no...he said you were a hoe and he didn't want anybody to see me with you because then they would think I was a hoe too"

"Really? A hoe..."? Now does that make sense? I'm telling you that's even more proof to you that he is hiding something." I replied cutting my eyes at Linda.

"That's what I'm thinking too but trying to down grade your character was so middle school to me. It does seem like he is hiding something. What is your friend doing later because I would like to talk to her?"

"She's in Paris right now...She's in the military and I think she may be stationed there."

"Wow...Well what's her name?"

I almost couldn't think of another name other than my own to tell her because I was the girl I was telling her about.

"Crystal?" Linda blurted out beating me to the punch

"Yeah, how did you know?" I replied surprised.

"Wow..." Linda replied as her eyes got watery and she gulped down another glass of wine.

"Let it out girl…" I insisted scooting closer to her and rubbing her back.

"He has called me that several times…"

"And what did you do when he called you that?"

"I confronted him about it and he told me that Crystal was the name he had for me when I acted a certain way in the bedroom." She said as the tears fell down her face.

"Wow…Pretty clever…but don't tell me you went for it?"

"What else was I supposed to do? He's my husband and I trust him…I can't just go off a hunch without any proof and start accusing him of things. I can't believe this shit!" Linda screamed resting her shoulder on my arm.

"Don't cry baby it happens to the best of us. But the question is what are you going to do now? Are you going to let him keep doing what he wants or are you going to get even?"

"Get even?"

"Baby…Listen my husband cheated on me the whole time we were together and I learned that the only way that I could hurt him as much as he hurt me was to leave him. As much as these men act like they don't want to be married or with just one person there biggest fear is losing control and being alone. The day I got up and decided to leave my husband, he panicked and almost lost his mind. He missed practices and games to find me and didn't stop until he did."

"So once he found you what did you do?"

"I came home and things got better for a little while but once he felt like he was in control again he started cheating again."

"Wow..."

"Yeah...I know...You think he would have got the hint the first time but he didn't."

"So what did you do?"

"Well one night he came home smelling like one of those sluts and I went off. We physically fought all night until I couldn't take it anymore...So I killed him."

"What? What do you mean you killed him? Like he is dead as we speak?" Linda replied looking up at me a little tense.

"Yes... He is dead as a deer in some headlights on the hood of a car."

"Wow! How did you kill him...?" She exclaimed sounding very interested.

"Well...He beat my ass around the whole house and it made its way to the kitchen where I was able to get hold of a kitchen knife and stab him until he stopped moving."

"Oh... My God...I think I remember hearing about something like that...But that was um.... Crystal Wilk's wasn't it?"

"They kept saying Crystal Wilk's but my name is Christina Wilk's." I replied trying to stay away from the name Crystal as much as possible.

"This is crazy…your husband was umm that big football player…Wow I remember it all now…It was on the news every now and then."

"Yeah…But anyway…what I'm getting to is you can't let him keep doing this to you. I know that it's impulse to go after our own kind but it's not Crystal's fault even if she knew. It's the man's fault…your man, Camry. He knew better than anybody that he was wrong. So if you're going to be mad at anybody be mad at him."

"You're right but what do you think I should do?"

"I don't know but I do know if you keep letting him cheat he will. Don't be surprised if he ends of knocking at my door one day looking for a repeat of the other night."

"I was worried about that…But you wouldn't do that to me would you Chrissy?" Linda asked looking deeply into my eyes.

"Baby…I want you more than I want him…I think that you would be better off with me anyway financially, sexually, and mentally, he doesn't deserve you…"

"Girl Stop…If I was in another body you could have me." She replied blushing.

"Linda…I wouldn't want you any other way." I replied kissing her on the lips.

She didn't stop me after the first, second, or third kiss…

"Wait no…I can't do this…" Linda said backing away from me.

"Baby don't...Don't go back home to him...Stay here with me I promise you won't have to worry about anything here...Money or anything...I'll protect you. Aren't you sick of all his mess?"

Linda stopped and looked down and took a deep breath.

"I don't know what to do...I'm not supposed to feel this way... I can't think...!" She replied as more tears began to fall down her face.

"Let me help you..." I replied kissing her again, this time on her neck then shoulder... "Do you want me to stop?"

Linda was silent for a minute as I continued to unbutton her shirt and continue to kiss her.

"No..."

"Are you sure?"

"No...But don't stop" She insisted lying back on the couch and embracing me with an onslaught of kisses...

26

It had been two days and I hadn't seen my wife. She kept telling me that she needed space and time to figure things out but wouldn't tell me where she was figuring things out at. Her absence only confirmed that she was cheating on me. She was probably somewhere in the islands with her new guy laid out on a beach enjoying the sun. I figured she was at the islands or something because she loved the sun and that's the only place I could see her going to ruin our marriage, I couldn't believe that she was acting this way towards me just when I thought our marriage was getting better.

Oddly enough I hadn't heard from Crystal too much either. She told me that she was sick and was taking some time out so she could get better which was very coincidental to me. In all my suspicion I drove to Crystals place to see if I could see Linda's car over there but to no avail. I called Linda's office and they were saying that she hadn't been coming to work. Something just wasn't right. I was trying to keep it cool and play the background but when I got a call from my friend Bill, my lawyer, I kind of lost all cool.

"What's up bro? Did you find anything?" I said answering Bill's call with my feet kicked up on my coffee table as I sat on my couch flicking through channels on my flat screen.

"Yeah...This woman you had me check into...Crystal Wilk's...She's a murderer."

"What?"

"She a psycho murderer....She's that chick who won that self-defense case a while back on Terrance Wilk's the big time football player, it was all over the news..."

"I think I remember her." I replied sitting up and taking a deep gulp of my own spit.

"Well yeah, that's her; It says she stabbed the guy 19 times with a steak knife."

"Damn!'

"Yeah...and Terrance was a pretty big guy to put down."

"Wow...So she beat the murder charge?"

"Yup...It says that she's on some pretty heavy meds too or was should I say. A bunch of anti-depressants and pain relievers..."

"So she's basically some drugged up nut that killed her husband..."

"Kind of...She is one year from having her masters in psychology so I would imagine she is one smart crazy killer. But do you mind me asking why?"

My heart kind of did this pause and then fluttered before I answered him.

"Look man...I got to go...thanks for the information talk to you later" I replied hanging up the phone in a hurry and trying to stop myself from panicking.

What the hell did I get myself into?

I fell in love with a nut? Why the hell didn't I just Google her sooner? I would have never thought she was that type of person just by her looks. Crystal is a very attractive woman so I guess that played as a good disguise in her case.

But the question was now that I knew this information what was I going to do with it? Do I back off or do I keep what I have going. I mean since she showed her face with my wife in my house I haven't seen much of her but I was thinking that we were still on ok terms. After all, love doesn't just go away. Especially with Linda being off with her lover I mean I was beginning to feel like I really didn't have much of a choice but to go with option B which was Crystal. Right? Where was Austin when I needed him? I couldn't call him and talk to him because his jaw was still wired but texting never stopped.

-Austin, bro, I need you- I texted to him in a dramatic fashion.

-What up?-

-I think Linda is cheating on me and I'm going to divorce her for Crystal-

-Lol-

-Man I'm serious-

-Dumb! Never leave dollars for change...it just don't make cents.-

-Like that did...-

-What makes you think she's cheating? Paranoia?-

-Hell no...She's been gone for a couple days and she won't talk to me...She will only text-

-So...-

-Bro this has been going on for a while-

-What's so special about crystal other than sex and money? Didn't she kill her husband?-

-You knew about that? Then why am I just finding out-

-Wow! You didn't know? Google! After you told me she was your ex I had to check her out I just hadn't had time to tell you-

-Yeah she did but it was self-defense-

-Are you defending a woman getting away with murder? Please don't it only makes you look desperate.-

-Well anyway...What should I do-?

-Get your wife back home... she is a good girl...Don't mess that up-

-I would if I knew where she was-

-You know, you just don't want to come to terms with it all...I have to go bro-

-Wait how did the whole Exvantage thing work out?-

-...I'm looking at the benefits of it right now bro...In a couple of months I'll have the benefit forever at the altar. All I can say is it had its benefits and it had its downsides-

I guess I was experiencing the downsides of things. My ex is turning out to be a real Pyscho and now I'm in love with her crazy ass. Austin was telling me to stay with Linda but how could I? As bad as I wanted the best of both worlds I knew I had to choose and despite how crazy Crystal was I still wanted to give her a try especially since it seemed my wife had moved on and found her someone else. It only made sense for me to go to the person that made me feel best.

....

Knock...Knock, Knock, knock

"Crystal open up I have to talk to you... I know you're sick but I don't care let me take care of you baby please" I shouted hoping that she was somewhere close in the house so she could hear me through her front door.

It only made sense to me to go after what I wanted and in this case, confusingly it was Crystal. I'm pretty sure that she wasn't as crazy as they were saying she was or making her seem. Even if she was I was willing to deal with it and try and make things work. I hadn't thought long on my choice but for right now it was what I wanted to do.

"Crystal! Baby please!" I shouted seeing both her cars in the drive way.

"Leave before I call the cops!" She shouted out of one of the windows of the large house.

"Call the cops? What are you talking about? Call them for what?"

"Get off of my property now...I told you not to come around here...We have nothing to talk about."

"Where is all of this coming from?" I shouted in disdain backing up from the door and looking up and around at the numerous windows to see which one she was yelling out of. "Crystal! Where are you?"

"Lower your damn tone and get the hell away from here. What are you doing here?" She said opening the door and stepping out with a kitchen knife in her hand.

"Crystal...what's? What's going on? What are you doing with that?"

"I'm cooking... I've already called the police so you need to go before they get here; I don't want to see anybody get locked up."

"Locked up...What...?"

"Don't come near me...Keep your distance..." She said raising the knife as if she was ready to use it on me."

"What are you going to do stab me? Do me like you did your husband?"

She looked at me hard enough to cut through me with her eyes."

"You know what you and my husband have in common? You're both dumb asses who are selfish and don't appreciate what you have right in your face."

"But I do Crystal...That is why I'm here so we can be together and do whatever it is you wanted to do...Build a family...Whatever." I replied reaching out for her.

"Don't touch me she yelled jerking her hand back...You're so clueless..."

"What?! What?!" I yelled beginning to get frustrated.

"I'm not talking about me dumb ass...I'm talking about your wife."

"My wife? You wanted me to leave her for you so now I'm here and you suddenly have a change of heart? You can't play with people's mind like that Crystal."

"Wow...A couple nights of meaningless sex and your willing to risk your 10 years of marriage? Pathetic! You think that I'm going to go be with a guy who does that so he can do the same to me? Hell no...Just get the fuck out of here boy..."

I was totally confused about everything. Where the hell is any of this coming from? Now I see where the whole Pyscho on medication thing came from because none of this is making any sense.

"You look confused...Do you want me to make it clear for you? Fine...Linda come on out baby."

"Linda?" I shouted seeing her poke her head out of the door.

"Linda what the fuck? What are you doing here?"

"I could be asking you the same thing..."

"So this is where you been? Here with her?" I replied as she opened the door a little more revealing that she had nothing but a black lace bra and pantie on.

"Yup...the whole time and this is where I'm going to stay I don't have time for the bull shit from you."

"What!! This is some bull shit! You better put on your clothes and get your ass out here now! What is wrong with you?" I exclaimed in disdain.

"I can't be with any man who can't appreciate me. Good bye Camry...I'll be sending those divorce papers to your house soon. Come on baby...Come back inside I'm waiting on you." She replied pulling Crystal who was standing guard in her black sweat pants and wife beater in front of me like she was ready to kill again.

"You better stay away from here boy or the next time I'm going to kill you..."

"Yeah...whatever..." I replied still trying to realize what was going on.

"Oh by the way, we are pregnant..." she replied as she went in the house and closed the door.

"Wait what?" I exclaimed as the door slammed...

"Pregnant? The both of you...? Fuck!'

27

Austin Wells

(6 months later)

Camry had finally swallowed his pride and told me everything that was going on with him. I found it absolutely funny but tragic what had been happening with him. For someone to be so intelligent he sure did get played like a dumb ass. He let his own experiment bite him in his ass and practically destroy his life. I don't understand how someone could give such great advice but not hear it their damn selves. If he would have kept a fine line between hoes and his home then maybe he would have been alright but he let his heart take a front seat right along with his dick and it all quickly crashed and burned. I would have never thought anything like this would have happened, not to him.

After a while it really seemed liked Linda and Camry were going to get a divorce. She was staying with Crystal and supposedly madly in love and Camry was spending a lot of time perfecting the practice of J.W.D. But as time went on the truth finally came out and Linda found out that Crystal was really Christina, Crystal supposed friend who Camry was cheating with. Linda was heartbroken in so many places she almost lost her mind, but instead of losing she ending up losing her baby in a miscarriage due to stress. She left Crystal and went back home to stay with her parents for a while before finally working things out with Camry and coming back home.

Crystal didn't take any of it to well. She didn't show her face too much but she made an appearance every now and then through a flattened tire or broken window or keyed car every other month. I knew she was crazy when Camry told me she had thrown a turkey through his back window of his Beemer. You have to be one strong bitch to do that. All in all, despite how mad and miserable she was she got what she automatically wanted...A baby, 6 months pregnant with Camry's child and counting. Whoever said hard work didn't pay off?

As for me...My body had finally healed and I had bought myself a new house to support my soon to be big family upon discovering Marie was pregnant with twins. Who knew that it could be possible for a relationship loser like me to finally be on the upside of love? I am finally a one woman man and I got the one who got away. How lucky am I?

Oh...and Mrs. Jenkins and her husband got a divorce but soon got back together. Once she found out what her husband did to me I guess it ignited a flame back in their marriage or something because they were in every magazine telling people how happy they were together and how to be successful in a marriage. Isn't that crazy?

I would see her every now and then around town but I would never speak. No pussy was worth my life... I was promoted once Marie's ex –fiance had quit. Mrs. Jenkins did do me a favor and let me keep my job that she got for me and all the extra things too. Not counting the Cadillac or bed, I had got over 30 grand cash from her...Did I fail to mention her husband paid my hospital bills so I wouldn't press charges?

All in all through all the mess I turned out all right. I got my girl and my life...I can't help but thank God because who's to